T0320417

Experiential Consumption and Marketing in Tourism within a Cross-Cultural Context

Advances in Tourism Marketing

Metin Kozak, Antónia Correia and Alan Fyall

The purpose of this series of cutting-edge research-informed edited books is to introduce the reader to a range of contemporary marketing phenomena in the domain of travel and tourism. Authored by leading academics in their fields of research interest, each book will bring together a selection of related themes with individual chapters contributing theoretical, methodological, policy-related and/or practical outcomes for the reader. Each book will be introduced and brought to a conclusion by the series editors who between them have many decades of research and publishing experience. The singular aim of this advanced series of scholarly texts is to stimulate and engage readers in the fast-changing, complex and increasingly interdisciplinary nature of tourism marketing, and serve as a catalyst for future intellectual, academic, and professional-driven research agendas. This series encourages critical, participatory and humanistic approaches to research and welcomes contributions from all over the world. In particular, the series welcomes contributions from a non-Western perspective as tourism becomes truly global in both its reach and impact.

Experiential Consumption and Marketing in Tourism within a Cross-Cultural Context

Editors:

Antónia Correia, Alan Fyall, Metin Kozak

(G) Goodfellow Publishers Ltd

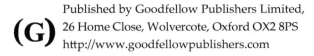

Published by Goodfellow Publishers Limited,
26 Home Close, Wolvercote, Oxford OX2 8PS
http://www.goodfellowpublishers.com

British Library Cataloguing in Publication Data: a catalogue record for this title is available from the British Library.

Library of Congress Catalog Card Number: on file.

ISBN: 978-1-911396-97-0

 Design and typesetting by P.K. McBride, www.macbride.org.uk

Printed by Baker & Taylor, www.baker-taylor.com

Cover design by Cylinder, www.cylindermedia.com

Contents

Part IV: Gastronomy Experiences

List of figures

List of tables

Author biographies

Fernando Almedia-García, Ph.D., is Professor in the Department of Geography, Faculty of Tourism, University of Malaga. His research is focused on tourism and regional residents' attitude towards tourism, sustainable development, economic development and tourism policy. He has published many papers on these subjects. He has collaborated in international projects with European, Latin American and East Asia universities. He leads the 'Territory and Tourism' Research Group. Email: falmeida@uma.es.

Zaid Alrawadieh, Ph.D., holds a Doctorate in Tourism Management from Istanbul University (Turkey) and a Master's Degree in Tourism and Environment from Pisa University (Italy). Currently, he lectures in the Department of Hotel, Restaurant and Catering Services at Istanbul University Cerrahpasa. His research interests include customer complaining behavior, tourist experiences, tourist behavior, and sharing economy in tourism and hospitality. Email: zaid.alrawadieh@istanbul.edu.tr.

Maria João Amante, Ph.D., holds a Doctorate and a Master in Psychology from the University of Coimbra. She is a Coordinate Professor at the Higher School of Education of the Polytechnic Institute of Viseu where she is the Director of the Department of Psychology and Science Education. She is a researcher at Center for Studies in Education, Technology and Health and has published several articles in international scientific journals. Email: majoa@esev.ipv.pt.

Robin M. Back, Ph.D., is an Assistant Professor at the Rosen College of Hospitality Management, University of Central Florida, USA following a lengthy career in the hospitality, tourism and wine industries. He has published a number of articles and book chapters in the areas of tourism, events and organizational leadership. He sits on the editorial board of the *Journal of Vacation Marketing*. His current research interests include wine tourism, wine marketing, and events, and he teaches wine and spirits related courses. Email: robin.back@ucf.edu.

Ali Bavik, Ph.D., is an Assistant Professor at the Institute for Tourism Studies (IFT), Macau. He completed his Ph.D. at the University of Otago and his undergraduate studies at Eastern Mediterranean University. His research interests are in the areas of hospitality marketing and management, specifically nepotism, organizational culture, consumer behaviour, job satisfaction, and employee performance management. Email: ali@ift.edu.mo.

Diego Bufquin, Ph.D., is an Assistant Professor at the Rosen College of Hospitality Management, University of Central Florida, USA, where he teaches hotel and restaurant management courses for both undergraduate and graduate students. He has published a variety of articles in the areas of hotel and restaurant management, more specifically in organizational and consumer behavior. He sits on the editorial boards of the *International Journal of Contemporary Hospitality Management* and the *Journal of Foodservice Business Research*. Email: diego.bufquin@ucf.edu.

Gurel Cetin, Ph.D., is an Associate Professor in Tourism Management Departmet at Istanbul University. He earned his Ph.D from business administration from Istanbul University in 2012, since than he has been teaching tourism management courses in several institutions. Dr. Cetin also has 15 years of practical experience in the hospitality and travel trade. His research interests include tourism marketing, destination management, sustainable tourism, tourist behavior and information technology in tourism. He is also the managing editor of *Journal of Tourismology*. Email: gurelc@istanbul.edu.tr.

Antónia Correia, Ph.D., is Professor of Tourist Behaviour and Tourism Economics, University of Algarve and Dean at the Faculty of Tourism and Hospitality at Universidade Europeia, both in Portugal. Research areas include consumer behaviour, tourism economics and modelling. She is also affiliated to CEFAGE and Coordinator of Tourism Research Line. She has published more than one hundred papers in tourism, leisure and economics journals. She is a member of the editorial boards of several leading journals including *Journal of Travel Research*, *Journal of Business Research*, *Tourism Analysis*, *Anatolia* and *Tourism Management Perspectives*, among others. E-mail: ahcorreia@gmail.com.

Rafael Cortés-Macías, Ph.D., holds a doctorate from the University of Malaga and is Professor of Human Geography, University of Malaga in the Department of Geography. He teaches undergraduate and graduate clases in tourism in the Faculty of Tourism. His research is conducted within the research group 'Territory and Tourism' (SEJ-402) with an emphasis on the study of the relationships between tourism, impacts and territorial planning, both within the national and international context. Email: rcortes@uma.es.

José António Filipe, Ph.D., holds a doctorate in Quantitative Methods by ISCTE-IUL. He also holds a Master in Management Sciences by ISCTE-IUL (Portugal) and graduated in Economics by ISEG/UTL - Instituto Superior de Economia e Gestão, Universidade Técnica de Lisboa

(Portugal). He is currently an Assistant Professor with Habilitation at ISCTE-IUL. Research Department of Mathematics in ISTA - School of Technology and Architecture, at ISCTE-IUL. His primary research areas are finance, economics, and mathematics among others. He has published 250 papers in scientific journals and conference proceedings, 30 book chapters, 10 books and 2 edited books. Email: jose-filipe@iscte.pt.

Catarina Frias is a Master's student in Tourism Management at the School of Technology and Management of Viseu, Portugal, where she is developing a thesis on Storytelling. She has a degree in journalism from the Faculty of Letters of the University of Coimbra. Email: catarina_frias@hotmail.com.

Alan Fyall, Ph.D., is Visit Orlando Endowed Chair of Tourism Marketing at the Rosen College of Hospitality Management, University of Central Florida, USA. He has published widely in the areas of tourism and destination marketing and management including 22 books. To date, he has examined 27 PhDs in the UK, India, France, South Africa, Australia, Hong Kong and Malaysia. He is Co-Editor of Elsevier's *Journal of Destination Marketing & Management* and sits on the editorial boards of many leading journals. His current research interests relate to sustainable tourism and coastal destination resilience. Email: alan.fyall@ucf.edu.

Shoji Iijima, Ph.D., is a Professor of University of the Ryukyus, Japan. He obtained his doctor's degree in Environmental Engineering from Okayama University. He has analyzed townscape environments, applying theories and methods employed in studies of light and visual environments. Regarding tourism, he has investigated visitors' evaluations of tourism destination environments. His methods include qualitative date collection through personal interviews as well as quantitative date collection through questionnaire surveys and experiments with visual stimuli. He has recently studied the features of spaces for tourists and locals in commercial spaces in tourism destinations. Email: ijimash@tm.u-ryukyu.ac.jp.

Fusun Istanbullu Dinçer, Ph.D., is a Professor and Founding Chair in the Tourism Management Department at Istanbul University. Her research interests include sustainable tourism, tourism marketing and tourist behaviour. She is also the Founding Editor in Chief of the *Journal of Tourismology*. Email: istanbul@istanbul.edu.tr.

Metin Kozak, Ph.D., is a Professor in the School of Tourism, Dokuz Eylul University, Turkey. He holds both Master's and Ph.D. degrees in

Tourism Management. His research focuses on consumer behaviour, benchmarking, destination management, and sustainability. He acts as the co–editor of *Anatolia: An International Journal of Tourism and Hospitality Research* and has been to several universities in the U.S., Europe and Asia as a visiting scholar and many conferences as a keynote speaker. Email: m.kozak@superonline.com.

Anna Leask, Ph.D., is Professor of Tourism Management at Edinburgh Napier University, UK. She has published widely in the areas of heritage tourism and visitor attraction management. She has examined 15 PhDs in the UK, Hong Kong and Australia. She is Associate Editor of Elsevier's *Journal of Destination Marketing & Management* and sits on the editorial boards of many leading journals. Her current research and teaching interests relate to destination and visitor attraction management, with recent focus on employee retention. Email: a.leask@napier.ac.uk.

Arlindo Madeira is a student in Tourism and Hospitality Management by ISCTE-Instituto Universitário de Lisboa/ Universidade Europeia, Portugal. Currently is a lecturer and researcher at Universidade Europeia, (Lisbon). Master of Marketing from Universidade Europeia (Portugal) and graduated in Hospitality Management from ISLA (Portugal). His current research interests are in wine tourism, gastronomy and hospitality management. Email: arlindo.madeira@universidadeeuropeia.pt.

Sérgio Moro, Ph.D., is Assistant Professor at Instituto Universitário de Lisboa (ISCTE-IUL), Lisboa, Portugal, and Sub-Director and Coordinator of the Information Systems Group of ISTAR-IUL. Sérgio is an interdisciplinary data scientist aiming to unveil patterns of knowledge through data-driven approaches in a wide range of domains, including marketing and tourism. His research appears in journals such as *Annals of Tourism Research, International Journal of Contemporary Hospitality Management, International Journal of Information Management, Journal of Business Research*, and *Computers in Industry*. He is member of the Editorial Panel of *Tourism Management Perspectives* for the year of 2019. Email: sergio.moro@iscte-iul.pt.

Bendegul Okumus, Ph.D., is an Assistant Professor at the University of Central Florida's Rosen College of Hospitality Management. Her research areas include food safety, healthy eating, culinary tourism, destination marketing, ethnic restaurants, restaurant selection and food waste. She has authored/co-authored numerous academic journal articles, book chapters and conference presentations. Email: bendegul.okumus@ucf.edu.

Cristina Oliveira is a PhD researcher in tourism management at ISCTE-IUL and Universidade Europeia, being affiliated in ISTAR-IUL, Lisbon, Portugal. She worked as a tourist accommodation manager, having won awards for customer relationship management, and quality lodging experience. Cristina taught courses on Business Communication and Negotiation Skills, and Management of Tourist Attractions in postgraduate and master programs. She has presented paper communications at international conferences as well as co-authored articles published in scientific journals such as *Journal of Hospitality Marketing and Management, Annals of Leisure Research, International Journal of Culture, Tourism, and Hospitality Research, Anatolia.* Email: crisphdturismo@gmail.com.

Mustafa Özdemir obtained his Master's degree in Tourism Management from Istanbul University. His main research interests include tourist guide, customer experience, guiding studies in tourism. He also has seven years of professional guiding experienced in the tourism and travel industry. Email: mstfozdemir87@gmail.com.

Jeong-Yeol Park, Ph.D., is an Assistant Professor at the Rosen College of Hospitality Management, University of Central Florida, USA. His research interests are potential travelers' purchasing behavior in online travel agents, and restaurant customers' behavior. His work was awarded the Martin Opperman Best Research Paper of the Year in 2015. He sits on the editorial boards of the *Journal of Destination Marketing & Management* and the *Journal of Hospitality and Tourism Insights*. Email: jeong-yeol.park@ucf.edu.

Carimo Rassal develops his teaching activity at the European University and at the University of the Algarve, Portugal, as an invited professor. A Ph.D. student in Tourism with a specialization in Management at the Faculty of Economics of the University of Algarve, Carimo develops his academic research at the Research Center of the University of Évora (CEFAGE) as researcher in the areas of Tourism, Hospitality and Gastronomy. With more than 25 years of professional experience, he regularly participates in consulting and training projects both nationally and internationally. Email: crassal@ualg.pt.

Cláudia Seabra, Ph.D., is Professor at the University of Coimbra, and invited Professor at the Polytechnic Institute of Viseu. With a Ph.D. in Tourism, she is undertaking her post-Ph.D. on "Terrorism and the EU 28: Impact on citizens and organizations". She has publications in the *Journal of Business Research, Tourism Management, European Journal of Marketing, Journal of Marketing Management, International Journal of Tourism*

Cities, and *Journal of Hospitality and Tourism Technology* among others. She is affiliated with the Geography and Spatial Planning Research Centre, the Nova School of Business & Economics, and the Center for Studies in Education, Technologies and Health. Cláudia develops her research in safety and terrorism, and cultural tourism. Email: cseabra@uc.pt.

Francisco Serra, received his Ph.D. in Economics and Management Sciences from the University of Huelva, Spain, in 2003. He was hired as an Assistant Professor in 1992 by the School of Management, Hospitality and Tourism of the University of the Algarve, in Portugal and holds now the position of Coordinating Professor. Since June 2016 he is the President of the Coordinating Commission for the Regional Development of Algarve, and of the Algarve, Alentejo and Andaluzia Euro region. From June 2012 to June 2016 he was the Director of the School of Management, Hospitality and Tourism of the University of the Algarve. He has conducted and supervised research in the fields of Hospitality Management, Tourism Development, Regional Economics and Systems Dynamics. Email: fserra@ualg.pt.

Carla Maria Alves da Silva, Ph.D., holds a Doctorate in Tourism from the University of Aveiro and a Master's degree in Social Sciences from ISCTE. She is an Associate Professor at the Higher School of Technology and Management of the Polytechnic Institute of Viseu (IPV), where she teaches in Tourism and Marketing degrees and in the Master of Tourism Management of which she is the director. She is a researcher at Center for Studies in Education, Technology and Health, and is a collaborator at the IPV's Digital Services Research Center and GOVCOPP - Competitiveness, Governance and Public Policy at the University of Aveiro. Email: csilva@estv.ipv.pt.

Naoi Taketo, Ph.D., is an Associate Professor of Tokyo Metropolitan University, Japan. He obtained his doctoral degrees from the University of Surrey, the UK, and Tokyo Institute of Technology, Japan. By adopting theories of environmental psychology and consumer behavior, he has investigated relationship among perceived physical features of destinations, visitors' impression, and goal-oriented mental states. His main target areas are public urban areas, such as historical districts and shopping streets. His methods include qualitative data collection through personal interviews with photographic stimuli and participatory photograph-taking research as well as quantitative data collection through slide experiments and questionnaire surveys. Email: naoi-taketo@tmu.ac.jp.

Akira Uehara is a PhD candidate of Tokyo Metropolitan University, Japan. He has studied the effects of perceived features of shops on tourists' evaluation of the shops, adopting theories and methods of tourism, consumer behavior, and man-environment research. Specifically, he focuses on the tourists' perception of environmental factors of tourist destination and its impact on their behavior. His main target areas are public urban areas, such as commercial spaces. His methods include quantitative data collection through questionnaire surveys and experiments with visual stimuli. He is currently researching impression and behavior of young tourists in the Tokyo Metropolitan area. Email: uehara-a.141950@outlook.com.

Ellis Urquhart, Ph.D., is a Lecturer in Tourism Management within the Business School at Edinburgh Napier University, UK. He specialises in visitor attraction management, co-creative experience design and technological mediation in the heritage sector and the wider attraction environment. Ellis teaches tourism management at both undergraduate and postgraduate levels at Edinburgh Napier University in addition to overseas programmes delivered in Switzerland and Hong Kong. He currently reviews for a range of tourism publications and sits on the editorial board of the *Journal of Tourism Futures*. Email: e.urquhart@napier.ac.uk.

Antonia Balbuena-Vázquez, Ph.D., holds a BA in Anthropology from the University of Granada, (Spain), a Ph.D. in Tourism from the University of Malaga, and is a member of the research group 'Tourism and Territory' (SEJ-402). Her main field of study is resident attitudes toward tourism. She is a researcher at the National University of Mexico (UNAM). Email: abalvaz@yahoo.es.

Carol Zhang, Ph.D., is Senior Lecturer in Marketing at Portsmouth Business School. Carol's research interests include nationalism, tourism marketing, tourism policy, cultural tourism, research methodology, and Chinese inbound and outbound tourism. As a critical tourism scholar, Carol has gained experience of using both qualitative and quantitative methodologies. She has published 7 journal articles in both English and Chinese peer-reviewed academic journals. Her recent publication, Politics and tourism promotion: Hong Kong's myth-making, is published in *Annals of Tourism Research*. Email: carol.zhang@port.ac.uk.

1 Introduction

Antónia Correia, Alan Fyall and Metin Kozak

Culture is the entangling web of symbols, sounds, rituals, rites and practices by which we become persons and by which we can grow. Culture is often the reason for travel, and both bargain and barrier in its consumption. Underpinned by globalization, tourism is both enabling and threatening culture and its practices, as business commodifies authentic differences. Sharing culture is the ultimate form of a touristic experience that should be unique, extraordinary, and memorable (Aho, 2001; Arnould & Price, 1993; Oh, Fiore & Jeoung, 2007; Pine & Gilmore, 1998, 1999) and worthy of being shared. Accordingly, MacCannell (1973) states that tourists are questing for the extraordinary in a novel space and time to which stimulation and emotional engagement are needed with the different elements of a context created by a service provider (Grupta & Vajic, 1999). Considering that experiences are composed of four different axes, namely education, escape, entertainment and aesthetics (Pine & Gilmore, 1998), experiential marketing is assumed as a critical tool to enact these experiences within the triad of place-host-guests interactions. These, in turn, end with the emotional attachment of the tourists with the destination and the willingness to share their experiences.

This book includes contributions that analyze and critique initiations to education, escape, entertainment and aesthetics experiences that ultimately reports on the facilitation, celebration and sharing of culture through tourism and how each is manifested in tourism marketing theory, policy and practice. The book contains case examples of the opportunities, best practices, aims, pitfalls and mistakes of those tourism businesses which have culture as their core experience as well as cases of where different tourists are engaged in exploring and learning about other cultures. In addition, the book contains chapters on the below themes of interest where culture has contributed strongly to their outcomes: the roles of tourists, locals and communities, events, business practices in facilitating and sharing cultural experiences, relationship marketing, experiential marketing, cross-border marketing, product differentiation and market segmentation, shopping experiences, storytelling and visual narrative analysis.

Part I of the book features six chapters, of which the first four cover the four realms of the destination experience: education, escape, entertainment and aesthetics and the last two the sharing propensity of tourists experiences. The first, Chapter 2 by Antonia Balbuena-Vázquez, Fernando Almeida-García and Rafael Cortés-Macías explores satisfaction and place attachment in a mature destination, that of Benalmádena in Spain. It approaches the tourists' experiences as an aesthetical activity where the contemplation should be driven by the locals. Therefore, this chapter presents information about residents' opinions regarding satisfactory and unsatisfactory aspects of tourism and determines levels of place attachment. The chapter goes on to identify what bothers and does not bother the residents of Benalmádena and how their views can, and should, be considered for the planning of the destination. Tourism as an industry clearly produces positive and negative effects on the local community. It is imperative, therefore, that residents are viewed as key actors whose views need to be taken into account if the development of successful tourism policies are to be achieved. The chapter sheds light on the fact, perhaps unsurprisingly, that tourists tend not to visit those destinations where they feel unwelcome or believe they will not be accepted. The chapter concludes that the level of support for tourism development from the host community would decrease if the community perceives that the total effects of tourism are negative.

Chapter 3 by Akira Uehara, Taketo Naoi and Shoji Iijima takes a slightly different direction, approaching experience as an entertainment activity, in that it evaluates the relationship between servicescapes and tourists' evaluation of shops; in the specific case context of Naha City. The chapter begins with an introduction as to how tourists' evaluation of shops is influenced by shops' features in various manners. For example, the chapter demonstrates how excessive interior manipulation (organization) shows negative effects on shops' touristic and active atmosphere while it also evidences how the disorderliness of interiors might have been sensed as touristic and active aspects of the shops, implying the importance of sustaining a certain degree of naiveté. Most telling is how shopkeepers' openness to tourists and the presentation of the local lifestyle in the interiors and exteriors of shops contributed to opportunities for tourists to fully experience more authentic local lifestyles. The chapter concludes that servicescape of shops should be considered, depending on whether the place intends to foster tourists' shopping activities or enhance their experience of local culture.

The experience theme, through an educational dimension, continues in Chapter 4, where Mustafa Ozdemir, Gurel Cetin and Fusun Istanbullu Dincer identify experiential components of guiding in package tours and measure their impact on tourist satisfaction. The authors determine and examine the role of tour guides and the contribution of guides' interpretation to the tourist experience and satisfaction, and identify experiential items of guided package tours on satisfaction and experience based on survey data informed by a qualitative phase. The chapter concludes by suggesting practical implications for tour operations, guiding associations' certification, educational institutions' curricula, and theoretical implications for the experience and tourism literature.

Chapter 5 by Claudia Seabra explores a darker side of tourism, that being the relationship between tourism and terrorism, and recalls that the escape dimension of the tourists' experience begs for a safe destination. Seabra discusses the means by which tourism and terrorism share many characteristics, including the fact that they frequently cross and go beyond national borders and involve citizens from different countries, and that terrorists increasingly appear to be using tourism and tourist sites to gain maximum publicity and support needed to achieve their goals. In many instances to date, tourists have been chosen as targets for their symbolic value, with terrorists turning them into valuable assets to be exploited.

Cristina Oliveira, Antónia Correia and Sérgio Moro explore a more positive experiential domain in Chapter 6, by explaining how sensory marketing offers an interesting approach to leveraging island tourism, and how the sensorial experience is perceived and shared by visitors. In particular, this chapter demonstrates how online reviews published on TripAdvisor for hotels, attractions and restaurants were used in identifying visitors' perspectives, with the chapter concluding that visual sense with a focus on beach, sea, sand, water and green work, although both auditory and olfactory senses of sea and water are not so explicit in the tourist reviews, albeit they still engrained in visitors' comments.

Chapter 7, the final chapter in Part I of the book, by Carimo Rassal, Antónia Correia and Francisco Serra investigates the effects of electronic word of mouth on service performance in hospitality through the service performance scope. The chapter furthers our understanding as to which attributes are relevant to the guest's overall assessment of a hotel experience and highlights findings that show the importance of: staff (language, assurance, responsiveness, reliability), rate promotions, hotel design and location, operational organization (facilities and services), room experience, food and beverage and price, in overall assessment of the hotel's service performance.

Part II of the book, on the theme of motivations and identity, includes two chapters with a strong Eastern connection. For example, Chapter 8 by Ali Bavik, Antónia Correia and Metin Kozak features a multi-group analysis of tourists' motivations to travel to Macau. It seeks to bridge the gap in the literature on the tourism market of Macau through a motivation-based clustering analysis to depict what goes beyond gambling motivations, and assesses empirical data collected through the development of a questionnaire survey that was conducted in Macau. The chapter introduces two clusters derived from the study findings, namely gamblers and non-gamblers, with culture, value for money, socialization, relaxation, and nightlife found to be the main drives of all tourist groups. Chapter 9 by Carol Zhang follows on by adopting an identity perspective in looking at being an outbound Chinese tourist. The chapter begins with an introduction to identity theory and tourism before providing an overview of research and government measures in dealing with uncivilised behaviours. It continues by exploring the way in which Chinese tourists reflect on the recent negative identity of the country before drawing out the dominant themes that underpin the reflections of Chinese tourists on the projected negative identities. Chapter 9 concludes by offering recommendations to the government and industry providers to deal with the increasingly negative perception of Chinese tourists.

Part III of the book explores a slightly different dimension, that of narratives and storytelling in the wider domain of tourist experiences. In Chapter 10, Ellis Urquhart and Anna Leask examine the management of co-creation narratives in the heritage sector, with a specific case focus on the Surgeon's Hall Museum in Edinburgh, Scotland. Urquhart and Leask bring together theoretical approaches to storytelling and narrative creation with co-creation of heritage experiences, before identifying and discussing management practices and associated opportunities for narrative co-creation. They propose that co-created narratives could lead to more engaging, individualised and memorable heritage visitor experiences. The chapter concludes with some experiential lessons for heritage management, including a need for narrative co-creation to be a considered within strategic heritage planning and operational decision-making. Similarly, Chapter 11, by Catarina Frias, Carla Silva, Maria João Amante and Cláudia Seabra, brings together the concepts of World Heritage sites, touristic experience and storytelling, identifies the dimensions of the pre-tourist storytelling experiences in World Heritage Historical Centers in Portugal, based on the information provided in their official websites, and discusses the findings with World Heritage Historical Center management entities.

Finally, **Part IV** introduces three chapters on the theme of gastronomy experiences in the wider tourism domain. The first, Chapter 12, by Gurel Cetin, Bendegul Okumus and Zaid Alrawadieh, takes a critical look at the role of gastronomy in destination marketing. Their chapter outlines the role of local food in tourism marketing and explores Istanbul, Turkey as a culinary destination. Chapter 13, meanwhile, by Diego Bufquin, Robin Back and Jeong-Yeol Park, takes a look at innovations in the wine tourism industry experience. The chapter assesses the effects of congruence perceptions – between a post-modernist hotel architecture, its surrounding landscape, visitors' self-image, and a winery's brand image – on winery visitors' arousal, delight and behavioral intentions. It then analyzes the relationships between substantive and communicative servicescape perceptions, and winery visitors' positive affect, satisfaction, and behavioral intentions, as well as the moderating effects of brand and architectural familiarity in order to investigate the influence of winery tourists' motivations and satisfaction on number of visits and revisit intentions. Finally, Chapter 14, by Arlindo Madeira, Antónia Correia and José António Filipe, takes a qualitative approach to understand memorable enogastronomic experiences. The chapter introduces those factors that make a memorable enogastronomic experience for tourists visiting a destination, and presents qualitative findings that reveal that gastronomy and wines play a major role in the way that visitors experience a destination and that some travellers would return to the same destination to savour its unique gastronomy.

The catalyst and primary source of material for this book was the international conference held in 2016 in Casablanca, Morocco. This book is the most expressive form of "the Art of Living together", the topic of the conference, with scholars attending from 20 different countries. The *Advances in Tourism Marketing* conference series, which started in 2005, have a long tradition of contributing to the body of knowledge with the publication of advances in tourism presented in the form of books and peer-reviewed journal articles. This particular book is shaped with material from the conference in addition to contributions from other authors from all over the world, that is by itself an exercise of experiential gathering that enriches the book! Finally, this book demonstrates that experiential marketing is a complex and multidimensional force to which tourists, locals, destinations, professionals and government are called to contribute. Furthermore, the contribution of all of them are not enough as emotions, senses and motivations of tourists moderate the form they experience and share the destination; this complexity and subjectivity bringing to light the fact that experiential marketing truly is an *art of living together*.

References

Aho, S. K. (2001). Towards a general theory of touristic experiences: Modelling experience process in tourism. *Tourism Review*, **56**(3/4), 33-37.

Arnould, E. J. & Price, L. L. (1993). River magic: Extraordinary experience and the extended service encounter. *Journal of Consumer Research*, **20**(1), 24-45.

Gupta, S. V. & Vajic, M. (1999). The contextual and dialectical nature of experiences. *New Service Development: Creating Memorable Experiences*, ed. J. Fitzimmons, M. Fitzimmons, 33-35.

MacCannell, D. (1973). Staged authenticity: Arrangements of social space in tourist settings. *American Journal of Sociology*, **79**(3), 589-603.

Oh, H., Fiore, A. M. & Jeoung, M. (2007). Measuring experience economy concepts: Tourism applications. *Journal of Travel Research*, **46**(2), 119-132.

Pine, B. J. & Gilmore, J. H. (1998). Welcome to the experience economy. *Harvard Business Review*, **76**, 97-105.

Pine, B. J. & Gilmore, J. H. (1999). *The Experience Economy: Work is theatre & every business a stage*. Harvard Business Press.

Part I:
Destination Experiences

2 Satisfaction and place attachement in a mature destination

Antonia Balbuena-Vázquez, Fernando Almeida-García and Rafael Cortés-Macías

---

The objectives of this chapter are to:

☐ Present information about residents' opinions regarding satisfactory and unsatisfactory aspects of tourism and to determine levels of place attachment;

☐ Identify what bothers and does not bother the people of Benalmádena and how such views can be considered for the planning of the destination;

☐ Demonstrate that tourism as an industry produces positive and negative effects on the local community;

☐ Identify residents as key actors who's views need to be taken into account if the development of successful tourism policies are to be achieved;

☐ Highlight that tourists tend not to visit those destinations where they feel unwelcome or believe they will not be accepted;

> ☐   Identify those causes that explain why residents support or do not support the tourism industry and its growth which, in turn, will help establish tourism development models that minimise negative impacts and maximise resident support for tourism;
>
> ☐   Conclude that the level of support of the host community would decrease if the community perceives that the total effects of tourism are negative.

Keywords: residents, opinion, satisfaction, dissatisfaction, place attachment, Benalmádena

Introduction

Mass tourism emerged in the sixties as the result of technological and social revolutions, such as the appearance of charter travel, the growing affluence of the middle classes of Western industrial countries and the progressive trend of leisure in wealthy countries (Dachary & Arnaiz, 2002), such that tourism became a sector that provided almost unlimited economic growth. With the oil crisis and the economic recession of 1974-1975, the positive effects of tourism were questioned, and it was concluded that this industry was not producing the benefits that were expected. During the seventies, the figure of the resident emerged, necessitating the first studies on the attitudes or opinions they had about the impacts of tourism (Andereck & Vogt, 2000).

In the middle of the eighties, the first symptoms of dysfunctionality of mass tourism began to show, as a result of the significant negative impacts that manifested in the tourist areas (De Kadt, 1991; Murphy, 1983). The concept of sustainability appeared, which includes, among other concepts, participation in the development processes by not only tourists and governments, but also all the stakeholders of the community affected by tourism (Pulido, 2008). As a consequence of these changes, it is claimed that the local community participates and forms part of tourism planning (Murphy, 1983), which results in a greater role for the resident.

For this reason, since the mid-seventies, there has been a dissemination of research that analyses the attitudes of residents (Sirakaya et al., 2002), considering their support as a key factor in the development and implementation of successful tourism policies. Resident participation is now widely regarded as a fundamental need for the sustainability of local development (Dyer et al., 2007). When a location becomes a tourist destination, the quality of life of local residents is affected by this development, since this process involves the arrival of a greater number of people, an increase in traffic, and demand for new infrastructures and facilities, among others. The success of any tourism project can be threatened to the extent that development is planned and carried out without the knowledge and support of the host population. Success in this industry depends on the attractions and services of the destination, and for this, the hospitality of local residents is required (Gursoy et al., 2002).

Residents can be an instrument that discourages the development of the tourism sector if the local community exhibits hostile behaviour towards tourists. A disgruntled, apathetic, distrustful community, full of anger, will transmit these feelings to tourists. And in general, tourists tend to be reluctant to visit places where they do not feel welcome (Yoon et al., 2001). The behaviour of residents towards tourists is important because most of them will avoid destinations where they do not feel welcome or accepted (Belisle & Hoy, 1980). There is a consensus in the literature on tourism that argues that the support of the host communities is essential and that this support is required both in the early stages of development and later, when it begins to consolidate (Kuvan & Akan, 2005). Knowing the causes that explain why residents support or do not support the tourism industry and its growth will help to establish development models that minimise negative impacts and maximise resident support for these initiatives (Williams & Lawson, 2001; Vargas et al., 2007). The level of support of the host community would decrease if it perceived that the overall effects of tourism are negative (Chen, 2000).

Place attachment plays an important role in supporting tourism development and adapting the local community to its impacts (Cheer & Lew, 2018). Tourism can be a positive factor that increases the level of attachment to the place in the community, due to an increase in local self-esteem, although it can also cause negative attitudes towards tourism (Kajan, 2014). The objective of this study is to collect information about residents' opinions regarding the satisfactory and unsatisfactory aspects of tourism and to identify the level of place attachment. The analysis in this study points out the aspects that cause discomfort in the local community, and provides a guide to highlight which aspects of tourist activity have to be encouraged and which ones have to be avoided.

Theoretical framework

Tourism, like other industries, is often used as a tool for national or regional development, characterised by generating a set of positive impacts on host communities, such as creating new employment opportunities (Andereck & Nyaupane, 2011; Diedrich & García, 2009); providing a source of currency (Var et al., 1985); improving local infrastructure, roads and public facilities (Andereck et al., 2005; Saveriades, 2000); contributing to improving the quality of life (King et al., 1993; McGehee & Andereck, 2004); stimulating cultural activities (Andereck & Vogt, 2000; Yoon et al., 2001); promoting exchange and cultural knowledge (Besculides et al., 2002; Dyer et al., 2007); preserving cultural values (Oviedo et al., 2008); protecting and improving historical buildings and archaeological sites (Akis et al., 1996; Liu et al., 1987); and helping to protect natural resources (Andereck & Nyaupane, 2011).

The main effects of tourism that are identified by the receiving communities are as follows:

♦ Tourism increases the cost of living (Liu & Var, 1986; Saveriades, 2000) and thus the price of housing (Aguiló et al., 2004) and the inability of a large part of the local population to acquire their first residence (Antón & González, 2008);

♦ It provides low wages and low quality (Jonhson et al., 1994) and seasonal jobs (Cerezo & Lara de Vicente, 2005);

♦ It leads to a lack of economic diversification;

♦ It causes massification (Andereck et al., 2005), traffic congestion (Dyer et al., 2007; Snaith & Haley, 1999) and parking problems (Sheldon & Abenoja, 2001);

♦ It increases crime (Haralambopoulos & Pizam 1996), drug use (Belisle & Hoy, 1980; Diedrich & García, 2009; King et al., 1993) and alcohol abuse (Milman & Pizam, 1988);

♦ It causes changes in the residents' way of life (Brunt & Courtney, 1999; Liu et al., 1987);

♦ It destroys cultural and historical resources, as well as natural resources (Aguiló et al., 2004; Yoon et al., 2001);

♦ It increases the volume of garbage (Andereck et al., 2005; Lankford, 1994; Snaith & Haley, 1999) and produces greater contamination (Johnson et al., 1994).

The benefits of tourism are undoubted. However, there is growing evidence that tourism has a negative impact on the lives of residents. Tourism development is usually justified on the basis of economic benefit, leaving negative social, cultural or environmental impacts in the background (Liu et al., 1987).

Until now, most research has not found that are very concerned about the negative aspects of tourism on a general level. In any case, some studies highlight concerns with one or more specific elements regarding the negative impacts of tourism (Andereck & Vogt, 2000), such as the increase in overcrowding at the destination (Andereck et al., 2005; Liu et al., 1987), the increase in garbage (Liu et al., 1987) and traffic congestion (King et al., 1993), among others. Some researchers underline important differences between the demographic characteristics of respondents in relation to positive or negative opinions about tourism in a destination. Other authors point out that sociodemographic variables do not contribute significantly to resident attitudes; in other words, that the existence of consistent relationships between demographic variables and attitudes is not confirmed. Nunkoo and Gursoy (2012) and Mason and Cheyne (2000) concluded, for example, that women were more opposed to tourism development than men. However, a study by Ritchie (1988) noted that while there may be some differences between men and women, there are a lot of common elements between both genders.

With regard to age, some studies indicate that elderly residents showed positive attitudes towards tourism (King et al., 1993, Tomljenovic & Faulknerm, 2000); on the other hand, elderly people have a less negative view of some of the impacts of tourism, such as those on the environment (Bujosa & Rosselló, 2007). In other research, more elderly residents perceive tourism with a more negative attitude (Haralambopoulos & Pizam, 1996). Civil status has not been a variable that has led to interesting results (Smith & Krannich, 1998), while the variable of being a native or non-native resident has provided significant value with respect to the 'non-native' condition, showing a more favourable attitude towards tourism (Davis et al., 1988).

Residents expressed greater support for tourism the higher their educational level (Haralambopoulos & Pizam, 1996; Hernández et al., 1996; Teye et al., 2002), although other authors obtained opposite results (Andriotis & Vaughan, 2003). The literature suggests that the opinions and perceptions of residents on the impacts of tourism are very varied (Dyer et al., 2007). In other words, the responses of the community are heterogeneous, such that these studies are characterised precisely by this diversity of opinions. In this sense, we can understand that societies are made up of people with very varied perceptions and with interests that do not necessarily have to be common in terms of the valuation of tourism. This discrepancy in the results of the research can be attributed to the specific characteristics of the population in the places where all the studies are carried out (Tosun, 2002).

Regarding place attachment, one of the most accepted definitions is proposed by Hidalgo and Hernández, who describes it as "a positive affective bond between a person and the place where he lives" (2001, p.274). Other authors have defined the attachment to the place as the social integration of an individual in the community, which reflects an emotional link between the person and their community (McCool & Martin, 1994). Tourism studies have often analysed the attachment to the destination from the perspective of the visitor, their satisfaction and loyalty to the place (Alegre & Juaneda, 2006; Ramkissoon et al., 2013). On the other hand, the attachment of the residents towards the place where they live and their relation to the satisfaction towards the tourist development has not been studied very much. Frequently, the attachment to the place in tourist spaces has been measured in relation to the time of residence and as a function of having grown up or been born in that community (Davis et al., 1988; Jurowski et al., 1997; McCool & Martin, 1994). Nonetheless, non-tourist studies have measured attachment to the place through other variables such as affection, identity, dependence, social ties and pride in that place (Hidalgo, 2014).

Methodology

Study area

Benalmádena is located in the South of Spain, in the province of Malaga, Andalusia and is one of the municipalities that constitutes the Western Costa del Sol. This municipality consists of three districts, or urban centres, that were differentiated some time ago. At the moment, this differentiation is confused due to the urban development that the municipality has experience since tourism took off at the beginning of the sixties (SOPDE, 1997). These urban districts are Benalmádena Pueblo (old village), Arroyo de la Miel and Benalmádena Costa. In Benalmádena, agrarian and livestock farming was dominant, although between the eighteenth and nineteenth centuries, the industrial activity of paper mills was also important (Balmaceda & Martín, 2004). Therefore, until the arrival of tourism, the economic structure of this municipality was based on agriculture. In 1961, the first hotel in Benalmádena was built, beginning an unstoppable spiral towards the tourist and real estate boom and giving rise to an important transformation of the land. In 2016, Benalmádena had 37 tourist establishments (25 hotels, 8 hotel-apartments, 4 hostels), which represents a total of 14,173 beds. These figures place this destination in third place with respect to the number of hotel beds in the Costa del Sol, behind Torremolinos and Marbella, and in fifth position regarding the supply of tourist apartments in the Costa del Sol (SIMA, 2016). The supply of second tourist accommodation is much wider than the offer of hotel beds. It is estimated that the destination offers some 59,000 tourist housing places (INE, 2017).

Figure 2.1: Benalmádena view. Source: Authors

Instruments

The results presented here are based on the data collected by a questionnaire given to a sample of 770 people during the months of June, October and December 2014. We used stratified random sampling, classifying the population of Benalmádena into strata or population groups, taking into account the homogeneity within the groups and the heterogeneity between them, so that each group is proportional to the total population. The categories selected for the multiple stratification were made based on the following variables: districts of the municipality, gender and age. The sampling error is 5% for the general results, with a confidence level of 95% and $p = q = 0.50$ (Table 2.1).

In the first part of the questionnaire, sociodemographic information was collected about gender, age, marital status, whether the participant was native to Benalmádena and the participant's level of education. In the second part, two open-ended questions were proposed: "describe the satisfactory aspect of tourism in Benalmádena" and "describe the aspect that bothers you the most or that dissatisfies you with tourism in this locality". These open-ended questions allowed the respondents to answer in their own words, without limiting the response options. The item chosen to measure the social attachment of the residents was as follows: "I am proud to live in Benalmádena", which has been previously used by different authors (Scannel & Gifford, 2010; Scopelliti & Tiberio, 2010). The sociodemographic responses were easily incorporated into the database. However, the open questions were more difficult to codify on labels given the great diversity of responses received. These were classified by groups that expressed the same opinion or could be interpreted in the same way, and in this manner, the labels that were awarded for each of the answers emerged.

Table 2.1: Technical summary of the research. *Source:* Authors

Population	Residents
Study sample	770
Study area	Benalmádena (Benalmádena Costa, Arroyo de la Miel and Benalmádena Pueblo)
Data collection period	June, October and December 2014
Type of sampling	Stratified sampling
Confidence level	95%
Error range	5

The collected data were organised, tabulated and analysed using the SPSS Version 19 program. The data was processed through the use of univariate and bivariate statistical tools.

Results

Resident profile

In this study, the sample consisted of residents, of which 49.1% were men and 50.9% were women. With regard to age, 20.5% of respondents are made up of those under 20 years of age; 39.5% of the group were from 20 to 44 years old; 26% were between 45 and 64 years of age and 14% were over 65 years of age. In reference to marital status, the majority of the group is made up of singles, at 52.1%, and 33% represent the married population, 9.4% the divorced or separated and 5.6% the widowed.

Table 2.2: Sociodemographic characteristics of residents. *Source:* Authors

Category	Indicators	Percentage
Gender	Male	49.1
	Female	50.9
Age	Under 20 years old	20.5
	From 20 to 44 years old	39.5
	From 45 to 64 years old	26.0
	More than 65 years old	14.0
Civil status	Single	52.1
	Married	33.0
	Divorced or separated	9.4
	Widow/Widower	5.6
Native Non-native	Native resident	13.6
	Non-native resident	86.4
Level of education	No education	4.5
	Primary education	18.2
	Secondary education	52.5
	University education	24.8

With respect to having been born in Benalmádena (condition of native or non-native), only 13.6% of the population residing in the municipality were born there, while 86.4% were born outside. Approximately half of the sample (52.5%) has an educational level of secondary education, 24.8% are university students, 18.2% have primary education and 4.5% are residents who have no education (Table 2.2).

The Chi-Square coefficient of Pearson has been carried out to determine the relationship between two sociodemographic variables, and we have detected a significant association between:

♦ Age and marital status (χ^2= 442,280; p = 0,000), residents under 20 are single;

♦ Age and level of studies (χ^2= 278,646; p = 0,000), residents under 20 years of age have secondary education;

♦ Civil status and native and non-native residents (χ^2= 8,681; p = 0,034), divorced or separated are 'non-native' of Benalmádena;

♦ Civil status and level of education (χ^2= 134,339; p = 0,000), single residents have secondary education;

♦ Native or non-native resident and level of education (χ^2= 14,491; p = 0,002), non-native residents have secondary education.

Satisfactory and unsatisfactory aspects of tourism

From a sample of 770 residents, 572 answered the question about satisfactory and unsatisfactory aspects of tourism, and a total of 198 people did not answer it (Table 2.3).

Table 2.3: Satisfactory aspects of tourism. *Source*: Authors

		Frequency	Valid %age
Valid responses	Promotes employment, the economy grows	263	46.0
	Stimulates cultural diversity, creates a good atmosphere	109	19.1
	Variety of hostelry and leisure offerings	72	12.6
	Improves public services and facilities	83	14.5
	Beaches	45	7.9
	Total	572	100.0
Lost		198	
Total		770	

The response that has had a higher valid percentage of response (46.0%) has been the one referring to "promotes employment, the economy grows", being the argument that preferably justifies the satisfactory aspects of tourism development in Benalmádena. Subsequently, in order of importance, the answers with the highest scores are the following: "stimulates cultural diversity, creates a good atmosphere", with 19.1%; "improves public services and facilities", with 14.5%; "has an interesting variety of hostelry and leisure offer", with 12.6% and lastly, residents value 'beaches' as a positive aspect of tourism (7.9%).

Only 487 people from Benalmádena answered the question "what aspect of tourism bothers or dissatisfies you in this locality", with 283 answers having been lost. This could have been because the residents were not interested in answering the open questions, or, in this particular case, they did not perceive any discomfort or dissatisfaction with tourism (Table 2.4). With regard to those who did answer the question, 28.3% of residents (valid percentage) mentioned that the "pollution, dirt, noise" that occurs in the locality is the aspect that bothers them the most; 21.8% respondents point out "overcrowding and seasonality" as problems, understanding this item in the sense that the high season produces congestion of tourists, and during the low season, the decrease in tourists causes unemployment. The "inadequate political management" represents 12.9%; "traffic and lack of parking" accounts for 10.3%; "discomfort of residents with some legal/illegal aliens" 9.2%; "excessive urban development" 8.8%; and lastly, "others" with 8.6%.

Table 2.4: Unsatisfactory aspects of tourism. *Source*: Authors

		Frequency	Valid %age
Valid responses	Overcrowding / seasonality	106	21.8
	Pollution (dirt, noise)	138	28.3
	Traffic, parking lots are insufficient	50	10.3
	Poor political management	63	12.9
	Upset of residents by some legal / illegal aliens	45	9.2
	Excessive urbanism	43	8.8
	Others	42	8.6
	Total	487	100.0
Lost	0	283	
Total		770	

The Chi-Square coefficient of Pearson has been carried out to determine the association between the sociodemographic variables and the satisfactory and unsatisfactory aspects of tourism, and the results are as follows:

♦ Age and satisfactory aspects: residents under the age of 20 (51.4%) value the fact that tourism generates employment and stimulates the economic growth of the destination.

♦ Native or non-native resident and satisfactory aspects: more than half of the natives (64.4%) have also mentioned as a positive aspect the generation of employment and the growth of the economy that is produced by tourism.

♦ Age and unsatisfactory aspects: almost the majority of those over 65 (40.9%) are bothered by pollution.

♦ Level of studies and unsatisfactory aspects: more than half of the respondents without studies (60.9%) are upset that tourism generates pollution.

Table 2.5: Chi square coefficient of Pearson. *Source:* Authors

Variables	Pearson Chi square contrast		
	c2	gl.	Sig. P.
Age and satisfactory aspects	24.875	12	0.015
Being native / non-native and satisfying aspects	14.261	4	0.007
Age and unsatisfactory aspects	50.595	18	0.000
Level of education and unsatisfactory aspects	47.328	18	0.000

Table 2.6: Place attachment

I am proud to live in Benalmádena	%	Native Resident	Non-Native Resident
Yes	83.7	92.3	82.4
No	4.5	1.9	4.9
I do not know	11.8	5.8	12.8

With regard to the level of place attachment to Benalmádena, we observe that it is very high in both natives and non-natives (Table 2.6). In the case of the natives, 92.3% of them feel proud of living in Benalmádena compared to only 1.9% who deny it. Among non-natives, the percentage of those who are proud is a little lower, 82.4%, although very high, with 4.9% of them do not feel attached. There are no significant differences between the two groups (Chi square = 2.17, p = 0.14). On the other hand, there is a significant relationship between "attachment to the place" and satisfactory aspects of tourism: of those residents who are proud of Benalmádena, the majority (50.8%) recognise the importance of tourism as a generator of employment and economic growth (Chi square = 37.945, p = 0.000).

Discussion and conclusion

The profile of the resident obtained in this investigation is: (i) under 20 years old; (ii) marital status: single, divorced or separated; (iii) level of studies: secondary; and (iv) non-native resident in Benalmádena.

In relation to the satisfactory aspects of tourism, the resident is aware of the economic benefit that tourism produces in the destination, which is why he has responded that it generates employment and benefits the local economy. Those under 20 years of age, as well as native residents, are the groups that have mentioned it the most. Younger residents could more easily find a temporary job than other age groups and therefore, they have evaluated the effect of tourism more favourably (Almeida-Garcia et al., 2016; Bujosa & Rosselló 2007). In the same way, the natives have responded that tourism generates employment and promotes the economic growth of Benalmádena. The natives have coexisted since the 1960s with tourism and have been able to convey the importance of tourism in the local economy, which is perhaps why they could be more aware of this benefit.

The most unsatisfactory aspect suggested was "tourism generates pollution, dirt and noise", which has been answered by the group that is over 65 years old and those that do not have education. These groups could have a more critical sense of this tourism effect or they could be more aware of this negative impact. In relation to age, these results are in line with the study by Haralambopoulos and Pizam (1996), which indicated that older residents had more negative attitudes towards tourism, in this case, towards the environmental impact. Regarding the level of education, the study reached the same conclusions as studies by Hernández and colleagues (1996) Kuvan and Akan (2005), which concluded that residents with lower levels of academic education are associated with the most critical view.

Residents in Benalmádena, both native and non-native, have very high levels of attachment to the place, although the population born in the municipality has a somewhat higher level. The level of attachment in Benalmádena is in line with the studies of McCool and Martin (1994), who identified that people living in destinations with a high level of tourism development have a stronger sense of attachment to the community. The new population that arrives in Benalmádena (more than half of the community has been living for less than 10 years) can quickly become attached to the community. These residents have previously made the choice to live in a place that provides them employment and climate comfort. Therefore, it is likely that residents with a high level of attachment have a fairly clear assessment of the positive and negative aspects of tourism development. This situation may be related to the notable development of tourism activity in a mature destination and the creation of greater social resilience in this type of destination. Most of the residents that are most proud of living in Benalmádena have answered that the main satisfactory aspect of tourism is related to the generation of employment and the increase of the local economy.

In summary, knowing the opinions of the residents on the effects of tourism in their city allows us to understand why the residents support or do not support tourist development. In this vein, new tourism models that minimise negative impacts and maximise support for tourism can be designed if the opinion of the local community is taken into account (Williams & Lawson, 2001; Vargas et al., 2007). The success of any tourism project can be threatened to the extent that it is planned and built without the knowledge and support of the host population.

Finally, the conclusions of this study could be summarised as follows:

◆ The profile of the typical resident in the destination is under 20 years of age, single, separated or divorced, with secondary education and not born in Benalmádena;

◆ The aspect of tourism that most satisfies the population of Benalmádena is the creation of employment and economic growth in the city;

◆ Residents noted that pollution, dirt and noise are aspects of tourism that bother them the most;

◆ Those under 20 years of age and Benalmádena natives are the groups that most mentioned as a satisfactory aspect the fact that tourism is the engine of the economy and a generator of employment.

◆ Those over 65 years of age and those who do not have education feel worried about or are bothered by the pollution generated by tourism.

◆ The Benalmádena population has a high level of place attachment.

Acknowledgements

This study is financed by the projects: "Tourism-phobia and tourism-philia. Conflicts between residents and tourism in the city of Malaga". Malaga University. Andalucía Tech; and "Transformations of the historic urban landscape induced by tourism: Contradictions and controversies, governance and governance" (CSO2016-75470-R). Ministry of Economy, Government of Spain

References

Aguiló, E., Barros, V., García, M.A. & Roselló, J. (2004). *Las actitudes de los residentes en Baleares frente al turismo*. Palma: Universidad de las Islas Baleares.

Akis, S., Peristianis, N. & Warner, J. (1996). Residents attitudes to tourism development: The case of Cyprus. *Tourism Management,* **17**(7), 481-404.

Alegre, J. & Juaneda, C. (2006.) Destination loyalty: Consumers' economic behavior. *Annals of Tourism Research,* **33**(3), 684-706.

Almeida-García, F., Peláez-Fernández, M.A., Balbuena-Vázquez, A. & Cortés-Macías, R. (2016). Residents' perceptions of tourism development in Benalmádena (Spain). *Tourism Management,* **54**, 259-274.

Andereck, K.L., Valentine, K.M., Knopf, R. C. & Vogt, C. A. (2005). Residents' perceptions of community tourism impacts. *Annals of Tourism Research,* **32**(4), 1056–1076.

Andereck, K.L. & Nyaupane, G.P. (2011). Exploring the nature of tourism and quality of life perceptions among residents. *Journal of Travel Research,* **50**(3), 248–260.

Andereck, K.L. & Vogt, C.A. (2000). The relationship between residents' attitudes toward tourism and tourism development options. *Journal of Travel Research,* **39**, 27-36.

Andriotis, K. & Vaughan, D.R. (2003). Urban residents' attitudes towards tourism development: The case of Crete. *Journal of Travel Research,* **42**(2), 172-185.

Antón, S. & González, F. (Coord.) (2008). *A propósito del turismo*. Barcelona: Editorial UOC.

Balmaceda, J.C. & Martín, M.C. (2004). *Félix Solesio. Fundador de Arroyo de la Miel*. Benalmádena: Excmo. Ayuntamiento de Benalmádena.

Belisle, F.J. & Hoy, D.R. (1980). The perceived impact of tourism by residents: A case study of Santa Marta, Colombia. *Annals of Tourism Research,* **7**(1), 83-101.

Besculides, A., Lee, M.E. & McCormick, P.J. (2002). Residents' perceptions of the cultural benefits of tourism. *Annals of Tourism Research,* **29**(2), 303-319.

Brunt, P. & Courtney, P. (1999). Host perceptions of sociocultural impacts. *Annals of Tourism Research,* **26**(3), 493-515.

Bujosa, A. & Roselló, J. (2007). Modelling environmental attitudes toward tourism. *Tourism Management,* **28**, 688–695.

Cerezo, J.M. & Lara de Vicente, F. (2005). El turismo como industria de España y de la Unión Europea. In G. López, J. Tomás & F. Lara de Vicente (Eds), *Turismo Sostenible: un enfoque multidisciplinar e internacional* (pp. 255-287). Córdoba: University of Córdoba.

Chen, J. S. (2000). An investigation of urban residents' loyalty to tourism. *Journal of Hospitality & Tourism Research, 24,* 5-19.

Cheer, J.M. & Lew, A.A. (Eds.). (2017). *Tourism, Resilience y Sustainability: Adapting to Social, Political y Economic Change.* London: Routledge.

Dachary, A.C. & Arnaiz, S.M. (2002). *Globalización Turismo y Sustentabilidad. Universidad de Guadalajara.* México: Editorial Pandora.

Davis, D., Allen, J. & Cosenza, R.M. (1988). Segmenting local residents by their attitudes, interests, and opinions toward tourism. *Journal of Travel Research, 28*(2), 2-8.

De Kadt, E. (1991). *Turismo: Pasaporte al desarrollo?* Madrid: Ediciones Endymion.

Diedrich, A. & García, E. (2009). Local perceptions of tourism as indicators of destination decline. *Tourism Management, 30,* 512–521.

Dyer, P., Gursoy, D., Sharma, B. & Carter, J. (2007). Structural modeling of resident perceptions of tourism and associated development on the Sunshine Coast, Australia. *Tourism Management, 28,* 409–422.

Gursoy, D., Jurowski, C. & Uysal, M. (2002). Resident attitudes. A structural modeling approach. *Annals of Tourism Research, 29*(1), 79-105.

Haralambopoulas, N. & Pizam, A. (1996). Perceived impacts of tourism: The case of Samos. *Annals of Tourism Research, 23,* 503–526.

Hernández, S., Cohen, J. & García, H. (1996). Residents' attitudes towards an instant resort enclave. *Annals of Tourism Research, 23,* 755–779.

Hidalgo, M. (2014). Operationalization of place attachment: A consensus proposal. *Studies in Psychology, 34*(3),251-259.

Hidalgo, M. & Hernández, B. (2001). Place attachment: Conceptual and empirical questions. *Journal of Environmental Psychology, 21,*273–281.

Instituto de Estadística y Cartografía de Andalucía (SIMA) (2016). *Sistema de Información Multiterritorial de Andalucía, SIMA.* Seville: Junta de Andalucía.

Instituto Nacional de Estadística (INE) (2017). Censo de Población y Viviendas 2011. Retrieved May 15, 2018, from http://www.ine.es/

Johnson, J.D., Snepenger, D.J. & Akis, S. (1994). Residents perceptions of tourism development. *Annals of Tourism Research, 21*(3), 629-642.

Jurowski, C., Uysal, M. & Williams, R. (1997). A theoretical analysis of host community resident reactions to tourism. *Journal of Travel Research, 36*(2),3-11.

Kajan, E. (2014). Community perceptions to place attachment and tourism development in Finnish Lapland. *Tourism Geographies, 16*(3),490-511.

King, B., Pizam, A. & Milman, A. (1993). Social impacts of tourism: Host perceptions. *Annals of Tourism Research, 20*(4), 650-665.

Kuvan Y. & Akan P. (2005). Residents' attitudes toward general and forest-related impacts of tourism: The case of Belek, Antalya. *Tourism Management,* **26**, 691–706.

Lankford, S.V. (1994). Attitudes and perceptions toward tourism and rural regional development. *Journal of Travel Research,* **32**(3), 35-33.

Liu, J. & Var, T. (1986). Resident attitudes toward tourism impacts in Hawaii. *Annals of Tourism Research,* **13**(2), 193-214.

Liu, J., Sheldon, P. J. & Var, T. (1987). Resident perception of the environmental impacts of tourism. *Annals of Tourism Research,* **14**, 17-37.

Mason, P. & Cheyne, J. (2000). Residents' attitudes to proposed tourism development. *Annals of Tourism Research,* **27**(2), 391-411.

McCool, S. & Martin, S. (1994). Community attachment and attitudes toward tourism development. *Journal of Travel Research,* **32**(3), 29-34.

McGehee, N. & Andereck, K. (2004). Factors predicting rural residents' support of tourism. *Journal of Travel Research,* **43**(2), 131–140.

Milman, A. & Pizam, A. (1988). Social impacts of tourism on Central Florida. *Annals of Tourism Research,* **15**(2), 191-204.

Murphy, P. E. (1983). Community attitudes to tourism, *Tourism Management,* **2**, 189-195.

Nunkoo, R. & Gursoy, D. (2012). Residents' support for tourism an identity perspective. *Annals of Tourism Research,* **39**(1), 243–268.

Oviedo, M. A., Castellanos, M. & Martin, D. (2008). Gaining residents' support for tourism and planning. *International Journal of Tourism Research,* **10**, 95–109.

Pulido, J. I. (2008). *El turismo rural.* Madrid: Editorial Síntesis.

Ramkissoon, H., Graham, L. & Weiler, B. (2013). Testing the dimensionality of place attachment and its relationships with place satisfaction and pro-environmental behaviours: A structural equation modeling approach. *Tourism Management,* **36**, 552-566.

Ritchie, J.R.B. (1988). Consensus policy formulation in tourism: Measuring resident views via survey research. *Tourism Management,* **9**(3), 199-212.

Saveriades, A. (2000). Establishing the social tourism carrying capacity for the tourist resorts of the east coast of the Republic of Cyprus. *Tourism Management,* **21**, 147-156.

Scannell, L. & Gifford, R. (2010). Defining place attachment: A tripartite organizing framework. *Journal of Environmental Psychology,* **30**, 1-10.

Scopelliti, M. & Tiberio, L. (2010). Homesickness in university students: The role of multiple place attachment. *Environment and Behavior,* **42**(3),335-350.

Sheldon, P.J. & Abenoja, T. (2001). Resident attitudes in a mature destination: The case of Waikiki. *Tourism Management,* **22**, 435-443.

Sirakaya, E., Teye, V. & Sönmez, S. (2002). Understanding residents' support for tourism development in the Central Region of Ghana. *Journal of Travel Research,* **41**(8), 57-67.

Smith, M.D. & Krannich, R.S. (1998). Tourism dependence and resident attitudes. *Annals of Tourism Research,* **25**(4), 783-802.

Snaith, T. & Haley, A. (1999). Residents' opinions of tourism development in the historic city of York, England. *Tourism Management,* **20**, 595-603.

Sociedad de Planificación y Desarrollo, (SOPDE) (1997). *El turismo residencial y de segunda residencia en la provincia de Málaga.* Málaga: Urania.

Teye, V., Sönmez, S.F. & Sirakaya, E. (2002). Residents' attitudes toward tourism development. *Annals of Tourism Research,* **29**(3), 668-688.

Tomljenovic, R. & B. Faulkner (2000). Tourism and older residents in a Sunbelt Resort. *Annals of Tourism Research,* **27**(1), 93-114.

Tosun, C. (2002). Host perceptions of impacts: A comparative tourism study. *Annals of Tourism Research,* **29**(1), 231–253.

Var, T., Kendall, K. W. & Tarakcioglu, E. (1985). Resident attitudes towards tourists in a turkish resort town. *Annals of Tourism Research,* **12**(4), 652-658.

Vargas, A., Plaza, M.A. & Porras, N. (2007). *Desarrollo del turismo y percepción de la comunidad local: Factores determinantes de su actitud hacia un mayor desarrollo turístico.* Madrid: XXI Congreso Anual de AEDEM.

Williams, J. & Lawson, R. (2001). Community issues and resident opinions of tourism. *Annals of Tourism Research,* **28**(2), 269–290.

Yoon, Y., Gursoy, D. & Chen, J.S. (2001). Validating a tourism development theory with structural equation modeling. *Tourism Management,* **22**(4), 363-372.

3 The relationship between servicescapes and tourists' evaluation of shops

Akira Uehara, Taketo Naoi and Shoji Iijima

The objectives of this chapter are to:

☐ Highlight how tourists' evaluation of shops is influenced by shops' features in various manners;

☐ Demonstrate how excessive interior manipulation (organization) showed negative effects on shops' touristic and active atmosphere;

☐ Evidence how the disorderliness of interiors might have been sensed as touristic and active aspects of the shops, implying the importance of sustaining a certain degree of naiveté;

☐ Highlight how shopkeepers' openness to tourists and the presentation of the lifestyle in the interiors and exteriors contributed to opportunities for tourists to experience local lifestyles;

☐ Demonstrate how the decorated interiors and assortment of touristic goods had negative effects on tourists' perception of the shops as places to experience local culture, whereas the organized interiors had positive effects on the same perception;

☐ Conclude that servicescape of shops should be considered depending on whether the place intends to foster tourists' shopping activities or enhance their experience of local culture.

Keywords: Servicescape, shopping, tourist behavior, experiences, perceptions.

Introduction

Shopping has been viewed as an important part of the tourism experience (Hsieh & Chang, 2006) and as a destination attraction (Timothy & Butler, 1995). It has been shown to be one of the major motivations for tourists (Turner & Reisinger, 2001; Wang, 2004). Apart from providing tourists with purchasing opportunities, shopping offers them a taste of local culture (Stobart, 1998). Experiencing a destination and its local culture has been pointed out as one of the key motives for shopping at a tourist destination; other motives include purchasing necessities and meeting social obligations (Murphy et al., 2011).

Retailers in an increasingly competitive marketplace find it more difficult to differentiate their stores solely on the basis of merchandise, price, promotion, and location (Baker et al., 1994). This implication highlights the importance of other factors, such as stores' environmental factors. Kotler (1973) argued that a store itself can offer a unique atmosphere or environment that may influence the consumer's patronage decision. Store environments have been found to be one type of input into the consumer's image of, or overall attitude toward, a store (Darden & Schwinghammer, 1985). Darden and Schwinghammer (1985) found that consumers' beliefs on the physical attractiveness of a store have a higher correlation with patronage intentions compared with merchandise quality, general price level, or selection.

The above observations on the importance of stores' physical environments can be understood with reference to the concept of man–environment research. Tourism phenomena, including tourist shopping, are argued to emerge from interacton between humans and environments (Walmsley & Jenkins, 1992). Man–environment research, a stream of environmental psychology, adopts transactionalism, which refers to a standpoint for emphasizing and examining the mutual relationship between humans and environments (Gifford, 2001). Such a stance takes importance particularly in understanding that tourists' shopping, in terms of their decision on their purchases at destinations, tends to be made *after* rather than *before* their arrival (Moore et al., 2012).

This chapter, which is the preliminary stage of a study on the effects of shops on tourists' evaluation of a destination, aims to elucidate the relationship between shops' characteristics and tourists' evaluation of the shops. The research relies on the concept of servicescape and measures the effects of shops' social, physical, and design factors on tourists' evaluation through an onsite participatory research method. This chapter pays particular attention to the taste of local life that tourists obtain from the shops. In light of the findings of Stobart (1998), it is meaningful to elucidate the features of shops that appear active and tourist friendly, which have been pointed out as significant factors in attracting tourists (Naoi et al., 2009) and ensuring that they experience local culture.

Literature review

Research on tourist-environment relationship in commercial spaces

Shopping in commercial spaces is one of the major motives of tourism (Choi et al., 1999; Cohen, 1995). Tourists purchase souvenirs and local specialties and pay for local dishes at restaurants. Timothy (2005) argued that tourists' shopping may not necessarily be only for purchasing goods but also for leisure activities. Butler (1991) classified tourists' shopping into two types: shopping for purchases and shopping as an activity that is secondary to excursions. Secondary shopping is regarded as observable, particularly when they visit a destination with primary attractions, such as cultural assets, rather than shopping opportunities. At such destinations, before or after visiting primary attractions, they may take opportunities to enjoy shopping at nearby shopping places with no predetermined plans about what and where to purchase.

While some parts of tourists' decision making, such as the length of their stay and their trip type, are usually done before their trip, others, such as those regarding tourists' onsite activities, are likely to be done after their arrival (Moore et al., 2012). Such tourists' onsite decisions may be affected by environmental factors. Gifford (2001), noted the possibility that spaces' characteristics may affect particular behaviors positively or negatively. This claim is regarded as applicable for relationships between tourists and destinations. Particularly, when tourists make an onsite purchase with no predetermined plans, their decision may be influenced by environmental factors, such as visually attractive signs, rather than information available at home. Moore et al. (2012) also suggested that tourists' onsite behaviors can be induced by not only pre-trip information, such as guide books, but also by the characteristics of visited environments.

The abovementioned man–environment research is considered as one of the academic areas on the relationship between tourists and places in commercial spaces. Approaches of this area have been intensively applied in the fields of civil engineering and architecture. Many studies in these fields have focused on the man–environment relationship in daily environments and analyzed the effects of environmental factors on individuals' movements (Hashimoto et al., 2009; Kiso & Monnnai, 2013; Tanaka et al., 2003). Meanwhile, few studies have focused on the relationship between tourists and places, and to the best of the current authors' knowledge, none of them have touched on the influences of detailed environmental factors on tourists' shopping.

Although there are previous tourism studies dealing with tourists' purchasing behavior, studies that asked respondents for evaluations of onsite environments are scarce. The dominant practices are face-to-face (Moore et al., 2012), mail (Fairhurst et al., 2007; Littrell et al., 2004), and web surveys (Choi et al., 2016). These studies examined tourists' pre-trip decision-making and their post-trip satisfaction, but not tourists' onsite evaluation of visited environments.

As for onsite studies on tourists' shopping experiences, Zaidan (2016) researched 527 foreign tourists' evaluation and perceived characteristics of luxury items sold at a shopping mall. Brida and Tokarchuk (2017) interviewed 886 tourists to investigate the relationship between their planned and actual expenditures. Suhartanto, Ruhadi, and Triyuni (2016) examined 563 visitors' perceptions and expectations of shopping attributes, including products' characteristics, services, convenience, and shop location. Despite the scope for investigation of tourists' characteristics owing to the large sample size, these studies have failed to shed light on the effects of environmental factors, such as individual shops' exteriors and interiors.

Turning further to consumer behavior studies on the effects of environmental factors on consumer buying behavior, there are studies that examined the effects of the layouts of a restaurant or the colors and brightness of lighting inside it (Ariffin et al., 2012) and the effects of music (Yalch & Spangenberg, 2000). However, most of them employed experimental settings. These have not been applied to on-site research, at least for investigating tourists' shopping. It is thus important to clarify the characteristics of shops that contribute to tourists' shopping and cultural experiences at non-tourist-oriented shops. Naoi et al. (2015) elucidated the features of touristic, non-touristic, and intermediary spaces in shopping districts, as perceived by local students. Uehara et al. (2017) further examined local students' perceptions of the characteristics of various spaces in a shopping district, focused on the relationship between the characteristics of commercial spaces and tourist activities undertaken by students there. However, these studies, which both pointed to the importance of non-touristic features for visitors' experiences, examined locals', and not tourists', perceptions of shopping places.

Characteristics of shopping places for tourists

Venues for tourists' shopping vary in form. While some shopping malls are designed primarily to accommodate tourists, other venues, such as supermarkets, do not cater particularly to tourists (Timothy, 2005). The latter can include tourist shopping habitats (Bloch et al., 1994), which vary according to the diversity of small shops reflected in their colors, scents, and sounds. These small businesses enhance the tourism experience by highlighting local customs and culture (Hsieh & Chang, 2006). The present study focuses on shopping streets, which are similar to tourist shopping habitats in that they comprise a variety of small shops owned by different owners. They were selected because, as explained in the next paragraph, differences between shops' touristic or non-touristic characteristics are the focus of this study.

The characteristics of shopping places can be summarized into three interacting spatial settings: landscape, streetscape, and servicescape. The landscape includes broader variables, such as scenery. The variables of streetscape concern the appearance of streets' features, such as paving, trees, signage, and street furniture. The servicescape includes social, physical and design, and ambient factors, such as product variety, shop keepers' attributes, shop layouts, and lighting (Murphy et al., 2011). The servicescape is perhaps the most pivotal to creating the environment of individual shops (Murphy et al., 2011).

This research is conducted based on the concept of servicescape. As the servicescape is the most specific to each shop and is likely to reflect the shop's characteristics intended for its target customers, including tourists and non-tourists, the focus on the servicescape is considered effective in capturing differences between touristic and non-touristic shops. However, it is difficult to measure ambient factors, such as hearing (sounds and tourists' voice) and smell (regional cuisine). This study thus focused on social as well as physical and design factors, which may affect tourists' evaluation of shops, to establish how these factors relate to tourists' evaluation.

On the characteristics of shopping spaces, Snepenger, Reiman, Johnson and Snepenger (1998) argued that the shifts in core clienteles from locals to tourists, in merchandise from mundane products to nonessentials and mementos, and in prices from affordable to unaffordable for most local residents may be viewed as signs that a shopping district is evolving into a tourist venue. Their claim accords with the findings of Naoi, Soshiroda, Iijima and Shimizu (2015), which analyzed local students' open-ended onsite evaluations of shops in the city center shopping streets in Naha City, Japan. Uehara, Naoi, and Iijima (2017) further conducted an onsite survey to analyze local students' perceptions of the characteristics of various spaces in the same shopping streets in Naha City, and then examined the relationship between the characteristics of commercial spaces and evoked tourist activities. However, the above studies examined only perceptions of spaces and not the influence of shops' characteristics on tourists' evaluation of shops.

Aims of this study

This study aims to elucidate the relationship between perceived shops' servicescape and tourists' evaluation of shops. This study puts particular emphasis on shops' touristic and non-touristic characteristics. The originality of this study lies in its attempt to examine the effects of tourists' onsite evaluation of shopping places from the perspective of the man–environment relationship. To highlight the environmental characteristics, this work adopted onsite research that asked participants to rate places actually visited.

Study sites

Several shopping streets near Kokusaidori Street, the main shopping street of Naha City, the prefectural capital of Okinawa Prefecture, Japan, were selected as the research area, because of the fame of the prefecture as a tourism destination and the mixture of touristic and non-touristic shops. Okinawa prefecture is in the subtropical climatic zone, whereas the four remaining main islands of Japan are in the temperate climatic zone (Kakazu, 2011). The prefecture ranked 2nd among Japan's 47 prefectures as a summer tourism destination (Japan Travel Bureau, 2009). Turning to the commercial aspects, many shops in these and other shopping streets close to Kokusai Dori Street have been used primarily for souvenir shops. However, Kinjyo's study (1996) reported a mix of shops targeting tourists and other locals.

As to the individual shops, Yamashiro et al. (2016) conducted an onsite survey that asked 10 local university students majoring in tourism to rate their impressions of the 186 shops in the same shopping streets on a 5 five-point scale. They selected 10 shops that were evaluated as touristic; 10, as particularly non-touristic; and another 10, as having both touristic and non-touristic characteristics.

Subjects

The sample comprised 16 university students majoring in architecture from Tokyo Metropolitan who were on their field trip. None of them had resided in the prefecture; 11 of them had visited Kokusai Dori Street before this study (four had visited once; seven had visited two to five times), five had never visited the street. There is a possibility that there is a difference between the subjects in their visiting experiences. This method was chosen to emphasize the structure of evaluating not only the subjects but also the perceived characteristics of the servicescape. However, the considerable time necessary for the implementation hampered the employment of general tourists. Indeed, this study's subjects may not be claimed to represent actual visitors in general because of the specific academic interest of the students.

Nevertheless, the students can be considered tourists because of the travel distance. By air, the students' travel time from Tokyo Metropolitan to Okinawa Prefecture took about two to three hours. Moreover, previous studies on man–environment that evaluate houses have often employed students majoring in architecture (Sanui & Inui, 1987; Maki et al., 1996). Moreover, the subjects were considered to be able to offer perspectives as tourists as none of them had ever resided in the prefecture; their specialty was also expected to help in offering insight into the features of the shops for this preliminary study. Thus, although the implied results may not be applied fully to tourists in general, they may still offer implications about tourists' evaluations, which can be tested by future studies.

Methods and materials

An onsite participatory study was conducted in shopping streets in Naha City, Okinawa Prefecture, Japan, from 11:00 to 13:00 on November 11, 2016. The areas surrounding Kokusai Street were selected. Although many shops in and adjacent to the street are primarily souvenir shops (Kim, 2009), other shops still sell local commodities and clothes. Sixteen university students, who were not from the prefecture, rated the designated 30 shops on 35 5-point bipolar scales.

Nine scales regarding the exteriors of the shops (Kimura & Yamamoto, 2005; Tanabe & Ooi, 2006; Tanaka et al. 2013) and nine other scales related to the interiors of the shops (Inagaki & Iijima, 2009; Takahashi & Oi, 2007; Fukuda & Yamada, 2007) were developed based on environmental psychological studies of shops. Eight scales concerning the assortment of merchandise and attitudes of staff were adopted from interpersonal impression studies (Kim et al., 2012; Yuksel, 2004; Swanson & Horridge, 2004) product attributes, and store attributes.

Table 3.1: Word pair and sources

Word pair	Sources
Exterior	
Exclusive – Inclusive	Tanabe & Ooi, 2006; Kimura & Yamamoto, 2005
Inconspicuous sign – conspicuous sign	Tanaka et al., 2013
Doesn't look old –Looks old	Tanaka et al., 2013
Hard to see people inside – Can see people clearly	Tanaka et al., 2013
Can't tell what kind of shop – Can tell what kind of shop	Tanaka et al., 2013
Outside color is dark – Outside color is bright	Tanaka et al., 2013
Unclear Okinawa decor – Clear Okinawa decor	Uehara et al., 2017; Tanaka et al., 2013
Not Okinawa style – Okinawa style	Uehara et al., 2017; Tanaka et al., 2013
Hard to go in – Easy to go in	Tanabe & Ooi, 2006
Interior	
Dim lighting – Bright lighting	Inagaki & Iijima, 2009
Cluttered – Organized	Tanaka et al., 2013
Dirty – Clean	Fukuda & Yamada, 2007
Simple – Decorated	Inagaki & Iijima, 2009; Tanaka et al., 2013
Unclear Okinawa decor – Clear Okinawa decor	Uehara et al., 2017; Tanaka et al., 2013
Not Okinawa style – Okinawa style	Uehara et al., 2017; Tanaka et al., 2013
Dark interior colors – Bright interior colors	Inagaki & Iijima, 2009; Tanaka et al., 2013
Chaotic – Sense of unity	Tanaka et al., 2013
Plain – Flashy	Tanaka, Uematu & Yanasse, 1989
Assortment of merchandise	
Aimed at locals – Aimed at tourists	Swanson & Horridge, 2006
Doesn't offer Okinawa speciality goods – Does offer Okinawa speciality goods	Swanson & Horridge, 2006
Prices seem cheap – Prices seem expensive	Choi et al., 2008; Yuksel, 2004
Attitude of staff	
Staff seem unfriendly – Staff seem friendly	Yamamoto, 1997; Choi et al., 2008
Seems hard to talk to staff –Seems easy to talk to staff	Choi et al., 2008
Don't feel positive towards staff – Feel positive towards staff	Choi et al., 2008
Staff seem gloomy – Staff seem cheerful	Choi et al., 2008
Staff seem unkind – Staff seem kind	Choi et al., 2008
Shop overall	
Ordinary – Extraordinary	Naoi et al., 2009
Can't experience Okinawa customs – Can experience Okinawa customs	Uehara et al., 2017
Gloomy – Cheerful	Kimura, 2014; Ogawa, 2016
Dull – Vibrant	Ogawa et al., 2016
Familiar – Original	Uehara et al., 2017
For locals – For tourists	Uehara et al., 2017; Naoi et al., 2009
Can't feel the Okinawa lifestyle – Feel the Okinawa lifestyle	Uehara et al., 2017
Conventional – Distinctive	Uehara et al., 2017
Unsettled – Calm	Ogawa et al., 2016

Nine scales related to the overall impressions of the shops were based on tourism studies on evaluations of destinations (Naoi et al. 2009; Ogawa et al. 2016; Uehara et al. 2017). Table 3.1 presents these scales.

Procedure

An onsite participatory study was conducted in the target shopping streets. The sessions were conducted on November 11, 2016. The subjects were asked to rate each of the 30 target shops using 35 5-point bipolar scales. The subjects were instructed to observe each shop for 30 seconds and then rate it.

Findings

Sixteen university students (10 males and 6 females in their 20s from Tokyo) rated the 30 shops on 35 5-point bipolar scales. The size of the data collected was 480. The size of the data used in the analysis after exclusion of the unusable responses was 308.

Factor analysis

Exploratory factor analysis (principal factor method with promax rotation) was conducted separately for the ratings on the scales regarding exteriors and interiors, assortment of merchandise, staff's attitudes, and overall evaluation, so that each factor had an Eigenvalue larger than 1.0. When a factor loading was positive, that factor is positively related to the rating closer to the word on the right side of each word pair. The largest absolute factor loadings exceeding .4 was understood as indicating sufficient loading onto a factor (Hair et al., 1992; Nunnally, 1978). Otherwise, the item was deleted in a stepwise manner. Table 3.2 presents the results of the factor analysis.

Exterior findings

The analysis generated two factors. The items 'Looks old,' 'Can see people clearly,' and 'Can tell what kind of shop' were deleted as they did not show sufficient loading. The distinctive items that loaded on the first factor were 'Clear Okinawa Décor' and 'Okinawa style.' The first factor was thus named 'Okinawa style (exterior).' The items that loaded distinctively on the second factor were 'Inclusive,' 'Conspicuous sign,' 'Outside color is bright,' and 'Easy to go in.' Therefore, the second factor was named 'Open (exterior).'

Table 3.2: Results of the factor analysis

Construct Item		1st factor	2nd factor	3rd factor	Variance explained	Eigen-value
Exterior appearance of the shop						
Okinawa-style (.940)[a]						
Okinawa decor unclear	/ Clear Okinawa decor	0.979	-0.042		43.525	3.005
Not Okinawa style	/ Okinawa style	0.843	0.039			
Open (.718) [a]						
Exclusive	/ Inclusive	-0.132	0.719		11.390	1.040
Inconspicuous sign	/ Conspicuous sign	0.025	0.666			
Outside color is dark	/ Outside color is bright	0.167	0.518			
Hard to go in	/ Easy to go in	0.137	0.486			
		Total variance explained			54.614	
Interior of the shop						
Decorated (.809)[a]						
Plain	/ Flashy	0.910	-0.028	-0.174	35.266	35.266
Simple	/ Decorated	0.781	0.004	-0.162		
Dark interior colors	/ Bright interior colors	0.582	0.096	0.200		
Dim lighting	/ Bright lighting	0.512	0.002	0.349		
Okinawa-style (.928)[a]						
Not Okinawa style	/ Okinawa style	0.012	0.960	0.007	17.455	1.951
Okinawa decor unclear	/ Clearly Okinawa decor	0.012	0.891	-0.018		
Organized (.722)[a]						
Cluttered	/ Organized	-0.148	-0.008	0.765	8.419	1.076
Chaotic	/ Sense of unity	-0.144	0.032	0.665		
Dirty	/ Clean	0.258	-0.064	0.611		
		Total variance explained			61.140	
The assortment of merchandise						
Goods for tourists (.715)[a]						
Aimed at locals	/ Aimed at tourists	0.747			55.831	1.559
Doesn't deal in Okinawa specialities	/ Deals in Okinawa specialities	0.747				
		Total variance explained			55.831	
The attitude of staff						
East to access staff (.910)[a]						
Seem hard to talk to staff	/ Seems easy to talk to staff	0.908			67.373	3.683
Staff seem unfriendly	/ Staff seem friendly	0.874				
Staff seem gloomy	/ Staff seem cheerful	0.781				
Staff seem unkind	/ Staff seem kind	0.767				
Don't feel positive to staff	/ Feel positive towards staff	0.763				
		Total variance explained			67.373	
Overall						
Touristic (.848)[a]						
Ordinary	/ Extraordinary	0.842	-0.022	-0.075	35.562	3.218
Conventional	/ Distinctive	0.743	-0.097	0.153		
For locals	/ For tourists	0.742	-0.019	-0.081		
Familiar	/ Original	0.740	0.117	0.031		
Activity (.798)[a]						
Gloomy	/ Cheerful	-0.001	0.894	-0.032	18.612	1.824
Dull	/ Vibrant	0.003	0.737	0.006		
Experiencing the Okinawa lifestyle (.761)[a]						
Can't feel the Okinawa lifestyle	/ Feel the Okinawa lifestyle	-0.079	0.002	0.881	9.117	1.072
Can't experience the Okinawa feel	/ Can experience the Okinawa feel	0.106	0.022	0.698		
		Total variance explained			63.292	

Interior findings

For this analysis, all items showed sufficient loading. This analysis generated three factors. The distinctive items that loaded on the first factor were 'Flashy,' 'Decorated,' 'Bright interior colors,' and 'Bright lighting.' This factor was named 'Decorated (interior)'. The items that loaded distinctively on the second factor were 'Okinawa style' and 'Clear Okinawa décor.' This factor was named 'Okinawa style (interior)'. The third factor was relevant to 'Organized,' 'Sense of unity,' and 'Clean,' and thus named 'Organized (interior)'.

Assortment of merchandise findings

The item 'Prices seem expensive' was deleted as it did not show sufficient loading. This analysis generated one factor, which was named 'Goods for tourists.'

Attitudes of the staff findings

All items showed sufficient loading. Analysis generated one factor. 'Seems easy to talk to the staff,' 'Staff seems friendly,' and 'Staff seems cheerful' were related to this factor, named 'Approachable staff'.

Overall evaluation findings

The item 'Calm' was deleted as it did not show sufficient loading. This analysis generated three factors. The distinctive items that loaded on the first were related to 'Extraordinary,' 'Distinctive,' 'For tourist,' and 'Original.' This factor was thus named 'Touristic.' The items that loaded distinctively on the second were 'Cheerful' and 'Vibrant.' Therefore, this factor was named 'Activity.' The third factor was relevant to 'Feel the Okinawa lifestyle' and 'Can experience Okinawa customs,' and was named 'Experiencing the Okinawa lifestyle.' The results are illustrated in Figure 3.1.

A stepwise multiple regression analysis was performed and used each factor's score of the overall evaluation as the dependent variables and the factors' scores of the remaining key variables as the independent variables. As a result, the ratings of 'Touristic' were found to be influenced positively by the scores of 'A shop's interior' (Decorated) and 'Assortment of merchandise' (Goods for tourists), as well as influenced negatively by the score of 'A shop's interior' (Organized) (Figure 3.2).

The scores of 'A shop's exterior' (Okinawa style and open), 'A shop's interior' (Decorated), 'Assortment of merchandise' (Goods for tourists), and 'Staff's attitude' (Approachable staff) positively influenced 'Activity,' whereas that of the 'A shop's interior' (Organized) negatively affected it (Figure 3.3).

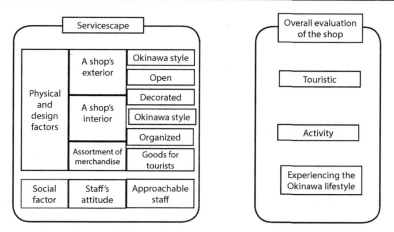

Figure 3.1: Results of the factor analysis

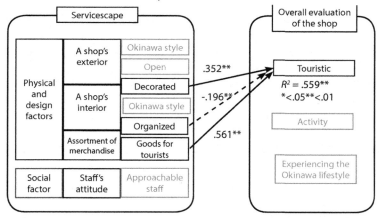

Figure 3.2: Results of the multiple regression analysis on 'Touristic'

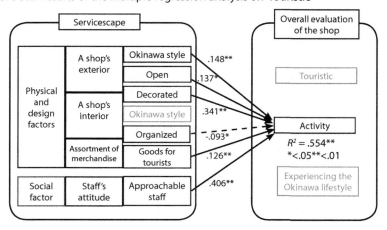

Figure 3.3: Results of the multiple regression analysis on 'Activity'

The score of 'Experiencing the Okinawa lifestyle' was positively affected by the scores of 'A shop's exterior' (Okinawa style), 'a shop's interior' (Okinawa style and Organized)' and 'Staff's attitude' (Approachable staff), and negatively affected by those of 'A shop's interior' (Decorated) and 'Assortment of merchandise' (Goods for touristic) (Figure 3.4). However, muticollinearity (VIF ≥ .5) was not observed (O'Bein, 2007).

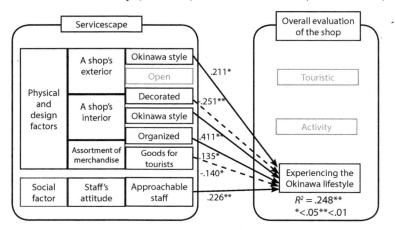

Figure 3.4: Results of the multiple regression analysis on 'Experiencing the Okinawa style'

Conclusion

The subjects' evaluation was found to be influenced by the features of the shops in various manners. First, commercial manipulations (interior decorations, products for tourists, and shopkeepers' openness to tourists) were found to contribute to the touristic and active atmosphere of the shops. A shop's exterior's openness and Okinawa style had a positive effect on the active atmosphere and were thus found to be beneficial in its formation. However, excessive manipulation (organization) of the shops' interiors was suggested to have a negative effect on their touristic and active atmosphere. The interiors' disorderliness might have been sensed as a touristic and active aspect of the shops, indicating the importance of sustaining a certain degree of quaintness.

Second, the presentation of the local lifestyle of the interiors and exteriors and shopkeepers' openness to tourists were contributing factors to providing tourists with opportunities to experience the local way of life. However, contrary to the effects of the decorated interiors and assortment of touristic goods on the shops' touristic and active senses, they were found to have a negative effect in that they may not offer tourist opportunities to experience the Okinawa lifestyle. In contrast, the organized interiors were suggested to have positive effects. Therefore, although the presentation of the local lifestyle and shopkeepers' openness to tourists are important for shops to function as places for tourists' shopping or appreciation of local culture, the decoration and organization of the interiors and assortment of touristic goods might be regarded as distracting from local authenticity. Thus, the servicescape of shops must be reconsidered carefully depending on whether the place intends to foster tourists' shopping activities or enhance their experience of local culture.

This chapter focused on the effects of detailed features of perceived servicescape on tourists' evaluation of the shops. These effects have been examined rarely in empirical investigations in the fields of tourism, consumer behavior, and man-environment research. Servicescapes may generate univalent impressions, which may have positive or negative effects on tourists' evaluation of shops depending on the evaluative dimension, such as touristic, active, or local-lifestyle-related sense. A focus on such complex tourists' evaluation of shops' servicescape is believed to offer practical insight for those who not only intend to attract visitors but also highly value the features that reflect the local lifestyle. In other words, this and future studies of a similar kind, which examine the man-environment relationship, may foster tourism that respects locals' values regarding their home places.

This study has two notable limitations, namely, the limited sample and target areas. As for the former, the scope of generalization of the results is limited because the sample is limited in terms of both size and variety. The limited target areas might also have resulted in the findings being not applicable to other cases, particularly as they may not consider the latter's environmental characteristics and the effects of tourists' experiences. In spite of these limitations, this study is significant because it examined complex and concrete characteristics of environments. For example, this study enabled the subjects to observe the attitudes of the staff and obtain their responses, the process of which is considered challenging when adopted in other types of experiments, such as slide experiments and general questionnaire surveys. Studies aiming for general conclusions that use large samples of actual tourists would be valuable. Nevertheless, considering the complexity of and diversity among tourism destinations and the complex human psychology and behavior, accumulating studies that focus on specific aspects of tourism destinations and tourists' responses would foster understanding of tourist psychology.

References

Ariffin, H.F., Bibon, M.F. & Abdullah, R.P.S.R. (2012). Restaurants' atmospheric elements: What the customer wants. *Procedia - Social and Behavioral Sciences*, **38**(December 2010), 380–387.

Baker, J., Grewal, D. & Parasuraman, A. (1994). The influence of store environment on quality and store image. *Journal of the Academy of Marketing Science*, **22**(4), 328–339.

Bloch, P.H., Ridgway, N.M. & Dawson, S.A. (1994). The shopping mall as consumer habit. *Journal of Retailing*, **70**(1), 23–42.

Brida, J.G. & Tokarchuk, O. (2017). Tourists' spending and adherence to shopping plans: The case of the christmas market in Merano, Italy. *Tourism Management*, **61**, 55–62.

Butler, R. W. (1991). West Edmonton mall as a tourist attraction. *Canadian Geographer*, **35**(3), 287–295.

Choi, M.J., Heo, C.Y. & Law, R. (2016). Developing a typology of Chinese shopping tourists: An application of the Schwartz Model of Universal Human Values. *Journal of Travel and Tourism Marketing*, **33**(2), 141–161.

Choi, W.M., Chan, A. & Wu, J. (1999). A qualitative and quantitative assessment of Hong Kong's image as a tourist destination. *Tourism Management*, **20**(3), 361–365.

Cohen, E. (1995). Touristic craft ribbon development in Thailand. *Tourism Management*, **16**(3), 225–235.

Darden, W.R. & Schwinghammer, J.K.L. (1985). The influence of social characteristics on perceived quality in patronage choice behavior. In *Perceived Quality: How Consumers View Stores and Merchandise*. Eds. J.Jacoby and J.Olson. Lexington, MA: Lexington Books, pp. 161–172.

Fairhurst, A., Costello, C. & Fogle Holmes, A. (2007). An examination of shopping behavior of visitors to Tennessee according to tourist typologies. *Journal of Vacation Marketing*, **13**(4), 311–320.

Fukuda, Y. & Yamada, Y. (2007). Impression of restaurants façade design during daytime and nighttime influencing on accessibility. *Summaries of technical papers of annual meeting Architectural Institute of Japan*. **7**, 41–42.

Gifford, R. (2001). *Environmental Psychology: Principles and practice (3rd ed.)*. Optimal books.

Hair, J.F., Anderson, R.E., Tatham, R.L. & Black, W.C. (1992). *Multivariate Data Analysis with Readings*. New York: Macmilian.

Hashimoto, Y., Ishiguro, K. & Monnnai, T. (2009). Survey of staying behavior as semiosis of man-environment system: Study on the semiosis of man-environment system in waterfront space in river Kamogawa, Kyoto (part1), *Transactions of AIJ, Journal of Architecture and Planning*. 705–706.

Hsieh, A.-T. & Chang, J. (2006). Shopping and tourist night markets in Taiwan. *Tourism Management*, **27**(1), 138–145.

Inagaki, T. & Iijima, S. (2009), Effects of gloss of finish and various elements on evaluation of the atmosphere and the choice of behavior. *Color Science Association of Japan*. **33**(4), 308–318.

Japan Travel Bureau. (2009). News release: *Kono Natu ni Ikitai nihon no Ryokosaki ha? [Where do you wish to visit in Japan this summer?]*

Kakazu, H. (2011). Sustainable island tourism: The case of Okinawa. In J. Carlsen & R. Butler (Eds), *Island Tourism: Sustainable perspectives (ecotourism)* (pp.171–185). Wallingford: CAB Intl.

Kim, S., Hirose, K., Imada, M., Yoshida, M., Matsuo, M. & Fujii, T. (2012) The association between personal attribution and interpersonal cognitive structure, *Information and Communication Engineers*, **112**(46), 97–102.

Kim, J. (2009). Retail system of Okinawa: The existence mechanism of commercial accumulation in Naha. *Okinawa. Regional Studies*, **5**,61–71.

Kimura, N. & Yamamoto, A.(2005). Comparative examination of townscape simulation technique: A case study in Wakamiya-oji, Kamakura-city, Japan. *Architectural Institute of Japan*. **F-1**, 239–240.

Kinjyo, H. (1996). The development of Naha Central Business District: On the store locations of Kokusai Shopping Street, *Shokei Ronshu*, **24**(1), 15–44.

Kiso, K. & Monnai,T. (2013). Modeling and simulations of human behavior semiosis based on protocol analysis: study on semiosis of human behavior afforded by architecture and urban space (part 3). *Transactions of AIJ, Journal of Architecture and Planning* **78** (687), 1003–1012.

Kotler, P. (1973). Atmospherics as a marketing tool. *Journal of Retailing*, **49**(4), 48–64.

Littrell, M.A., Paige, R.C. & Song, K. (2004). Senior travellers: Tourism activities and shopping behaviours. *Journal of Vacation Marketing*, **10**(4), 348–362.

Maki, K., Inui, M. & Nakamura, Y. (1996). Individual difference in streetscape evaluation. *Journal of Architecture, Planning and Environmental Engineering (Architectural Institute of Japan)*, **483**, 55–62.

Moore, K., Smallman, C., Wilson, J. & Simmons, D. (2012). Dynamic in-destination decision-making: An adjustment model. *Tourism Management*, **33**(3), 635–645.

Murphy, L., Moscardo, G., Benckendorff, P. & Pearce, P. (2011). Evaluating tourist satisfaction with the retail experience in a typical tourist shopping village. *Journal of Retailing and Consumer Services*, **18**(4), 302–310.

Naoi, T., Airey, D., Iijima, S. & Niininen, O. (2009). Evaluating historical districts: Exploring the use of photographs and slide experiments. *Tourism Analysis*, **14** (5), 587–603.

Naoi, T., Soshiroda, A., Iijima, S. & Shimizu,T. (2015). Local students' perceptions of spaces for tourists and locals in a shopping district: Photo-based research, *Marketing Places and Spaces (Advances in Culture, Tourism and Hospitality Research, Volume 10)*, 1–18.

Nunnally, J.C. (1978), *Psychometric Theory*, McGraw-Hill, NewYork.

O'Brien, R. M. (2007). A caution regarding rules of thumb for variance inflation factors. *Quality & Quantity*, **41**(5), 673–690.

Ogawa, M., T. Naoi. & Iijima, S. (2016). Effects of people in photographs on potential visitors' evaluations. In. M. Kozak & N. Kozak (Eds.), *Tourist Behavior: an International Perspective*, pp.168–176. Wallingford, UK: CABI

Sanui, J. & Inui, M. (1987). Subgrouping approach to the structural model of place evaluation: a study on the construct system associated with place evaluation: 2. *Journal of Architecture, Planning and Environmental Engineering (Architectural Institute of Japan)*, **374**, 54–60.

Snepenger, D.J., Reiman, S., Johnson, J. & Snepenger, M. (1998). Is downtown mainly for tourists? *Journal of Travel Research*, **36**(3), 5–12.

Stobart, J. (1998). Shopping streets as social space: Leisure, consumerism and improvement in an eighteenth-century county town. *Urban History*, **25**(01), 3–21.

Suhartanto, D., Ruhadi. & Triyuni, N. N. (2016). Tourist loyalty toward shopping destination: The role of shopping satisfaction and destination image. *European Journal of Tourism Research*, **13**(August), 84–102.

Swanson, K.K. & Horridge, P.E. (2004). A structural model for souvenir consumption, travel activities, and tourist demographics. *Journal of Travel Research*, **42**(4), 372–380.

Takahashi, H. & Oi, N. (2007). The aesthetic sense of values and evaluation structure in interior space. *Architectural Institute of Japan*. **615**, 59–64.

Tanabe, E. & Ooi, N. (2006), Easiness of entering commercial stores recognized from their façade designs *Architectural Institute of Japan*, **2**(45), 29–32.

Tanaka, K., Naoi, T. & Ai, H. (2013). Extraction and comparison of the objects of the tourist's gaze in a tourist areas and its circumference areas. *Proceeding of JITR Annual Conference*, **28**, 285-288.

Tanaka, M., Takeuchi, Y., Nishizawa, S. & Yamashita, T. (2003). Studies on the environmental behavior of the actual situation around moving and staying. *Transaction of AIJ, Journal of Architecture and Planning*, **572**, 49–53.

Timothy, D. (2005). *Shopping Tourism, Retailing and Leisure*. Tonawanda, NY: Multilingual Matters.

Timothy, D. J. & Butler, R. W. (1995). Cross-boder shopping. A North American perspective. *Annals of Tourism Research*, **22**(1), 16–34.

Turner, L.W. & Reisinger, Y. (2001). Shopping satisfaction for domestic tourists. *Journal of Retailing and Consumer Services*, **8**(1), 15–27.

Uehara, A., Naoi, T. & Iijima, S. (2017). Relationship between the characteristics of commercial and evoked tourist activities: Investigation about slide evaluation and their tourist activities image by university students majoring in tourism. *Man-Environment Research Association,* **38**(2), 1–10.

Walmsley, D.J. & Jenkins, J.M. (1992). Tourism cognitive mapping of unfamiliar environments. *Annals of Tourism Research*, **19**(2), 268–286.

Wang, D. (2004). Hong Kongers' cross-border consumption and shopping in Shenzhen: Patterns and motivations. *Journal of Retailing and Consumer Services*, **11**(3), 149–159.

Yamashiro, K., Uchima, M., Uehara, A. & Iijima, S. (2016). A study on tourism attractions of shopping street as to tourism destination. *Proceedings of JITR Annual Conference* **31**, 177–180.

Yalch, R. F. & Spangenberg, E. R. (2000). The effects of music in a retail setting on real and perceived shopping times. *Journal of Business Research*, **49**(2), 139–147.

Yuksel, A. (2004) Shopping experience evaluation: a case of domestic and international visitors. *Tourism Management,* **25**, 751–759.

Zaidan, E. A. (2016). Tourism shopping and new urban entertainment: A case study of Dubai. *Journal of Vacation Marketing*, **22**(1), 29–41.

4 Experiential components of tour guiding in package tours

Mustafa Ozdemir, Gurel Cetin and Fusun Istanbullu Dincer

The objectives of this chapter are to:

☐ Identify experiential components of guiding in package tours and measure their impact on tourist satisfaction;

☐ Determine and examine the role of tour guides and the contribution of guide's interpretation to the tourist experience and satisfaction;

☐ Identify experiential items of guided package tours on satisfaction and experience based on survey data informed by a qualitative phase;

☐ Explore the most salient guiding attributes among 26 experiential guiding items;

☐ Suggest practical implications for tour operator operations, guiding associations' certification, educational institutions' curricula and theoretical implications for experience and tourism literature.

Keywords: Guide experience, customer experience, tourist experience, tour guides, package tours, professional guides.

Introduction

Customer experience has been discussed as an important factor for organizational success. Positive experiences have the potential to create loyal customers and hence are acknowledged as a source of competitive advantage (Cetin et al., 2014). Organizational strategies have also evolved aiming to provide customer experiences rather than merely selling products and services (Pine & Gilmore, 1998). The evolution of customer experiences is more evident in the tourism industry (Karayilan & Cetin, 2016). Various research studies have confirmed that positive memorable experiences correlate with positive tourist behaviors (Buonincontri et al., 2017). Tourism is also defined as travelling for experiencing something different, escaping daily routines, living temporarily in a novel time and space, and a quest for the extraordinary (MacCannell, 1973).

Increasing welfare and growing economies make people financially richer but often poorer in time. Yet, fast changing lifestyles, intense work loads, the desire to award oneself and increasing expectations of people about using their scarce spare time more effectively result in travelers to seek experiential activities (Cetin, 2012). One of these experiential products in tourism are package tours. Guided package tours offer customers the chance to experience different destinations in a time effective and convenient way, and include major tourism services (e.g. lodging, transportation, sight-seeing, food and beverage). These package tours are also usually accompanied by a local (guide) who leads the way while informing the tourists (Mintel, 2010; Ryan, 1995; Sheldon & Mak, 1987). Mediated by a guide, package tours remove cultural and language barriers, striking a desirable balance between cultural exploration and familiarity. Experienced in the local way of doing things and familiar with the local itinerary, tour guides therefore are important front-line employees in organized package tours shaping tourist experiences in a destination (Wang et al., 2000). Guides' mediatory or interpretation roles and skills help tourists acquire unique and memorable experiences from the guided tour as well as from the destination. These positive experiences also play an important role in promotion of the destination through word of mouth (Cetin & Yarcan, 2017). As cultural brokers, guides also bring cultures together and minimize cultural distance.

Despite the importance of guides in the tourism system, their roles in creating positive tourist experiences have been neglected in the literature. Because package tours include various other tourism services they also offer a suitable background to study overall tourist experiences.

This study attempts to first identify experiential components of guiding in package tours through in-depth interviews with guided package tour participants. After these experiential items are identified, their importance and impact on satisfaction is measured using a questionnaire. The background of the study begins with defining the concept of customer experience and its importance, then tourist experiences are discussed and package tours and guides' role in tourist experiences are explored in the third section. Methodology describes the qualitative and quantitative stages of data collection, sampling and analysis. Findings and implications are discussed in the final two sections.

Customer experiences

Customer experiences have been approached from several dimensions in the literature. An experience can be defined as the fact or state of having been affected by an event or a stimulus which is subjectively unique, extraordinary, memorable, and that creates a desire to be shared by others (Aho, 2001; Arnould & Price, 1993; Merriam & Webster, 1993; Oh, Fiore & Jeoung, 2007; Pine & Gilmore, 1998, 1999). Furthermore, Hirschman and Holbrook (1982) discuss the concept of experience as personal events defined as "the state filled with emotion". According to Schmitt (1999), experiences are private events that occur in response to stimulation and that involve the entire being as a result of observing and participating in an event. Yuan & Wu (2008) defined the concept of experience as an ultimate outcome gained by consumers as a result of consuming the product and service. Experience is also defined as the positive emotional state of customers after having any sensation or knowledge acquisition resulting from some level of interaction with different elements of a context created by a service provider (Gupta & Vajic, 1999).

The markets are also discussed to be transforming from physical products and services to experiences. Pine & Gilmore (1999) offered the concept of the experience economy which replaced the delivery-focus of traditional rational approaches, with a customer-focused experiential hedonic perspective. Explaining the costumer behavior better, experiential marketing became a popular approach in marketing literature (Tsai, 2005). As a result, trying to reach and keep customers with traditional marketing methods started to lose importance and experiential marketing gained popularity. Customer experiences were categorised into four realms: education, escape, entertainment and esthetics (Pine & Gilmore, 1998). Organizations offering such features in their products and services create memorable experiences. These experiences in turn emotionally connect the customer to the brand and transform them into loyal customers (Williams & Buswell, 2003).

The tourist experience

Tourism is an experience intensive activity and it has been at the forefront of staging experiences (Cetin et al., 2014). As Sternberg (1997) asserted, "tourism primarily sells a 'staged experience' and tourism's central productive activity is the creation of the touristic experience". Visiting a particular tourist destination is typically motivated less by the elaborated physical characteristics of the site than by the powerful mental and emotional images the tourist has for the expected experience at the destination. Hence, the tourist seeks unique experiences beyond solely consuming touristic products and services offering functional value. This new quest for unique and memorable experiences requires the tourism service providers to adopt their products and services to create positive experiences (Oh et al., 2007).

Tourist experiences can be defined as extra-ordinary events that create positive emotional perceptions during a vacation. According to Pine and Gilmore (1998) experiences are economic offerings and they create a value for the customer. They also categorize experiences under four realms. Educational experiences are supposed to develop customers intellectually, esthetic experiences relate to appreciation of beauty and arts, escapist experiences refer to the desire to breaking-out from daily routines, and entertainment-related experiences express a state of joy and positive emotions. Cetin and Walls (2016) also stress that functional and physical features of products or services, because they might easily be copied, are not able to create sustained competitive advantage in tourism unless these are accompanied with unique experiences.

The tourist experience in guided tours

Previous studies focusing on tourist experiences were conducted in different service settings such as hotels, cruises, attractions, museums, restaurants and so on (Ali et al., 2016; Prebensen et al., 2017). Yet, because these studies have focused on individual services, they do not offer a comprehensive reflection. The variety of services and facilities included in package tours might provide a more holistic representation of tourist experience. Kucukaslan (2009) refer to the guided package tour as a social learning activity that includes visiting and experiencing various places, in a safe and convenient environment at a reasonable cost. Because these tours are usually guided by locals, they also offer local know-how, efficiency and safety (Cetin & Yarcan, 2017). The package tour was estimated to make 40% of the market by 2015 (Mintel, 2010).

As package tours are usually conducted in groups and involve various services (e.g. transportation, accommodation) in various different places, a representative of the tour organizer also accompanies the participants. This representative is responsible for coordinating different stakeholders and service providers, making payments on behalf of the tour operator, arranging timing, ensuring group cohesion, knowledge provision, mediation between tourists and the local culture and solving problems (Kizilirmak & Cetin, 2014; Tanguler, 2002). As a mediator of local culture, guides might also affect participant experiences in the destination and customize services according to cross-cultural issues (e.g. food) (Morgan & Xu, 2009). Despite their importance in tourism system, tour guides and their impact on tourist experiences have been overlooked.

Tour guides are not only responsible for information dissemination but also flow of the tour as promised by the tour organizer (Cetin & Yarcan, 2017). In package tours, tourists are captive within the prearranged spaces and timing, as are the guides, who stay with the group during most of the tour. Representing the tour operator, tour guides are also considered as frontline employees mediating between customers, service providers and the locals (Ap & Wong, 2001). Thus, tour guides become an important factor affecting package tour experiences. Tour guide representing locals also create an image of the destination (Huang et al., 2010) and remove most barriers associated with language (Wang et al., 2000) and unfamiliarity.

During a package tour the tourist absorbs the group activity while actively participating through interactive engagement in his/her mind and body (Oh et al., 2007) and thus improving his/her skills and knowledge by actively participating in educational activities in destinations. Moreover, Ap & Wong (2001) asserted that a tour guide's specialized linguistic knowledge contributes to the transformation of the travel experience into an educational experience. Furthermore, the tourist affects the overall experience and tour guides' performance, while actively participating the tour activity. The purpose of tourist participation in the tour activity thus becomes a temporary escape from daily life, to which the tourists return, feeling refreshed after experiencing the extraordinary (Pine & Gilmore, 1998).

The tourist also passively observes the activities and performance of the guide by utilizing his/her five senses at destinations (Oh et al., 2007). Moreover, the tour guide does not only possess specialized knowledge of the destination but also needs to convey the information in an understandable fun way. Therefore, guides need to have a good sense of humor to turn information processing into an enjoyable activity (Cohen et al., 2002). For example, the tour guide's archeological presentation of the ancient city of Troy might be more enjoyable when accompanied by mythological stories about Troy being occupied in a Trojan horse, tricking the defenders (Sahin &Yılmaz, 2009). A tour guide's ability to highlight the most important aspect of sites, attractions, cross-cultural issues, food, museums and so on allows participants to have the time to experience other things on their own (Oh et al., 2007) as well.

Tour guides also work as the mediator between the tourists' and hosts' cultures. According to Cohen (1985), the mediating function of a tour guide includes two components: social mediation and cultural brokerage. Social mediation involves helping tourists construct and thus makesense of their experiences, linking tourists to the local population and to tourist sites and facilities, and making the host environment non-threatening for the tourist. Cultural brokerage, as suggested by Cohen (1985), mainly involves provoking thought and helping tourists connect with host culture (Ham, 2002; Tilden, 1977). Cultural mediation is considered by Cohen as a primary role of the professional tour guide, and the second component of guide's mediatory role, and it is seen as vital to the quality of tourist experiences and a memorable tour (Cohen, 1985).

As a result of mutual interaction between tourists and local guides, tourists are living authentic experiences (Cetin & Okumus, 2018) gained by direct participation in package tour, and the tour guide has to be knowledgeable about the country's history, culture and architecture (Kuon, 2011) and so on. In this context, while participating in a package tour, tourists have been going through intellectual, authentic, entertaining and educational experiences. Besides, the staged tourist experience might be considered as a theatre scene which heavily depends on the performance of guide's professional representation and interpretation (Kuon, 2011). And thus being involved in the interaction with local culture the tourists live unique and memorable experiences during the package tour activity. Various studies discussed that the reason for selecting package tours by tourists is to have a guide who would provide detailed and artistic information about the destinations (Quiroga, 1990; Wang, Hsieh & Huan 2000).

Tanguler (2002) claimed that main tourist motivation in participating in guided package tours is to feel safe, to make use of the services of a specialized guide, to learn how to travel, to see different places and to shop and relax while doing so. Goldsmith and Waigand (1999) claimed that the tourists who have a quest for learning new things and making friends want to participate in guided package tours. Icoz (2000) claims that information conveyed by specialized tour guides is absorbed easier by tourists. Tetik's (2006) study conducted in Kusadasi revealed that tourists select guided package tours in order to learn the cultural and historical values and norms of Turkish people (Sahin, 2012). Consequently, guides and their services have important role in creating tourist experiences in package tours (Cohen et al., 2002).

Methodology

The primary aim of this study is to identify guide-related experiential factors and their impact on positive tourist behaviors in guided package tours. The first objective of identifying the experiential attributes of a guided tour was accomplished using a qualitative study. In-depth one-to-one interviews with 32 respondents who joined a package tour in Istanbul were conducted between April-June 2015, electronically recorded and transcribed for content analysis. Informants were asked about their definition of package tour experiences, their motivations to attend the tour, the guides' role in the overall package tour experience and the dimensions of their experiences. The open-ended questions used in the interview were created based on extensive literature as well as on a review of the literature on tourist experiences (Kuon, 2012). Though the interviews also explored the socio-demographic and trip characteristics, the primary enquiry was how tour guides contribute to tourists' experiences.

All interviews recorded were transcribed in the language (English) used in the interviews, coded, categorized and summarized for emerging patterns and themes that would inform the survey to be used at the quantitative stage (Kuon, 2012). Results were also compared with literature on the roles and responsibilities of guides and an item pool of 58 experiential items was created. The initial survey including these items was tested on 31 respondents and based on their feedback and analysis of the data, items that were perceived as irrelevant and with weaker loadings were removed from the survey. A total of 26 items were than used in the final version of the survey. 500 surveys were distributed between May-June 2016 in Istanbul to tourists participating in a guided package tour. A total of 151 valid questionnaires were collected. Istanbul can be considered as a suitable context to study guiding experiences as the city offers various heritage sites that are popular among cultural tourists (Cetin & Walls, 2016). Research findings are discussed in next section.

Findings

Among the 151 tourists participating in this survey, 90 were female. The majority of them (73) were married, 137 were university graduates and 91 of them were above the age of 35. The length of the package tour was more than a week for 112 of the respondents, the rest joined shorter package tours. Table 4.1 details the list of items and their importance as perceived by the respondents. Based on the respondent ratings, the highest rated items are guide's knowledge of local life-style, enjoyable personality of the guide, guide making the tour more fun to attend, guide's enthusiasm, and learning a lot from the guide. Thus the entertainment and educational experiences were rated more important, than the escapist and esthetic experiences provided by the guide.

Table 4.1: Descriptive statistics of experiential items in a guided package tour

Guided package tour experiential Items	Mean	Satisfaction
Guide was knowledgeable of local's lifestyle.	4.59	0.43**
The personality of the tour guide made us enjoy the trip.	4.55	0.60**
Guide made the tour more fun to attend.	4.54	0.61**
Guide was enthusiastic about his job.	4.50	0.56**
I learned a lot listening to the guide.	4.48	0.56**
Guide was able to identify various characteristics of the destination.	4.47	0.58**
Guide was able to communicate in an effective way.	4.45	0.58**
Guided tour was more educational than regular tours.	4.43	0.53**
Interesting facts provided by the guide made me learn new things.	4.42	0.54**
Guide told us stories that were both educational and entertaining.	4.41	0.47**
Guide behaving like a friend made the tour more enjoyable.	4.40	0.46**
Guide led us to places that we would not go individually.	4.39	0.61**
Guide possessed sophisticated knowledge.	4.38	0.58**
Guide's communication skills were adequate.	4.38	0.64**
Guide experience has made me learn something of importance.	4.37	0.55**
Guide's language skills were adequate.	4.37	0.58**
Guide was able to represent the locals.	4.37	0.61**
Guide's personal appearance was neat and appropriate.	4.36	0.57**
Guide's stories and personal tales made me to enjoy the site.	4.35	0.55**
Guiding tour was entertaining.	4.34	0.38**
Guide's interpretation made me imagine the history.	4.32	0.52**
Guide has changed my previous image of the destination.	4.31	0.53**

Guide interpretation has made me appreciate design details at tourist attraction.	4.29	0.51**
Guide's interpretation allowed us to see various artistic details.	4.27	0.52**
Guide interpretation raised my curiosity to learn new things.	4.26	0.47**
Guide improved my sense of escape, from the daily routine.	4.21	0.62**

**Correlation is significant at p<0.01 level (two tailed).

Table 4.1 also displays each factor's relationship with satisfaction. All items had a positive correlation with satisfaction on p<0.01 level. Factors with a higher relationship with guided tour satisfaction levels of respondents were listed as: guide's communication skills (r = 0.64), guide's contribution to sense of escape (r = 0.62), guide's representation of locals (r = 0.61), guide's ability to show the unseen (r = 0.61), guide's ability to create a fun environment (r = 0.61) and guides having an enjoyable personality (r = 0.60). In order to identify which experiential items have a linear impact on satisfaction from the guided tour, a regression analysis was also utilized. As shown in Table 4.2, the variance in satisfaction (R^2 = 0,64), can be explained by five factors out of 26 items. These are guide's communication skills (β = 0.21), sense of escape from daily routine (β = 0.35), guide's interpretation made us see various artistic details (β = 0.24), learned a lot listening to the guide (β = 0.14) and guide made the tour more fun to attend (β = 0.14).

Table 4.2: Results of regression explaining the impacts of experiential items on satisfaction.

Independent variables	B	SE	B	T	Sig.
Constant	0.01	0.27		0.52	0.95
Experiential Components					
Guide's communication skills were adequate.	0.22	0.06	0.21	3.74	0.00**
Guide improved my sense of escape from daily routine.	0.22	0.05	0.35	4.81	0.00**
Guides interpretation made us see various artistic details.	0.22	0.06	0.24	3.97	0.00**
I learned a lot listening to the guide.	0.18	0.06	0.14	3.00	0.00**
Guide made the tour more fun to attend.	0.17	0.07	0.14	2.50	0.01**

Note: B = Coefficient; SE = Standard Error; β = Standardized Coefficient; t = t-Value; Sig. = Significance, Dependent Variable: Satisfaction; R = 0.797; R^2 = 0.635; Adjusted R^2 = 0.625; Standard Error = 0.422.

Insignificant items were excluded in this table.

*Significant at p<0.05 level. **Significant at p<0.01 level.

Conclusion

Despite the fact that package tours constitute a significant part of the tourism industry, with tour guides important stakeholders within the tourism system, the impact of tourist guides on package tour experiences has been neglected in academic research. Mediating between the guests, hosts, suppliers and the tour operator, tour guides are responsible for the flow of the tour, information dissemination, group cohesion, coordination, timing and so on. Hence they have an important role in the creation of positive guest experiences and satisfaction (Cetin & Yarcan, 2017). They also represent the tour operator and locals to tourists. This study, using a mix of methods, identified 26 guiding attributes that affect the guest experiences in package tour environment and measured their importance and relationship with satisfaction. Findings confirm the importance of guiding attributes on package tour satisfaction.

The communication skills of the guides, their personality, ability to create a sense of escape, represent the locals and show the unseen were items with larger loadings. Communication skills, ability to create a sense of escape, to be able to interpret various artistic details, ability to teach and creating a fun environment were identified as the factors that explain the variance satisfaction levels. These findings have implications for the design of package tours and selection of tour guides. The contents of the package tours should include more authentic items that would make tourists feel that they are in a different place. Guides also need to have extensive and attractive knowledge about the destination. Their personality is also significant; although intellectual needs are important for participants, entertainment and fun were also mentioned. An enjoyable and humorous personality might also be considered as important guide attributes.

Concerning theoretical contributions, this study confirmed that educational, entertainment, escapist and esthetic experience attributes might be used in a guided package tour environment to measure satisfaction. Yarcan (2007) also discusses sophisticated knowledge and information dissemination as important guide features. Cohen (1979) discusses spending quality time away from daily life as the main motivation for travel, which refers to escape. Guides' animator role was also mentioned as important by Wong and Wang (2009), referring to the entertainment sphere. Finally, esthetic details and the importance of arts and harmony were discussed by Cetin and Dincer (2014). Another implication is the training and education of the guides. The majority of respondents complained about gaps in curricula in tour guiding education and lack of standards among the guides themselves. Guiding as a profession, certification and remuneration are also related to the structure of the industry as an external factor that needs a collective effort to change. Ap and Wong (2001) stress the role of governments and the tourism industry to solve the challenges guides face in their profession.

There are various limitations to this study. The study was conducted in Istanbul, which is a cultural destination (Okumus & Cetin, 2018). Although the majority of guided package tours are designed as cultural tours there might be other motivations involved. For example, in an adventure tour different guide attributes might emerge as more important. Importance of information dissemination and knowledge of local culture might be replaced by path finding and knowledge of flora and fauna in a nature based tour package. Karamustafa and Cesmeci (2006) claim that tour guides should be empowered to adjust the tour program based on external and internal factors. Thus the group dynamics might also affect the tourist experience. Yarcan (2007) dicuss that tour guides should be informed about the profile of the group and involved in the development of the itinerary by tour operators for a more successful operation. Future studies would use the experiential items suggested in this study to group them into various groups of tour guide attributes (e.g. inherited, developed) and apply them into different settings. In summary:

♦ The study explored the role of guides in tourist experiences during package tours.

♦ The study revealed that all educational, esthetic, entertainment and escapist experiences are relevant in package tours.

♦ The communication skills of the guides, their personality, ability to create a sense of escape, represent the locals and show the unseen were experiential guiding characteristics with larger loadings.

♦ Communication skills, ability to create a sense of escape, ability to interpret various artistic details, ability to teach and creating a fun environment were identified as the guide-related roles that explain the variance satisfaction levels.

♦ The local knowledge of the guide listed highest among mean values which also refer to the importance of cross-cultural issues.

♦ The study offers various important implications on guiding profession, training and hiring professional tour guides.

References

Aho, S.K. (2001). Towards a general theory of touristic experiences: Modeling experience process in tourism. *Tourism Review,* **56**(3 & 4), 33-37.

Ali, F., Amin, M. & Cobanoglu, C. (2016). An integrated model of service experience, emotions, satisfaction, and price acceptance: an empirical analysis in the Chinese hospitality industry. *Journal of Hospitality Marketing & Management,* **25**(4), 449-475.

Ap, J. & Wong, K. K. F. (2001). Case study on tour guiding: Professionalism, issues and problems. *Tourism Management,* **22**, 551-563.

Arnould, E. J. & Price, L. L. (1993). River magic: Extraordinary experience and the extended service encounter. *Journal of Consumer Research,* **20**(1), 24-45.

Buonincontri, P., Morvillo, A., Okumus, F. & van Niekerk, M. (2017). Managing the experience co-creation process in tourism destinations: Empirical findings from Naples. *Tourism Management,* **62**, 264-277.

Cetin, G. (2012). Konaklama Isletmelerinde Musteri Deneyiminin Sadakat ve Tavsiye Davranisina Etkisi (In Turkish). Master Thesis, Istanbul University, Institute of Social Sciences.

Cetin, G., Akova, O. & Kaya, F. (2014). Components of experiential value: Case of hospitality industry. *Procedia-Social and Behavioral Sciences,* **150**, 1040-1049.

Cetin, G. & Dincer, F.I. (2014). Influence of customer experience on loyalty and word-of-mouth in hospitality operations. *Anatolia,* **25**(2), 181–194.

Cetin, G. & Okumus, F. (2018). Experiencing local Turkish hospitality in Istanbul, Turkey. *International Journal of Culture, Tourism and Hospitality Research,* **12**, 223-237.

Cetin, G. & Walls, A. (2016). Understanding the customer experiences from the perspective of guests and hotel managers: Empirical findings from luxury hotels in Istanbul, Turkey. *Journal of Hospitality Marketing & Management,* **25**, 395-424.

Cetin, G. & Yarcan, S. (2017). The professional relationship between tour guides and tour operators. *Scandinavian Journal of Hospitality and Tourism,* **17**(4), 345-357.

Cohen, E. (1979). A phenomenology of tourist experiences. *Sociology,* **13**(2), 179-201.

Cohen. E. (1985). The tourist guide: The origins, structure and dynamic of a role. *Annals of Tourism Research,* **12**, 5-29.

Cohen, E., Ifergan, M. & Cohen, E. (2002). A new paradigm in guiding the Madrich as a model. *Annals of Tourism Research,* **29**(4), 919-932.

Goldsmith, C.S. & Waigand, H. (1989). *Building Profits with Group Travel*, San Francisco: Dendrobium Books.

Gupta, S. & Vajic, M. (1999). The contextual and dialectical nature of experiences. In J. Fitzsimmons & M. Fitzsimmons (Eds.), *New service development*, pp. 33-51. Thousand Oaks, CA: Sage.

Ham, S. (2002). Meaning making: The premise and promise of interpretation. Keynote address to Scotland's First National Conference on Interpretation, Royal Botanic Gardens, Edinburg.

Hirschman, E.C. & Holbrook, M.B. (1982). Hedonic consumption: Emerging concepts, methods and propositions. *Journal of Marketing*, **48**(3), 92-101.

Huang, S., Hsu, C. & Chan, A. (2010). Tour guide performance and tourist satisfaction: A study of the package tours in Shanghai, *Journal of Hospitality & Tourism Research*, **34**(3), 3-33.

Icoz, O. (2000). Seyahat Acentaları ve Tur Yönetimi, Turhan Kitabevi, Ankara.

Karamustafa, K. & Çeşmeci, N. (2006). Paket Tur Operasyonunda Turist Rehberlerinin Karşılaştıkları Yönetsel Sorunlar Üzerine Bir Araştırma. *Anatolia: Turizm Arastirmalari Dergisi*, **17**(1), 70-86.

Karayilan, E. & Cetin, G. (2016). Tourism Destination: Design of Experiences. In *The Handbook of Managing and Marketing Tourism Experiences*. Sotiriadis, M. & Gursoy, D. (Eds.) Emerald Group Publishing Limited, pp. 65-83.

Kizilirmak, I. & Cetin, G. (2014). The characteristics of Ahilik in Grand Bazaar and implications on tourism experience. In Bansal, S., Walia, S. & Rizean, A. (eds.), *Tourism Present and Future Perspective*. New Delhi: Kanishka Publishers, pp. 282-289.

Kucukaslan, N. (2009). *Seyahat Isletmelerinde Tur Planlaması ve Tur Yönetimi*. Istanbul: Alfa Aktüel Yayıncılık.

Kuon, Vannsy (2011). *The Pursuit of Authenticity in Tourist Experiences: The Case of Siem Reap-Ankgor, Cambodia*, Master Thesis of Tourism Management of Lincoln University.

MacCannell, D. (1973). Staged authenticity: Arrangements of social space in tourist settings. *The American Journal of Sociology*, **70**(3): 589-603.

Merriam-Webster. (1993). *Merriam-Webster's Collegiate Dictionary* (10 ed.). Springfield, MA: Merriam-Webster, Inc.

Mintel. (2010). Package Holidays - UK - July 2010 Retrieved 1 September 2010, from http://academic.mintel.com/sinatra/oxygen_academic/search_results/show&/display/id=479781

Morgan, M. & Xu, F. (2009). Student travel experiences: Memories and dreams. *Journal of Hospitality Marketing and Management*, **18**(2/3), 216-236.

Oh, H., Fiore, A.M. & Jeoung, M. (2007). Measuring experience economy concepts: Tourism applications. *Journal of Travel Research,* **46**, 119-132.

Okumus, B. & Cetin, G. (2018). Marketing Istanbul as a culinary destination. *Journal of Destination Marketing & Management, 9, 340-346.*

Quiroga, I (1990). Characteristics of package tours in Europe. *Annals of Tourism Research,* **17**, 185-207.

Pine, J. & Gilmore, J.H. (1998). Welcome to the Experience Economy. *Harvard Business Review,* 97-105.

Pine, B.J. & Gilmore, J.H. (1999). *The Experience Economy: Work is Theatre and Every Business a Stage.* Boston: Harvard Business Press.

Prebensen, N. K., Chen, J. S. & Uysal, M. S. (Eds.). (2017). *Co-creation in Tourist Experiences.* Taylor & Francis.

Ryan, C. (1995). Learning about tourists from conversations: The over-55s in Majorca. *Tourism Management,* **16**(3), 207-215.

Schmitt, B. (1999). *Experiential Marketing.* New York: The Free Press.

Sheldon, P.J. & Mak, J. (1987). The demand for package tours: A mode choice model. *Journal of Travel Research,* **25**, 13-17.

Sternberg, E. (1997). The iconography of the tourism experience. *Annals of Tourism Research,* **24**(4): 951–69.

Sahin, K. & Yilmaz, G., (2009). Tourism quest and planning based on natural sources in the City of Samsun. *Uluslararası Sosyal Araştırmalar Dergisi.* 2(7), 218-231.

Sahin Sen, S. (2012). *Turist Rehberlerinin Kültürlerarası İletişim Yeterlilikleri: Alman, İngiliz ve Rus Turistlerin Algılamaları,* Doktora Tezi, Balıkesir Üniversitesi Sosyal Bilimler Enstitüsü.

Tanguler, A. (2002). *Profesyonel Turist Rehberliği ve Profesyonel Turist Rehberlerinin Seyahat Acentası ve Müşteri İlişkileri: Kapadokya Örneği.* Hacettepe Üniversitesi Sosyal Bilimler Enstitüsü.

Tetik, N. (2006). *Türkiye'de Profesyonel Turist Rehberliği ve Müşterilerin Turist Rehberlerinden Beklentilerinin Analizi (Kuşadası Örneği),* Yüksek Lisans Tezi, Balıkesir Üniversitesi Sosyal Bilimler Enstitüsü, Balıkesir.

Tilden, F. (1977). *İnterpreting our Heritage.* Chapel Nill, NC: Univeristy of North Carolina Press.

Tsai, S. (2005). *Integrated Marketing as Management of Holistic Consumer Experience.* Business Horizons.

Wang, K.-C., Hsieh, A.-T. & Huan, T.-C. (2000). Critical service features in group package tour: An exploratory research. *Tourism Management,* **21**, 177-189.

Williams, C. & Buswell, J. (2003). *Service Quality in Leisure and Tourism.* Oxon: CABI Publishing.

Wong, J.-Y. & Wang, C.-H. (2009). Emotional labor of the tour leaders: An exploratory study. *Tourism Management*, **30**, 249-259.

Yarcan, S. (2007). Profesyonel Turist Rehberliğinde Mesleki Etik Üzerine Kavramsal Bir Değerlendirme, *Anatolia: Turizm Araştırmaları Dergisi*, **18**(1), 33-44.

Yuan, Y.-H.E. & Wu, C.K. (2008). Relationships among experiential marketing, experiential value, and customer satisfaction. *Journal of Hospitality & Tourism Research*, **32**(3), 387-410

5 Terrorism and tourism revisited

Cláudia Seabra

The objectives of this chapter are to:

☐ Demonstrate that international terrorism and tourism share some characteristics in that they cross and go beyond national borders, involve citizens from different countries and use the latest travel and communication technologies;

☐ Show how terrorists often use tourism in order to gain the publicity and support needed to achieve their goals;

☐ Highlight that tourists are often chosen as targets for their symbolic value with terrorists turning them into valuable assets to be explored.

Keywords: terrorism, tourism industry, safety, security, risk perception, terrorism attacks

---

Introduction

Tourism activity is perhaps the best example of the experience economy (Quan & Wang, 2004), as the experience is the core product in the travel industry (Tsaur et al., 2007). Tourists are customers emotionally as well as rationally compelled (Schmitt, 1999), concerned with accomplishing pleasurable and memorable experiences. More than products, tourists desire satisfying experiences (Tsaur et al., 2007). Terrorism and the perceived risk associated with attacks can damage the image of destinations and therefore can affect negatively tourism experiences and behaviors (Seabra et al., 2014).

Tourism demand is particularly sensitive to tourists' concerns about their safety, health and well-being (Blake & Sinclair, 2003). However, although natural disasters have a significant impact on tourists' behaviors, terrorist attacks have a more intimidating role for tourists (Sönmez, 1998). In fact, risk perceptions on personal safety can be a crucial factor influencing the image, and the choice of a destination. Some studies go even further, confirming that a terrorist act can influence negatively not only the image of the affected destination, but also of the neighboring sites, leading to a negative global image in an entire region (Kozak et al., 2007). In addition, past research concluded that risk perception in travelling is crucial in travel planning behavior independently of tourists' cultural background and country of origin (Seabra et al., 2013). In fact tourists from countries with different levels of safety consider travel safety as a critical issue and that it influences directly international trip decisions and behaviors, especially in what regards to terrorism and political instability risk (Seabra et al., 2018).

Terrorism has become an important and recurring topic in the public discourse in the 21st century. In its domestic and international form, it is carried out by revolutionary groups and vigilantes, being a constant in modern societies (Feichtinger et al., 2001). In these last few decades, terrorism has entered in the media discourse – and at the same time into public opinion – causing a feeling of general insecurity and unsafety in people's daily life everywhere, anytime (Seabra et al., 2014). In fact, terrorists are very conscious of the importance of public opinion, planning their attacks accordingly by "choosing the time, location or target that will make the strongest impact on the public" (Malečková & Stanišić, 2014: 632). Terrorists continue to select vulnerable and defenseless targets (Atkinson et al., 1987) to achieve their goals.

Tourists have been examples, in recent years, of this vulnerability and represent targets that have become more and more desirable (Seabra et al., 2014). A terrorist attack targeting tourists can help its authors to achieve several objectives: advertising, economic threat, and ideological opposition to tourism, among others (Sönmez, 1998). The awareness of the human costs associated with the recent terrorist events and the redirection of economic resources, presumably driven by perceived risks associated with future terrorist incidents, have led to a concentration of efforts, by various tourism organizations, to improve their understanding of terrorism and of its consequences on this industry (Blomberg et al., 2004).

The tourism industry is one of the activities that suffer most from terrorist activity. "The adverse economic effects of terrorism on the tourism sector are felt by all countries where terrorist attacks occur, regardless of whether or not these incidents are aimed at tourists" (Institute for Economics & Peace, 2016: 67). Terrorism targeting the tourism sector represents heavy costs directly by decreasing tourist arrivals and receipts, which will affect and cause a decrease in those countries' GDP; indirectly employment in tourism and other related industry sectors will decrease as well (Institute for Economics & Peace, 2016).

In this context, the increased exposure to significant political, economic, social and technological losses and the terrorist threat lead to a higher vigilance from tourism companies and managers so they might be able to deal with impending crises. The understanding of the terrorism phenomenon and of its impacts makes it possible to develop more effective strategies to stop or reduce the severity of their impacts, both on the economy and on society (Ritchie, 2004). Based on an extensive literature and data analysis, this chapter's main goal is to make an important contribution to science and management by analyzing the terrorism phenomenon, specifically its connection with the tourist industry. It is our aim to update the pioneer work of Sönmez (1998) and help to connect the dots between terrorism and tourism, answering the question: what connects tourism and terrorism?

Terrorism: A puzzling phenomenon

Terrorism is a puzzling phenomenon that has attracted researchers' attention in various study fields. Hoping to understand and control these occurrences, as well as their adverse effects, governments, organizations and academic communities have made efforts to understand it. However, this is not a simple task. The topic is so troublesome and studied in so many perspectives that conceptually there is no universally accepted definition for terrorism (Poland, 1988). The often-quoted cliché that "one person's terrorist is another person's freedom fighter" shows the different points of view and the definition problems that this concept entails (Sönmez & Graefe, 1998b). The definition of terrorism has raised quite a buzz among researchers and organizations over the years. There is no unanimity on the definition only "the lack of consensus in the literature on the determinants of terrorism" (Savun & Phillips, 2009: 879). The following table systematizes some of the various definitions that have been proposed over the last three decades for the terrorism concept.

Table 5.1: Definitions of terrorism

National Consortium for the Study of Terrorism and Responses to Terrorism[1] (2016)
The threats or actual use of illegal force and violence by a non-state actor to attain a political, economic, religious, or social goal through fear, coercion, or intimidation.
Fenstermacher, Kuznar, Rieger and Speckhard (2010)
Fundamentally, terrorism occurs when non-state organizations employ violence for political purposes and when the target of that violence is civilian (or military in non-combat settings), and the immediate purpose is to instill fear in a population.
Scheffler (2006)
Terrorism is a prima facie evil, and that the use of terrorist tactics is presumptively unjustified, it may sometimes be a response to policies that are also unjustified and which may be as objectionable as the terrorist response itself.
Goldblatt and Hu (2005)
Illegal usage of force or acting of violence against persons or their properties in order to intimidate its own Government, the citizenship or any other segment of society.
Tavares (2004)
Terrorist activities are expressions of the demand for change of certain groups who are dissatisfied with the political status-quo and who have abandoned the constitutional means.
UN Security Council (2004)
Criminal acts, including those carried out against civilians, committed with the intent to cause death or serious bodily injury, or taking of hostages, with the purpose to provoke a state of terror in the general public or in a group of persons or particular persons, intimidate a population or compel a government or an international organization to do or to abstain from doing any act.
Fullerton, Ursano, Norwood and Holloway (2003)
The most powerful way to generate psychological fear, apprehension and disruption in the functioning of societies and communities.
Radu (2002)
Any attack or threat of attack against unarmed targets with the objective of influence, change or condition major policy decisions. The attacks are mostly against large civilians targets to create fear.
Enders and Sandler (2002)
Use of threat or use of premeditated violence or unusual brutality by sub-national groups to achieve political, religious or ideological goals through intimidation of a huge audience, usually not directly involved with the politicians that terrorists aim to influence.
Hirsch, Kett and Trefil (2002)
Acts of violence committed by groups that view themselves as victimized by some notable historical wrong. Although these groups have no formal connection with governments, they usually have the financial and moral backing of sympathetic governments. Typically, they stage unexpected attacks on civilian targets, including embassies and airliners, with the aim of sowing fear and confusion.

European Union (2002)
Terrorism acts given their nature or context, may seriously damage a country or an international organization where committed with the aim of: seriously intimidating a population; or unduly compelling a Government or international organization to perform or abstain from performing any act; or seriously destabilizing or destroying the fundamental political, constitutional, economic or social structures of a country or an international organization.
Chomsky (2001)
Coercive measures against populations in an effort to achieve political and religious goals.
Pizam and Smith (2000)
Persistent and systematic strategy practiced by a country or political group against another country or group through campaigns of violence to achieve political, social or religious goals.
Treaty on Cooperation among the States Members of the Commonwealth of Independent States in Combating Terrorism (1999) [2]
Terrorism is an illegal act punishable under criminal law committed for the purpose of undermining public safety, influencing decision-making by the authorities, or terrorizing the population and taking (many) forms: Violence or threat against natural or juridical persons; Destroying... property... so as endanger people's lives, causing substantial harm to property (...); Threatening the life of a statesman or other public figure for the purpose of putting an end to his State (...); Attacking a representative of a foreign States or ... of an international organization.
Stern (1999)
Act of violence against individual noncombatants with the purpose of intimidating or influencing audiences.
League of Arab States (1998)
Any act or threat of violence, whatever its motives or purposes, that occurs in the advancement of an individual or collective criminal agenda and seeking to sow panic among people, causing fear by harming them, or placing their lives, liberty or security in danger, or seeking to cause damage to the environment or to public or private installations or property or to occupying or seizing them, or seeking to jeopardize national resources.
Smith (1998)
Politically motivated activity of small groups, directed to individuals in order to 'strike terror' in their midst, and thus control the opposition. The activity is local and of short duration.
US Department of State (1996)
An act of premeditated, politically motivated violence perpetrated against unarmed civilian targets by sub-national groups or clandestine agents, which aim to influence an audience and international terrorism as an action that involves citizens or territory of more than one country.

United Nations (1994)
Criminal acts intended or calculated to provoke a state of terror in the general public, a group of persons or particular persons for political purposes are in any circumstance unjustifiable, whatever the considerations of a political, philosophical, ideological, racial, ethnic, religious or any other nature that may be invoked to justify them.
Koopman (1993)
Acts of severe violence and unusual conspiracy directed against people or properties.
International Law Commission of the United Nations (1991) [2]
(International terrorist) An individual who as an agent or representative of a State commits or orders the commission by another individual of any of the following shall, on conviction thereof, be sentenced [to…]: Undertaking, organizing, assisting, financing, encouraging, or tolerating acts against another State directed at persons or property and of such a nature as to create a state of terror in the minds of public figures, groups of persons, or the general public.
USA Legal Code [3] (1992)
International terrorism means activities that: a) involve violent acts or acts dangerous to human life that are a violation of the criminal laws of the US or of any State, or that would be a criminal violation if committed within the jurisdiction of the US or of any State; b) appear to be intended (i) to intimidate or coerce a civilian population; (ii) to influence the policy of a government by intimidation or coercion; or (iii) to affect the conduct of a government by mass destruction, assassination, or kidnapping; and c) occur primarily outside the territorial jurisdiction of the US (…)
Domestic terrorism means activities that: a) involve acts dangerous to human life that are a violation of the criminal laws of the US or of any State; b) appear to be intended: (i) to intimidate or coerce a civilian population; (ii) to influence the policy of a government by intimidation or coercion; or (iii) to affect the conduct of a government by mass destruction, assassination, or kidnapping; and c) occur primarily within the territorial jurisdiction of the US.

1   In Institute for Economics & Peace, 2016.

2   In Kuznetcov & Kuznetcov (2013)

3   In Cornell Law School (2018)

The definition of terrorism has raised quite a buzz among researchers and organizations over the years. However, and despite the variety of definitions, there are certain common aspects:

◆ **A crime**: The violence or threat of violence against people or property;

◆ **The actors**: non state, illegal organizations

◆ **The forms**: domestic and international;

◆ **Main tools**: crime, violence, terror, threat, intimidation, extortion, kidnapping…;

◆ **The main motivations:** political, economic, religious, or social;

♦   **The main objective**: to influence the decision of governments, social groups, national or international organizations.

Over the time, the definitions are more complex, reinforcing the ideological message's importance that terrorists want to spread. In the end, terrorism has been considered as the primary security threat for West in 21th Century (Robertson, 2002 in Korstanje, 2015).

Terrorism: Evolution and globalization

Against all expectations, the end of the Cold War was not the beginning of peace. There has been a proliferation of armed conflicts around the world in recent years. The global configuration and geopolitics changed after the fall of the Berlin Wall and is largely related to the evolution of terrorism we see today (Cutter & Wilbanks, 2003). The economic, social, technological and cultural globalization influenced the evolution of terrorism in national and transnational contexts. Since the late 1960s, terrorist attacks have become more and more severe, better organized, more specialized, more violent, and geographically dispersed (Reisinger & Mavondo, 2005). The Palestinian attack in 1972 during the Munich Olympics that caused the death of 11 Israeli athletes and reached an audience of 800 million viewers (Schmid & DeGraaf, 1982) catapulted terrorism into the international scene (Sönmez & Graefe, 1998b) and changed the face of terrorism from that point. Since the 70s terrorism has changed and has evolved into a new reality.

In the 1980s and 1990s, researchers predicted a substantial increase of terrorist attacks in future (D'Amore & Anuza, 1986; Jenkins 1987, 1988). Experts speculated that terrorist groups would continue to select vulnerable targets, the attacks would be indiscriminate, and that terrorism would become more institutionalized and geographically wider as a method of armed conflict. On the other hand, they argued that, thanks to media coverage, the public would be subject to more terrorist attacks than ever (Atkinson et al., 1987). Some authors have even said that extraordinary security measures would become a permanent way of life and that terrorism would become almost a routine and something 'tolerable' (Jenkins, 1988). Indeed, terrorism numbers showed that they were right. Terrorism attacks increased from 650 events in 1970 to more than 15,000 in 2016, in total there were more almost 160,000 terrorist events in the last 45 years (START, 2017).

Many researchers believe that during the 1990s the world entered a new phase of terrorism dramatically different from its previous incarnations. It is called by some the "new terrorism" (Jenkins, 2001), or "new types of terrorists post-Cold War" (Hudson, 1999), "a new type of terrorists" (Stern, 1999), "new terrorists' generation" (Hoffman, 1999), or simply a "new wave of terrorism" (Rapoport, 2001). Generally, the argument is the same: terrorism changed its main characteristics (Bergesen & Han, 2005):

1. The organization has changed into a network. Terrorist organizations left the structured shape supported by a group of trained members to move on to a more flexible and anonymous structure.

2. Between the 1960s and the 1980s, terrorist groups clearly took a nationality, now new organizations and transnational groups have emerged, like Al-Qaeda or ISIS, with members of various nationalities and cells outside the origin country or region.

3. The identities of transnational terrorist groups are more difficult to recognize, since the responsibility for the attacks is not always claimed.

4. The terrorists' demands are vaguer, sometimes nonexistent.

5. There seems to be a change in terrorist motivations: once clearly political, they are now clearly religious. The so-called religious or 'sacred' terrorism demonstrates the prevalence of religion in the origins of the new terrorism, particularly in Islamic fundamentalism, Christian, messianic Zionism, religious cults.

6. Terrorist organizations became propaganda machines choosing specific targets based on their strategic value to spread as far as possible their message (Seabra et al., 2012).

In sum, terrorism is now an organized movement of transnational, flexible and anonymous structures that inflict attacks to send a message with various motivations, mainly religious or ideological.

Terrorism and tourism: The links

Terrorism suffered a process of profound change accompanied by a strong globalization (Bergesen & Han, 2005; Hoffman, 2002), turning it into an international issue and reality. When a terrorist incident involves citizens, targets institutions or governments from another country, terrorism assumes an international nature. According to the European Union (2002), terrorism events may, in fact, seriously damage a country by intimidating the population and destabilizing its political, constitutional, economic or social structures. Even more, the actions carried out in one country inflict costs to people and property in other countries (Enders & Sandler, 2004).

Tourism, being the most important international movement of people, has been regarded as a source of strategic targets by terrorist organizations. In fact, and paradoxically, international terrorism and tourism share some characteristics. Both cross national boundaries, involve citizens from different countries and use new technologies associated with travel and telecommunications (Schlagheck, 1988; Sönmez & Graefe, 1998a). The words tourism and terrorism can be placed at opposite ends of a continuum of quality of life. Tourism suggests life, relaxation, fun, while terrorism readily recalls feelings of death, destruction, fear and panic (O'Connor, Stafford & Gallagher, 2008).

Terrorists find in tourism destinations' infrastructures and consumers important targets, since they guarantee the achievement of several goals and purposes (Sönmez et al., 1999). Since the 1980s, researchers have found several links between terrorist activity and tourism and have tried to explain those connections. Although several authors describe the goals of terrorists differently, they agree that terrorist organizations have much to gain by attacking tourists (Sönmez, 1998). It is possible to find four main reasons to explain the relationship between tourism and terrorism: strategic goals achieved by terrorists; ideological goals achieved by terrorists; tourists are easy targets; and terrorism fear is cross-cultural.

Strategic goals achieved by terrorists

Attacking tourists provides terrorists with international media attention and limits the ability of particular political elites to control the media messages content (Baker, 2014). The involvement of citizens from other countries means international coverage for the terrorist cause. When tourists are kidnapped or killed, the situation is immediately dramatized in the media, which helps make the conflict globally visible. The terrorists achieve the exposure they need and media raise their audiences (Seabra et al., 2012). Terrorists also use tourists and tourism facilities to fund their campaigns. Large groups of citizens who speak another language allow camouflage and shield while offering various opportunities for the choice of targets. Terrorists may circulate among tourists and make financial transactions without raising suspicion. Also tourists are crime targets to achieve great amounts of money: through robberies and kidnappings, terrorists get the funds they need to carry out their activities (Richter & Waugh, 1986).

On the other hand, the perception that tourism development does not really benefit the local population and that, instead, it exploits and destroys indigenous cultures and industries, can lead to violence (Richter & Waugh, 1986). The failure of tourism entrepreneurs in the design, location and management of their projects in a way that would ensure the support of the community can lead to a violent opposition (Lea, 1996). So, the fact that tourists are foreigners can increase the support of locals and also decrease the risk of involving domestic targets (Richter & Waugh, 1986).

Finally, the tourism sector is an important economic activity and terrorist attacks cause a decline in foreign exchange inflows, allowing terrorists to impose indirect costs and gain political advantage on the targeted governments and countries (Hall & O'Sullivan, 1996). For many countries such as Egypt, Israel, Greece, Sri Lanka and Indonesia, the tourism industry is an extremely important activity for the GDP and that is why the terrorists have come together to stop the national economy and their governments (Aziz, 1995; Paraskevas & Beverley, 2007). When attacking tourists to achieve ideological goals, they punish local citizens for supporting their national governments and they also increase their power and legitimacy, making local governments more fragile (Hall & O'Sullivan, 1996).

Ideological goals achieved by terrorists

Tourists are regarded as having symbolic value as indirect representatives of hostile or opposed governments (Richter, 1983; Richter & Waugh, 1986; Sönmez & Graefe, 1998a) Tourists are effective tools to convey a message of ideological opposition (Sönmez et al., 1999). Tourism means capitalism and consumption, so an attack on that activity represents an ideological opposition to the Western values (Lepp & Gibson, 2003). Also, tourists usually come from developed countries, which in the terrorist perspective are seen as responsible for the situation of poverty those countries have to face (Korstanje & Skoll, 2014). The loss of attractiveness of the targeted tourism destination means an enormous loss of income for the local government, thus sending a message of ideological opposition to the tourism activity (Blake & Sinclair, 2003; Sönmez, 1998).

Cultural, socio-economic and communication discrepancies between tourists and residents can create resentments (Aziz, 1995; Lea, 1996). Sometimes, tourists are regarded as a movement of aliens, a form of neo-colonialism or a threat to their social rules, established values and religious beliefs (Wahab, 1996). The cultural, social, religious habits and tourist consumption are so different from the residents in certain destinations that they can be considered as an insult and generate situations of violence (Richter, 1983). Certain behaviors displayed by tourists that are contrary to the locals' culture, such as eating pork in an Islamic country, drinking alcohol, gambling and the choice of different dress styles can be seen as offensive. The difference between local poverty and tourists' pride and wellness evident in their own clothing, accessories and equipment may cause unavoidable shocks (Aziz, 1995).

Some studies have concluded that terrorism attacks on tourism may be seen as an attempt to protect the local status quo against modernity, because the mere contact with the tourists that bear the marks of this change can speed up the process (Wahab, 1996). The terrorist attacks on tourists can thus be considered as justifiable acts carried out to protect sacred beliefs, social norms, value systems and religious beliefs (Tarlow, 2005).

Tourists are easy targets

Tourists are vulnerable and easy targets for terrorists because they are obvious in their behavior and appearance, they move in large groups, are relaxed and not cautious at all (Ryan, 1993). Traditional targets (politicians and embassies) are less attractive to terrorists because security measures may be increased in order to ensure their safety, while tourists, by contrast, are soft targets (Lehrman, 1986). In fact, tourists are chosen as targets due to several practical reasons (Richter & Waugh, 1986):

1. They are easily identifiable: the tourists have habits, behaviors, specific dress codes which are sometimes different from the locals' (Aziz, 1995).
2. Usually, they carry many electronic devices like camcorders, cameras, cell phones that identify themselves as tourists.
3. They attend crowded public places such as museums, city centers and other tourist attractions.
4. The nature of tourism services places tourists in settings like hotels, tourist attractions or markets that can easily be placed under attack (Brunt, Mawby & Hambly, 2000).

Terrorism fear is cross-cultural

Risk perception in travelling is more pronounced and is cross-cultural, and terrorists are very aware of this fact (Seabra et al., 2012). Many studies proved that consuming and purchasing tourism services implies high levels of perceived risk of all kinds (Hugstad et al., 1987) and that 'uncertainty avoidance' is constant in all nationalities and cultures (Hofstede, 1980; Reisinger & Crotts, 2010; Seabra et al., 2013). This is mainly due to the intangibility and low standardized level of the tourism offer (Zeithaml, 1981). Tourism consumption is emotional since consumers plan the buy for a long time, idealizing experiences that generally involve a series of individuals (Seabra et al., 2007) expecting intangible outputs, mostly an experience of leisure and pleasure (Quan & Wang, 2004).

Although tourists associate multiple types of risk to travel purchase and consumption, the risk of terrorism is very specific (Seabra et al., 2014). In fact, previous research proves that tourists from different countries fear terrorism and turmoil due to its unpredictability and they are likely to cancel or delay their trip if they feel that such events might occur (Seabra et al., 2013). This kind of risk is transversal to citizens of all countries of origin. Recent research concludes that travelers from countries with different levels of peace fear terrorism in the same way and that it affects tourists' behavior and safety perceptions when planning and consuming an international trip (Seabra et al., 2018).

Conclusions and implications

Although terrorism has been a political weapon since the beginning of history, the form of struggle in contemporary periods has an impact and frequency never witnessed before. Terrorism today is almost a commonplace (Combs, 2017). The main goal of terror is to provoke an emotional fear, more than to obtain a military defeat. Terrorists achieve that goal by choosing high profile civilian targets or national society's symbols. Terrorism can generate deeper fear and anxiety, causing changes in individual and organizations' behavior (Spilerman & Steckov, 2009) mainly by the message's power (Seabra et al., 2012). Tourists are chosen as targets for their symbolic value: they represent Western capitalism, consumption, and values such as wealth, freedom of choice and independence (Richter & Waugh, 1986). For terrorists the symbolism, high profile, and media coverage brought by international tourists makes them too valuable to be left out of their terrorist acts (Sönmez et al., 1999).

With the present work, our main goal was to update the research on the connections between terrorism and tourism. Once more, it was possible to prove that those two phenomena are intrinsically bounded. Terrorism clearly benefits from attacks on tourism, and tourism activity is severely hampered by such attacks. Tourists are rational but also emotional consumers who desire pleasant and memorable experiences (Tsaur et al., 2006), destinations that want to attract tourists should pursue strategies to build their image and create conditions that enable positive and memorable tourism experiences (Kim et al., 2012). However, the tourist industry's strong exposure to terrorist incidents has been recognized by researchers. Few people travel to places where they feel threatened (Seabra et al., 2014). The social nature of terrorism leads, in many individuals, to the fear of traveling, especially abroad, and specifically to destinations perceived as unsafe. The violence affects directly the image of a country, both internally and internationally, destroying the functioning of society and interfering with the free flow of people and ideas (Pizam et al., 1997).

The vulnerability of the tourism sector has become quite visible during the terrorist events that marked the beginning of the 21st century (Henderson & Alex, 2004). Terrorist attacks have been responsible for most of the tourist crises in recent times. As a consequence of these crises, there are strong drops in the local tourism industry and in the arrival of tourists (Sönmez et al., 1999). Terrorism attacks have a dramatically negative effect on tourism industry demand levels. In fact, the tourism sector and the vast industry that supports it are particularly sensitive to shocks and external factors that are beyond the control of their managers (Evans & Elphick, 2005; McKercher, 1999). It is probably impossible to control terrorism, but nations cannot ignore it. Governments, companies and tourism institutions need to focus their attention on this threat in order to create effective marketing strategies (Hall & O'Sullivan 1996). Most terrorist attacks are difficult to prevent. They are different and difficult to solve with simple formulas, however, tourism destinations' managers should be prepared in order to build and implement their own specific action plan. In light of the social and global complexities, no target is immune to negative occurrences and to think that 'it only happens to others' may be dangerously immature and may be catastrophic (Sönmez, 1998). Crises resulting from terrorist attacks, which have become increasingly frequent, put an enormous pressure on staff and managers (Ritchie, 2004). Marketers, especially, need to understand tourists' behavior and their decision-making mechanisms in order to join forces and resources with managers in an attempt to attract tourists in a world where fear is global (Yeoman et al., 2006).

Acknowledgements

This work is part of a Post-PhD project financed by FCT - Fundação para a Ciência e Tecnologia, I.P. under the project SFRH/BPD/109245/2015, and is also funded under the project UID/Multi/04016/2016. Furthermore we would like to thank the Instituto Politécnico de Viseu and CI&DETS for their support.

This work was funded by Fundação para a Ciência e Tecnologia (UID/ECO/00124/2013 and Social Sciences Data Lab, Project 22209), by POR Lisboa (LISBOA-01-0145-FEDER007722 and Social Sciences Data Lab, Project 22209) and POR Norte (Social Sciences Data Lab, Project 22209).

References

Atkinson, S., Sandler, T. & Tschirart, J. (1987). Terrorism in a bargaining framework. *The Journal of Law and Economics,* **30**(1), 1-21.

Aziz, H. (1995). Understanding terrorist attacks on tourists in Egypt. *Tourism Management,* **16**, 91-95.

Baker, D. (2014). The effects of terrorism on the travel and tourism industry. *International Journal of Religious Tourism and Pilgrimage,* **2**(1), 58-67.

Bergesen, A. & Han, Y. (2005). New directions for terrorism research. *International Journal of Comparative Sociology,* **46**, 133-151.

Blake, A. & Sinclair, M. (2003). Tourism crisis management: US response to September 11. *Annals of Tourism Research,* **30**(4), 813-832.

Blomberg, S., Hess, G. & Orphanides, A. (2004). The macroeconomic consequences of terrorism. *Journal of Monetary Economics, 51,* 1007-1032.

Brunt, P., Mawby, R. & Hambly, Z. (2000). Tourist victimization and the fear of crime on holiday. *Tourism Management,* **21**(6), 417-424.

Chomsky, N. (2001). A leading terrorist state. *Monthly Review,* **53**, 10-19.

Combs, C. (2017). *Terrorism in the Twenty-First Century.* London: Routledge.

Cornell Law School. (2018). *18 U.S. Code § 2331 - Definitions.* Retrieved 14.03.2018 from Legal Information Institute: https://www.law.cornell.edu/uscode/text/18/2331

Cutter, S. & Wilbanks, T. (2003). *The Geographical Dimensions of Terrorism.* New York: Routledge.

D'Amore, L. & Anuza, T. (1986). International terrorism: Implications and challenge for global tourism. *Business Quarterly,* **4**, 20-29.

Enders, W. & Sandler, T. (2002). Patterns of transnational terrorism, 1970-1999: Alternative time-series estimates. *International Studies Quarterly,* **46**, 145-165.

Enders, W. & Sandler, T. (2004). After 11 Sept: Is it all different now? *The Lisbon Conference on Defence and Security (1-2 July). IDN.* Lisbon: Lisbon Conference on Defence and Security, Instituto da Defesa Nacional.

European Union. (2002). Terrorism for legal/official purposes definition. *Art.1 of the Framework Decision on Combating Terrorism.* Brussels: European Union.

Evans, N. & Elphick, S. (2005). Models of crisis management: An evaluation of theirs value for strategic planning in the international travel industry. *International Journal of Tourism Research,* **7**, 135-150.

Feichtinger, G., Hartl, R., Kort, P. & Novak, A. (2001). Terrorism control in the tourism industry. *Journal of Optimization Theory and Applications,* **108**(2), 283-296.

Fenstermacher, L., Rieger, K.T. & Speckhard, A. (2010). Protecting the homeland from international and domestic terrorism threats:. In L.

Fenstermacher, L. Kuznar & A. Speckhard (Edits.), *Current Multi-Disciplinary Perspectives on Root Causes, the Role of Ideology, and Programs for Counter-Radicalization and Disengagement* (p. 178). White Paper: Counter Terrorism.

Fullerton, C., Ursano, R., Norwood, A. & Holloway, H. (2003). Trauma, terrorism, and disaster. In R. Ursano, C. Fullerton & A. Norwood (Edits.), *Terrorism and Disaster* (pp. 1-22). Cambridge: Cambridge University Press.

Goldblatt, J. & Hu, C. (2005). Tourism, teorrorism, and the new World for event leaders. *EReview of Tourism Research,* 3(6), 139-44.

Hall, C. & O'Sullivan, V. (1996). Tourism, political stability and violence. In A. Pizam & Y. Mansfeld (Edits.), *Tourism, Crime and Security Issues* (pp. 105-123). Chichester: Wiley.

Henderson, J. & Alex, N. (2004). Responding to crisis: Severe acute respiratory syndrome (SARS) and hotels in Singapore. *International Journal of Tourism Research,* 6, 411-419.

Hirsch, E., Kett, J. & Trefil, J. (2002). *The New Dictionary of Cultural Literacy.* New York: Houghton Mifflin Company.

Hoffman, S. (2002). Clash of globalizations. *Foreign Affairs,* **81**, 104-115.

Hofman, B. (1999). *Inside Terrorism.* New York: Columbia University Press.

Hofstede, G. (1980). Culture and organizations. *International Studies of Management & Organization,* **10**(4), 15-41.

Hudson, R. (1999). *Who Becomes a Terrorist and Why: The 1999 government report on profiling terrorists.* Guilford, CT: The Lyons Press.

Hugstad, P., Taylor, J. & Bruce, G. (1987). The effects of social class and perceived risk on consumer information search. *Journal of Services Marketing,* **1**(1), 47-52.

Institute for Economics & Peace. (2016). *Gobal Terrorism Index: Measurig and Understanding the Impact of Terrorism.* Sidney: Institute for Economics & Peace.

Jenkins, B. (1987). The future course of international terrorism. In A. Kurz (Ed.), *Contemporary Trends in World Terrorism* (pp. 150-159). New York: Praeger.

Jenkins, B. (1988). Future trends in international terrorism. In R. Slater & M. Stohl (Edits.), *Current Perspectives on International Terrorism* (pp. 246-266). London: MacMillan.

Jenkins, B. (2001). Terrorism and beyond: A 21st century perspective. *Studies in Conflict and Terrorism,* **24**, 321-327.

Kim, J.H., Ritchie, J.B. & McCormick, B. (2012). Development of a scale to measure memorable tourism experiences. *Journal of Travel Research,* **51**(1), 12-25.

Koopman, R. (1993). The dynamics of protest waves: West Germany, 1965 to 1989. *American Sociological Review, 58,* 637-658.

Korstanje, M. (2015). The spirit of terrorism: Tourism, unionization and terrorism. *PASOS. Revista de Turismo y Patrimonio Cultural, 13*(1), 239-250.

Korstanje, M. & Skoll, G. (2014). Points of discussion around 09/11: Terrorism and tourism revisited. *e-Review of Tourism Research, 11*(1/2), 1-17.

Kozak, M., Crotts, J. & Law, R. (2007). The impact of perception of risk on international travellers. *International Journal of Tourism Research, 9*(4), 233-242.

Kuznetcov, A. & Kuznetcov, V. (2013). The legal definition of terrorism in the United States and Russia. *World Applied Sciences Journal, 28*(1), 130-134.

Lea, J. (1996). Tourism, realpolitik and development in the South Pacific. In A. Pizam & Y. Mansfeld (Edits.), *Tourism, Crime and International Security Issues* (pp. 123-142). New York: Wiley.

League of Arab States. (1998). The Arab convention for the suppression of terrorism. *Council of Arab Ministers of the Interior and the Council of Arab Ministers of Justice.* Cairo: League of Arab States.

Lehrman, C. (1986). When fact and fantasy collide: Crisis management in the travel industry. *Public Relations Journal, 42,* 25-28.

Lepp, A. & Gibson, H. (2003). Tourist roles, perceived risk and international tourism. *Annals of Tourism Research, 30*(3), 606-624.

Malečková, J. & Stanišić, D. (2014). Changes in public opinion and the occurrence of international terrorism. *Peace Economics, Peace Science & Public Policy, 20*(4), 631–653.

McKercher, B. (1999). A chaos aproach to tourism. *Tourism Management, 20,* 425-434.

O'Connor, N., Stafford, M. & Gallagher, G. (2008). The impact of global terrorism on Ireland's tourism industry: An industry in perspective. *Tourism and Hospitality Research, 8*(4), 351-364.

Paraskevas, A. & Beverley, A. (2007). A strategic framework for terrorism prevention and mitigation in tourism destinations. *Tourism Management, 1,* 1-14.

Pizam, A. & Smith, G. (2000). Tourism and terrorism: A quantitative analysis of major terrorist acts and their impact on tourism destinations. *Tourism Economics, 6*(2), 123-138.

Pizam, A., Tarlow, P. & Bloom, J. (1997). Making tourists feel safe: Whose responsibility is it? *Journal of Travel Research, 3*(3), 23-28.

Poland, J. (1988). *Understanding Terrorism.* Englewood Cliffs: Prentice-Hall.

Quan, S. & Wang, N. (2004). Towards a structural model of the tourist experience: An illustration from food experiences in tourism. *Tourism Management,* **25**(3), 297-305.

Radu, M. (2002). Terrorism after the Cold War: Trends and challenges. *Orbis,* **46**(2), 275-287.

Rapoport, D. (2001). The fourth wave: September 11 in the history of terrorism. *Current History,* December, 419-424.

Reisinger, Y. & Crotts, J. (2010). The influence of gender on travel risk perceptions, safety, and travel intentions. *Tourism Analysis,* **14**, 793-807.

Reisinger, Y. & Mavondo, F. (2005). Travel anxiety and intentions to travel internationally: Implications of travel risk perception. *Journal of Travel Research,* **43**, 212-225.

Richter, L. (1983). Tourism politics and political science: A case of not so benign neglect. *Annals of Tourism Research,* **10**(3), 313-315.

Richter, L. & Waugh, W. (1986). Terrorism and tourism as logical companions. *Tourism Management,* **7**(4), 230-238.

Ritchie, B. (2004). Chaos, crises and disasters: A strategic approach to crisis management in the tourism industry. *Tourism Management,* **25**(6), 669-683.

Ryan, C. (1993). Crime, violence, terrorism and tourism: An accidental relationship or intrinsic relationship? *Tourism Management,* **14**(3), 173-183.

Savun, B. & Phillips, B. (2009). Democracy, foreign policy, and terrorism. *Journal of Conflict Resolution,* **53**(6), 878-904.

Scheffler, S. (2006). Is terrorism morally distinctive? *Journal of Political Philosophy,* **14**(1), 1-17.

Schlagheck, D. (1988). *International Terrorism.* Lexington MA: Lexington Books.

Schmid, A. & DeGraaf, J. (1982). *Violence as Communications: Insurgent terrorism and the western news media.* Beverly Hills: Sage.

Schmitt, B. (1999). Experiential marketing. *Journal of Marketing Management,* **15**(1-3), 53-67.

Seabra, C., Abrantes, J. & Kastenholz, E. (2012). TerrorScale: A scale to measure the contact of international tourists with terrorism. *Journal of Tourism Research & Hospitality,* **1**(4), 1-8.

Seabra, C., Abrantes, J. & Kastenholz, E. (2014). The influence of terrorism risk perception on purchase involvement and safety concern international travellers. *Journal of Marketing Management,* **30**(9-10), 874-903.

Seabra, C., Abrantes, J. & Lages, L. (2007). The impact of external information sources in expectations formation and future use of media. *Tourism Management,* **28**(6), 1541-1554.

Seabra, C., Dolnicar, S., Abrantes, J. & Kastenholz, E. (2013). Heterogeneity in risk and safety perceptions of international tourists. *Tourism Management*, **36**, 502-510.

Seabra, C., Kastenholz, E., Abrantes, J.L. & Reis, M. (2018). Peacefulness at home: Impacts on international travel. *International Journal of Tourism Cities*. https://doi.org/10.1108/IJTC-10-2017-0050

Smith, V. (1998). War and tourism: An american etnography. *Annals of Tourism Research*, **25**(1), 202-227.

Sönmez, S. (1998). Tourism, terrorism and political instability. *Annals of Tourism Research*, **25**(2), 416-456.

Sönmez, S. & Graefe, A. (1998a). Influence of terrorism risk on foreign tourism decisions. *Annals of Tourism Research*, **25**(1), 112-144.

Sönmez, S. & Graefe, A. (1998b). Determining future travel behavior from past travel experience and perceptions of risk and safety. *Journal of Travel Research*, **37**(2), 171-177.

Sönmez, S., Apostolopoulos, Y. & Tarlow, P. (1999). Tourism and crisis: Managing the effects of terrorism. *Journal of Travel Research*, **38**(1), 13-18.

Spilerman, S. & Stecklov, G. (2009). Societal responses to terrorist attacks. *Annual Review of Sociology*, **35**, 167-189.

START - National Consortium for the Study of Terrorism and Responses to Terrorism. (2017). *Global Terrorism Database*. Retrieved 15.02.2018, from http://www.start.umd.edu/gtd/

Stern, J. (1999). *The Ultimate Terrorists*. Cambridge, MA: Harvard University Press.

Tarlow, P. (2005). Dark tourism: The appealing 'dark' side of tourism and more. In M. Novelli (Ed.), *Niche Tourism: Contemporary Issues, Trends and Cases* (pp. 47 -58). Oxford: Elsevier.

Tavares, J. (2004). The open society assesses its enemies: Shocks, disasters and terrorist attacks. *Journal of Monetary Economics*, **51**, 1039-1070.

Tsaur, S., Chiu, Y. & Wang, C. (2007). The visitors behavioral consequences of experiential marketing: An empirical study on Taipei Zoo. *Journal of Travel & Tourism Marketing*, **21**(1), 47-64.

United Nations. (1994). *Measures to eliminate international terrorism (Agenda item 108): UN General Assembly Resolution 49/60*. Retrieved 14.03.2018, from United Nations: http://www.un.org/en/ga/sixth/71/int_terrorism.shtml

United Nations Security Council. (2004). *Meetings coverage and press Releases*. Retrieved 14.03.2018, from United Nations: https://www.un.org/press/en/2004/sc8214.doc.htm

US Department of State. (2003). *Department of State – Diplomacy in Action.* Retrieved in 30/04/2019, from https://www.state.gov/j/ct/rls/crt/2002/html/19977.htm

Wahab, S. (1996). Tourism and terrorism: Sinthesis of the problem with emphasis on Egypt. In A. Pizam & Y. Mansfeld (Edits.), *Tourism, Crime and International Security Issues* (pp. 175-186). New York: Wiley.

Yeoman, I., Munro, C. & McHahon-Beattie, U. (2006). Tomorrow's: World, consumer and tourist. *Journal of Vacation Marketing,* **12**(2), 174-190.

Zeithaml, V. (1981). How consumer evaluation processes differ between goods and services. In J. Donelly & W. George (Edits.), *Marketing of Services* (pp. 186-190). Chicago: American Marketing Association.

6 Exploring the senses from the visitors' perspectives of the Cape Verde Islands

Cristina Oliveira, Antónia Correia and Sérgio Moro

The objectives of this chapter are to:

☐ Explain how sensory marketing offers an interesting approach by which to leverage island tourism;

☐ Highlight research aimed at understanding how the sensorial experience is being perceived by visitors;

☐ Demonstrate how online reviews published on TripAdvisor for hotels, attractions and restaurants were used in identifying visitors' perspectives;

☐ Highlight results that show visual sense with a focus on beach, sea, sand, water and green work. Although both auditory and olfactory senses of sea and water are not so explicit in the tourist reviews, they still engrained in visitors' comments.

Keywords: Island tourism; sensory marketing; tourist experience; online reviews.

Introduction

Jafar Jafari stated in 1974 that at that time almost every nation in the world realized the potential and importance of tourism as an economic and prosperous industry (Jafari, 1974). Although islands suffer from general scarcity and difficult access to resources, they are also usually attractive as they are associated with the image of granting unique and exclusive destination experiences to tourists who visit (Nunkoo & Gursoy, 2012), thus emphasizing the importance of studying tourists' experiences in islands.

Senses are one of the dimensions of customer experience (Schmitt, 1999). Schmitt (1999) argued that as a tactical and powerful strategy tool, sensory marketing can add value, differentiate tourism products as well as motivate tourism customers. Sensory marketing research is still very emergent (Hultén et al., 2009; Krishna, 2010; Lindstrom, 2005), being even more recent the study of sensory dimension in tourist experience (Agapito et al., 2013). The review of the literature on sensory experience in tourism suggests that this is still an understudied subject. The role of the five senses for the tourist experience was previously researched in urban and nature destinations (Pan & Ryan, 2009), in historic (Stancioiu et al., 2014), rural (Markwell, 2001), rural costal (Agapito et al., 2014), and wildlife (Ballantyne et al., 2011) contexts. Hence, so far there are only few studies addressing the sensory aspects related to tourist experience.

Sensory experiences can only be physically lived within the destination. Based on comments of previous visitors this netnographic research identified the five senses comprised in a single experience to ensure a holistic understanding of senses to memorize and engage in the experience. More specifically, this research analyzed and identified conclusions of sensory features that are more relevant in the destination Cape Verde. The intended contribution of this chapter is to identify sensory experiences that are stimulated when visiting Cape Verde.

This chapter is thus organized as follows. First, a review of literature on island tourism is conducted, being coupled by contextualization of both small island developing states (SIDS) and Cape Verde, since this archipelago constitutes the setting of the data collection. Second, the focus turns to previous studies performed on senses in tourism. Third, the methodology used in this research is explained. Fourth, results are analyzed and reported with regard to the five senses extracted from online reviews of the islands of Cape Verde. Finally, the conclusion stresses the most relevant findings, acknowledges the limitations of the study and suggests directions for future research.

Literature review

Tourism in islands

In the past, islands used to rely on agriculture, fishing and eventually handicrafts as pillars of their economy (Markwick, 2001). The recognized scarcity of resources turned attention to tourism as a solution to bring more diversification, employment and infrastructure (Sharpley, 2003). Nonetheless, tourism activities have also brought negative impacts to islands, and are seen as such by their local communities (Ko & Stewart, 2002). Indeed, islands have suffered from wearing out of their limited resources and fragile environments (Harrison, 2001). Although there should be put into practice serious sustainability criteria for further progress, it is not usually integrated in the development options of interest groups (Briassoulis, 2003).

Normally, most islands suffer from insufficient features related to transportation, food and lodging that make them more expensive than they would be if located in mainland (Mitchell & Reid, 2001). However, the singularity of islands, whether in terms of weather, climate and scenery can enable tourists to enjoy different and amazing experiences. Nevertheless, islands are challenged by a permanent tension between attractiveness and scarcity for each dimension experienced by tourists (Klint et al., 2012).

Previous studies researched island tourism from several perspective layers, whether on islands as tourist destinations (Del Chiappa & Presenza, 2013), tourism development (Seetanah & Sannassee, 2015) or sustainable tourism (Canavan, 2014) among others. Individual islands that have been researched include Aruba (Rivera et al., 2016) where it was identified attributes for a mobile app to the Island; Barbados (Cashman et al., 2012), on water use scarcity; Cyprus (Kilic & Okumus, 2005), on staff productivity management; and transport infrastructure development in the Mauritius (Khadaroo & Seetanah, 2007). Archipelagos that were studied included the Azores (Moniz, 2012) where repeat visitors were analyzed; international tourism and trade in Canary Islands (Santana-Gallego et al., 2011); and in Madeira (Almeida et al., 2014) the promotion of tourism in the rural areas as a mean of growth. Finally, in terms of regions, like Asia/Pacific, the Caribbean, and Europe, Park (2011) studied cruise tourism viability for the American-affiliated Pacific Islands (AAPI) region.

Small Island Developing States (SIDS)

Although there are a number of touristic well established, fully functioning and popular islands in the world (for example Honolulu, Santorini, Crete, Cyprus, Capri, Bora Bora, Bali, Phuket, Cozumel, Oahu and Kauai), there are also a number of small islands that are still going through development. SIDS (Small Island Developing States) were first recognized as a distinct group of developing countries at the United Nations Conference on Environment and Development in June 1992 (UNCED, 1992). An unofficial list of small island developing states classified by geographic regions appear in the United Nations Department of Economic and Social Affairs UNCTAD website. Cape Verde was then classified as a SIDS:

https://sustainabledevelopment.un.org/topics/sids/list

Islands are becoming even more attractive destinations with the number of international tourists visiting SIDS increasing by almost 300% in the decade up to 2011, from over 12 million to 41 million (UNWTO, 2012). So, Taleb Rifai, previous Secretary General for the UNWTO, stated that tourism development planned and managed in a sustainable way will bring huge economic benefits as well as development to Small Islands (UNWTO, 2012). He also added that tourism has already helped Cape Verde and the Maldives to move up from least developed countries.

The UNWTO, in its 2012 world report (Rio +20), explained that international tourism is an essential economic source that promotes growth, foreign exchange, income redistribution, poverty alleviation and job opportunities in SIDS. As they are becoming more known in the globe, SIDS strategic development needs to ensure their sustainable growth. They have a number of challenges to deal with, whether environmental, climate change, natural disasters to external economic shocks and dependency of imports.

To support their development, international summits and conferences were established. Also the Barbados Program of Action (1994) was developed to assist SIDS in their sustainable development efforts. Later in 2014 an action platform was developed to support and monitor implementation of pledges and commitments of partnerships. The 2030 United Nations agenda is a balanced economic, social and environmental plan of action for sustainable development. A worldwide collaborative partnership was established. Among other things the plan seeks to eradicate poverty as the basis for sustainable development. All countries and stakeholders will make part of it in a collaborative partnership. They will give special attention to Small island Developing States in pursuing sustainable development. (https://sustainabledevelopment.un.org/post2015/transformingourworld)

Cape Verde

Cape Verde was discovered and colonized by Portuguese explorers, establishing in the 15th century the first European settlement in the tropics. Only in 1975, Cape Verde achieved its independence from Portugal. This archipelago forms part of the Macaronesia eco-region. Due to the lack of natural resources, its developing economy is mostly service-oriented. However, there has been a growing focus on tourism and on foreign investment (UNWTO, 2014).

In the last official census conducted in 2013, the population was 512,000, with almost half (236,000) Cape Verdeans living on the main island of Santiago, where the capital city, Praia, has about 25% of Cape Verde's citizens (INE, 2013). As of 2018, the total population of Cape Verde is just over half a million (circa 553,000) with nearly 64% of the inhabitants living in urban areas. The total land area is 4,039 km2, with a density of 137 people per km2 (worldpopulationreview.com). Cidade Velha in Santiago is classified as an Intangible Heritage of Humanity by Unesco since 2009, for being the birthplace of the Creole nation. (http://www.guiadecaboverde.cv/index.php/category/circuitosroteiros

According to INE (2016), the most visited islands are Sal (293,000), Boa Vista (203,000), Santiago (72,000) and São Vicente (38,000). The main source tourist markets are the UK (131,000), Germany (71,000), Portugal and France (64,000 each), Benelux (62,000) and Italy (46,000). In the SIDS of the archipelago of Cape Verde (UM, 2016) which has ten islands in the Atlantic Ocean off the northwest coast of Africa, there are four islands (Brava, Fogo, Santo Antão, São Nicolau) being promoted by its destination marketing organization (DMO) as islands of the senses (www.guidadecaboverde.cv). The other six are not communicated in such way: three (Boavista, Maio, Sal) are promoted as islands of the sun; two (Santiago, São Vicente) communicated as islands of the essence; one (Santa Luzia) is an inhabited island.

The islands of the senses are promoted to foster intimate contact between tourists and nature, emphasizing uniqueness and true experiences with the people and culture of Cape Verde. The four islands are associated with the awakening of all senses and are said to share the conditions for the practice of nature-based tourism or ecotourism in its purest state being sought after by visitors who seek unique sensory experiences. Specifically, tourists can: (1) climb the imposing mountains of Santo Antão, with the Cova in the background; (2) challenge the famous volcano of Fogo, with the Manecon wine as host; (3) stroll through the natural park of Monte Gordo, under a green blanket of trees, in São Nicolau; (4) contemplate the stunning landscape of Fajã d'Água on the island of Flores (Brava).

The islands of the sun are communicated as offering beaches of white sand to lose sight on the horizon, some deserted, virgin in pure state. Waters are tepid and translucent, sometimes a turquoise blue to remind tourists of true gemstones. Visitors are able to dive with fish and let the body go to the waves while the sun shines high, practically 365 days a year. They provide activities aimed for travelers who do not dispense unique moments by the sea or long walks by the sand, while picking up shells. Tourist may surf some waves, paddle, or venture into windsurfing or kitesurfing. These islands are targeted to those in love with the sun and the sea.

Finally, the islands of the essence are where tourists can find a good part of the history, culture and traditions of Cape Verde. The two largest cities of the archipelago, Praia (Santiago) and Mindelo (São Vicente) are located in these islands, as the mythical Old City (Santiago), birthplace of the Creole nation, the first capital of the country, classified as Intangible Heritage of Humanity by Unesco since 2009. These islands are expected to have visitors being carried away in a unique trip between past and present, full of unforgettable experiences, such as the *morabeza* (a word that defines the art of well-being), to relive the history, listen to the music, know the traditions, and taste the flavors of these two islands that are a true invitation to sensations.

Senses in tourism

Senses have been stimulated for centuries in vast variety of ways as Howes & Classen (2014) discuss. Nowadays marketers communicate meaning on a visual channel using frequently color, size, and styling (sight). Music and other sounds affect consumer's feeling and behaviors, and can also bring sound symbolism (hearing). Like color, odor can also stir emotions and memory, with scent marketing being a form of sensory marketing (smell). Consumers' taste receptors contribute to their experience of many products and services (taste). Cultural factors also determine desirable tastes, hence influencing how consumers experience the actual taste. Sensations that reach the skin stimulate or relax consumers, thus giving the haptic (touch) sense an important role in consumer behavior.

Human senses are the basics of human nature. Sensorial experiences trigger psychological arousal whether positively or negatively. Thus, human senses are stimulated while there is a direct interaction with a service or a product. Thus, human's five traditionally recognized senses, sight, hearing, taste, smell, and touch, allow tourists to achieve a complete and real experience on their travel.

The importance of a tourism destination being promoted by the senses is expressed by different authors (Dann & Jacobsen, 2002; Pollard et al., 1998). The sensory appeal construct is defined as a need to experience tourism through sensation or feeling by tourists, perceived through specific sense modes, such as touch, smell, taste, sight, hearing or the sense of balance (Urry, 2002). Tussyadiah et al. (2012) stated that tourists seek benefits from the experiential consumption of destinations, whether social, physical or cultural. Ditoiu et al. (2014) argued that as the basis of the tourism is experiential, the tool to use for the sensory brand of destination is sensory marketing. Thus, bodily sensory experiences produce the most objective, complete and real dimension of a tourist impression, including all senses: sound, visual, touch, smell and taste (Bitner, 1992; Howes & Marcoux, 2006; Pine & Gilmore,1998; Urry, 2002; Walls et al., 2011). Rickly-Boyd & Metro-Roland (2010) also argued that symbolic elements can initially bring tourists to a destination, but it is the experience in loco that will shape their final opinion. For Stăncioiu et al. (2014) sensory marketing enhances the experience with a more positive image besides helping the development of the destination itself.

Table 6.1 lists authors who studied senses applied to consumer and tourist behavior. It aggregates information by sense, and organizes it by author. Thus, one can identify how many and who already studied each of the senses, as well as which were the senses researched in each of the previous studies. On the one hand, hearing has been the most researched sense (20 studies), followed by sight and smell (19 studies each), taste (14 studies) and then touch (13 studies). On the other hand, out of the twenty-four studies addressing sensory dimensions of tourism experiences, only nine considered all the five senses. Indeed, two studies focused on four senses, thus always leaving one out, six studies researched three senses, four studies looked at two senses, and other six studies solely addressed one sense.

Table 6.1: Authors who studied senses - empirical studies on the multi-sensory dimensions of tourism experiences. Source: Authors

Authors (24)	Sight	Hearing	Smell	Taste	Touch
Agapito et al. (2012)	x	x	x	x	x
Agapito et al. (2014)	x	x	x	x	x
Agapito et al. (2017)	x	x	x	x	x
Davis & Thys-Senocak (2017)			x		
Ditoiu et al. (2014)	x	x	x	x	x
Govers et al. (2007)	x	x	x	x	
Gretzel & Fesenmaier (2003)	x	x	x		
Gretzel & Fesenmaier (2010)	x	x	x		
Hung, Zheng, Carlson, Giurge (2017)	x	x			
Jaworska (2017)		x		x	x
Kastenholz et al. (2012)	x	x	x	x	x
Kim and Perdue (2013)	x				x
Kim & Eves (2012)		x	x	x	x
Kim et al. (2013)		x			
Lee, Gretzel and Law (2010)	x	x		x	
Markwell (2001)	x	x	x	x	x
Mateiro et al. (2017)	x	x	x	x	
Pan and Ryan (2009)	x	x	x	x	x
Rickly-Boyd & Metro-Roland (2010)	x	x	x		
Small et al. (2012)		x	x		x
Son & Pearce (2005)	x	x	x	x	x
Stăncioiu et al. (2014)	x	x	x	x	x
Steptoe et al. (1995)	x		x		
Wu et al. (2016)	x		x		
Total	19	20	19	14	13

Table 6.2 shows sensory elements classified according to the five senses that have been most researched in previous studies. First, the importance of land/landscape, mountain and rocks is revealed in their association to visual, olfactory and tactile senses; nature adds an auditory sensory dimension to it. Second, wind, rain, water and sea are altogether associated with four senses (visual, auditory, olfactory and tactile) with the same set of senses being stimulated by animals. From a gastronomic perspective, food and wine are quite comprehensive in addressing visual, olfactory and gustatory senses.

Table 6.2: Sensory elements most used in previous studies

Visual elements

Aboriginal culture; ambience; animals; architecture; Ayers Rock; bathroom amenities; beach; beautiful; black Church; Brâncuşi masterpieces; casino; castle; cleanliness; coast; colours; conservation; Constanţa; Cozia Monastery; Craiova; Danube; Desert; Dracula; emerald water; exterior; flags; forest; good weather; Great Barrier Reef; green fields; grey from stones; hotel interior; interesting wildlife; ivory sands; landscape; local culture; local people; luxury; Mamaia; market; mills; modern; monasteries; monuments; mountain; Muierii Cave; natural light; nature; open space; Outback; overall atmosphere; overall hotel exterior; past; people appearance; people attitude; physical heaviness; rain forest; restoration; river valley; roads; rocks; room quality; sad video; shopping; sky; stone houses; stream; street (busy/lively/people in the street); Sydney Opera House; Târgu Jiu; the Gate of the Kiss; topography; unfamiliar food appearance; water

Auditory elements

accent; animals; bells; birds; boats; club; concert; Dracula; festival; fire; insects; language; local music; Mamaia; manele; money; nature sounds; noise; ocean sound; people; pleasant; pleasant sound; quietness; river water; Sârbă (dance); seagulls; sizzling; stream; Street sounds; traffic; trains; water; wind

Olfatory elements

aerosols; agarwood; algae; ambergris; animals; antiques; aroma; Asian food; autumn leaves; blossomed linden tree; burned; church; clean; clean air; cologne; countryside; Danube Delta; enjoyable; evil scented; fireplace smoke; fish; flowers; fresh air; geothermal smells; goat; grass; herd; honey; incense; lake; land; local food; man-made smells; nature; odourless; Olt River; perfume; pine trees; pleasant; rain; resin from wood; Retezat National Park; salt water; scallion; sea breeze; sea smell; sulphur; sweet scent; Turkish coffee; unfamiliar food smell; wine

Gustatory elements

anchovies; aromatic plants; bread; bulz; cheese; ciorba; clove; coconut panna cotta; crusted horseradish; delicious; different taste; Dobrogea pies; fish; flavoured; food; fruit; good; goulash; green mango salsa; harissa couscous; honey; ice cream; Kurtos Kalacs; local beverage; local food; New Zealand scallops with grilled eel; pleasant texture; red radish; salmon; salty; sarmale; sausages; scallion sea food; Sibiu salami; star anise compote; sweet; tasty; unfamiliar food taste; unfamiliar food texture; Varză (cabbage) à la Cluj; wakame salad; wine

Tactile elements

animals; Bran Castle; brick; caressed; ceramics; chilly; clean air; coarse; cold; comfortable bed; coolness; Danube; endless column; enjoyable; flowers; food; grass; Horezu ceramics; humidity; land; mountain; palpable feeling of euphoria; plants; pleasant temperature; Poiana Braşov (sport activity); pressure; rocks; rough textures; sand; sea; sea breeze; sea coast; sea water; shells; snow; soft; tactile maps; trees; vegetation; warm temperature; wind; wood

Methodology

The method used for this research stems from the fact that a research gap was found in studying the importance of senses in tourist experience in islands as destinations. In addition, lack of studies was also found both in SIDS as well as in Cape Verde in this regard, and even more so when considering online reviews as a proxy of tourism experience.

This research was also associated with the business context in which this country´s destination marketing organization (DMO) promotes the islands of its archipelago according to three different clusters: islands of the Senses (4 islands: Brava, Fogo, Santo Antão, São Nicolau), islands of the Sun (3 islands: Boa Vista, Maio, Sal), and islands of the Essence (2 islands: Santiago, São Vicente). In order to cover all the experience from a holistic perspective accommodation, restaurants, and attractions were analyzed. A web scraping script was developed to extract all online reviews from the nine inhabited Cape Verde islands (Moro et al., 2018). Table 6.3 illustrates the sample of posts extracted from TripAdvisor in October 2018 in all the islands of the archipelago of Cape Verde.

Table 6.3: Units and online reviews analyzed in TripAdvisor for Cape Verde islands

Sense Islands

Island	Attractions	Accommodation	Restaurants
Santo Antão	10 (413 reviews)	57 (2,028 reviews)	20 (793 reviews)
Fogo	5 (222 reviews)	30 (614 reviews)	8 (220 reviews)
São Nicolau	6 (16 reviews)	7 (73 reviews)	4 (18 reviews)
Brava	NA	12 (53 reviews)	1 (3 reviews)

Sun Islands

Island	Attractions	Accommodation	Restaurants
Sal	55 (11,226reviews)	218 (29,180reviews)	92 (18,395 reviews)
Boa Vista	34 (4,306 reviews)	84 (24,279 reviews)	49 (5,127 reviews)
Maio	3 (41 reviews)	39 (185 reviews)	10 (209 reviews)

Essence Islands – History/Culture/Traditions

Island	Attractions	Accommodation	Restaurants
Santiago (Praia and Old City)	50 (1,470 reviews)	45 (2,371 reviews)	68 (2,603 reviews)
São Vicente (Mindelo)	13 (reviews)	52 (reviews)	32 (970 reviews)

A comprehensive software package used for the analysis of networks was UCINET (www.analytictech.com) which integrates the NetDraw program that works as a visualization tool for drawing diagrams of networks. This social network analysis software facilitates both quantitative or qualitative analysis of social networks, describing features of a network either through numerical or visual representation that is important to understand network data and convey the result of the analysis.

Findings

Sensory elements were identified in the online reviews about the nine islands of Cape Verde. Those were referred a total of 2,230,533 times. Overall, visual elements accounted for a massive share of 84%, followed by gustatory (7%), auditory (5%), olfactory (2%) and tactile (1%). Interestingly, whereas in the islands of the Sun both auditory (5.2%) and tactile (1.4%) senses were slightly above average, in the islands of the Essence visual sense was higher (86%), and in the islands of Senses gustatory (8%) and olfactory (3%) senses registered higher percentages (Table 6.4).

Table 6.4: Senses in online reviews of Cape Verde in each group of islands

Senses/ Islands	Sun	Essence	Senses	Total
Visual	84.2%	85.8%	83.8%	84.2%
Gustatory	7.0%	6.2%	8.2%	6.9%
Auditory	5.2%	4.4%	4.0%	5.2%
Tactile	1.4%	1.2%	1.3%	1.4%
Olfactory	2.3%	2.5%	2.6%	2.3%
Total	100.0%	100.0%	100.0%	100.0%

The visual sense reported by tourists is addressing beach, sea, sand as well as water and swimming pool, and the overall welcoming climate of the Cape Verde islands, e.g. sunshine (Figure 6.1). The destination is characterized as providing the sense of spacious and large. The outcome of these sensations is classified as fantastic, excellent and beautiful. The visual sensory elements which characterize the islands of the Sun include 'spacious', 'fantastic' and 'excellent'. In turn, whereas the islands of the Essence are more related to 'town' and 'night' the islands of the Senses are connected with 'green', 'safe' and 'nice'.

The following are illustrative examples of reviews:

"In my last day of visit I did the sea experience and we were so lucky to see two beautiful humpback whales and also flying fish, dolphins and a sea-eagle".

"We travelled for about two hours altogether on top of the boat which is very slow, for about five minutes viewing an underwater shipwreck with some shoals of pretty fish swimming around it and a further five minutes looking at a statue dimly through dirty windows."

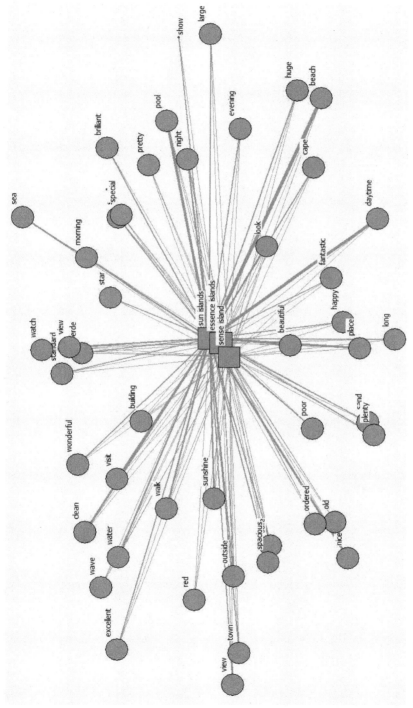

Figure 6.1: Visual sense in online reviews of groups of islands in Cape Verde

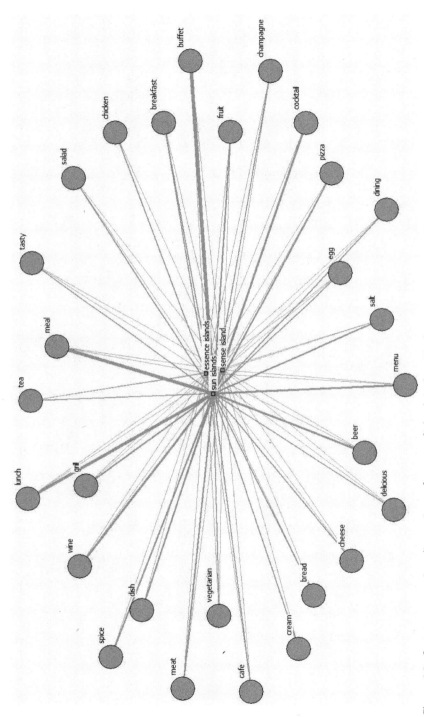

Figure 6.2: Gustatory sense in online reviews of groups of islands in Cape Verde

Within the gustatory sense, in terms of food and beverage tourists emphasize meat, chicken, salad and vegetarian food while the most stressed drinks are wine, beer, cocktail, champagne, coffee and tea (Figure 6.2). With regard to overall meals, reviewers underline breakfast and lunch related with buffet, and snacks. Adjectives such as delicious and tasty are used quite often. 'Buffet', 'snack' and 'tea' are gustatory sensory elements more associated with the islands of the Sun, 'meat', 'bread' and 'delicious' linked with the islands of the Essence, and 'lunch', 'beer' and 'spice' with the islands of the Senses.

Here are some examples of reviews:

"We had a really tasty meal, the cocktails were great, I highly recommend trying the cookies which wasn't on the menu but was suggested by our friendly waiter."

"A refreshingly cool sports bar with darts, pool, sports TV, excellent service and good wine and beer! We were made to feel at home and treated as friends. One of the reasons we shall be returning again to Santa Maria!"

"I can really recommend the time traveler tour, a lot to see and experience in a half day. Tamara is a lovely person and had answers to all our questions. Small groups so it's possible to personalize, if you are for example looking for something special to buy. We found the best coffee thanks to her!"

"We haven't tasted a bad house wine since we have been in Cape Verde"

'Music' 'entertainment' and 'party' are overall present in the auditory sense analysis in all three groups of islands of Cape Verde, although there is clearly more emphasis in the Sun islands (Figure 6.3). While the islands of the Essence are identified as more focused on 'street' and associated 'enjoyment', the islands of the Senses bring about 'quietness . In terms of foreign languages, English, French and Italian are the ones that are heard more frequently or with more intensity in Cape Verde.

The following reviews constitute examples:

"Nice place, friendly live music, nice ambience, prices ok. Worth a visit."

"The live music gave it a brilliant vibe too, we will be back. If you get the opportunity, definitely visit here"

"So clean, fine and quiet. Definitely the most beautiful beach in the island."

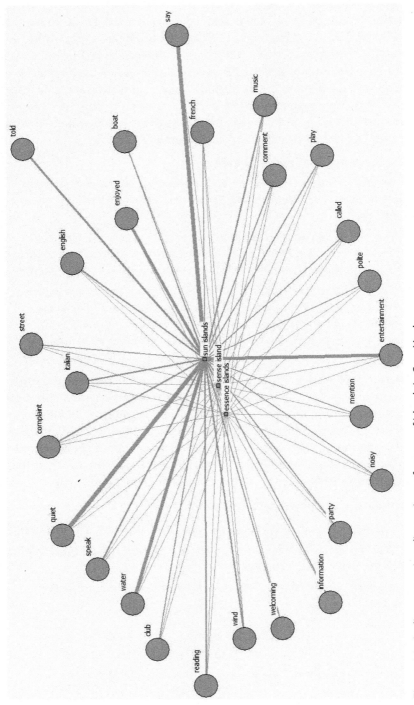

Figure 6.3: Auditory sense in online reviews of groups of islands in Cape Verde

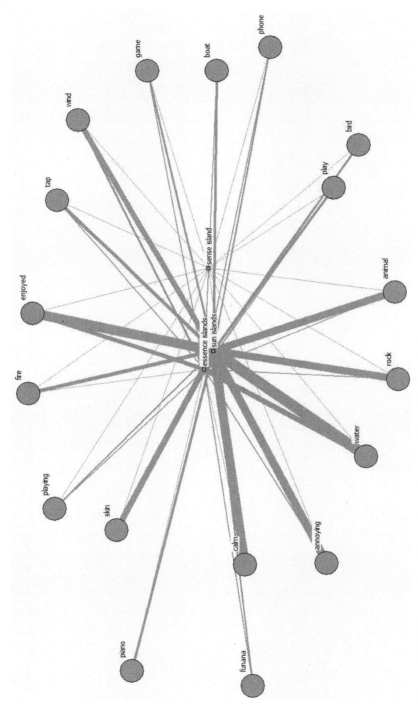

Figure 6.4: Tactile sense in online reviews of groups of islands in Cape Verde

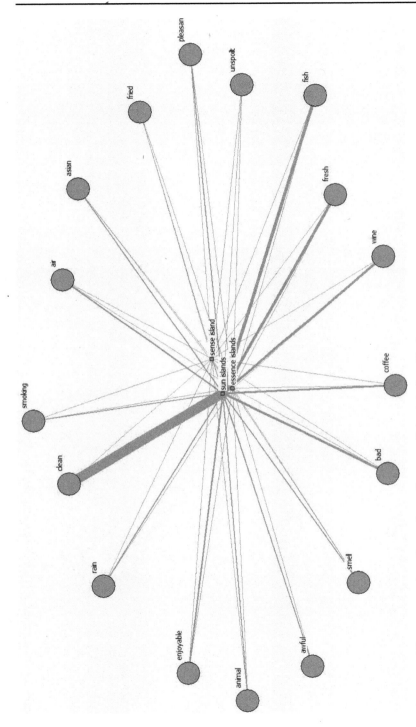

Figure 6.5: Olfactory sense in online reviews of groups of islands in Cape Verde

With regard to the tactile sense, both cold water and windy are the two most striking elements (Figure 6.4). More specifically, the element that is emphasized in the islands of the Sun is 'water', whereas 'playing' and 'piano' are stressed in the Essence islands, and 'wind' and 'animal' in the islands of the Senses. It is interesting to understand that although the word *Funana* represents a music and dance genre from Cape Verde, it is used in the tactile sense referring to staying in a hotel named Riu Funana, in Sun Island, Sal, "that is less windy and has a lot more activity on the beach". Here are examples of those reviews:

"The boat tour was unpleasant because the wind was cold the sea quite rough, and it was quite cloudy that day. It was unbelievable that they continue to be able to fill the boat up with such a poor offering. I wished I had looked on trip adviser before going on this!"

"I'm an animal lover and love petting them so didn't mind the cats and dogs roaming around but I'm sure it must put some people off."

Finally, the olfactory sense is rather focused on gastronomy since fish and steak are given relevance as well as wine and coffee (Figure 6.5). The Sun islands are matched with 'clean'. Further, the Essence islands are related with 'wine ' and 'coffee ', and the Sense islands with 'air', 'fish' and 'fresh'. It is also interesting to see that some negative adjectives 'awful' and 'bad' were stressed in the olfactory sense but the reviews show that they actually had a positive intention.

Examples of online reviews:

"Lunch was organised in a local restaurant of a Capeverdian chef trained in Switzerland and it was great to try the different dishes of goat, fish and chicken with different sides"

"I've been to more developed holiday destinations in Europe with vast numbers of awful restaurants compared to here. And there's something quite refreshing, exciting, and old school about making a find like CapeFruit in such an unspoiled and beautiful area."

"Have never been to a place quite like this but that's not a bad thing it's a great thing!"

"Food looked and smelled good"

"Just enjoyed the most beautiful lunch here on Christmas day. The setting is really peaceful and it has a lovely laid-back hippie vibe. The staff are really friendly too. My husband and I enjoyed some cold beers (at 200 CVEs each) and two tuna wraps, that were delightful and tasted very fresh. They were very filling too. The place is very clean and you get the sense that quality ingredients and high standards are very important to the owner. A must for anyone travelling to Santa Maria."

Conclusion

Sensorial analysis is essential to help the planning of the management marketing strategies of a destination. Sensorial marketing gives full comprehension of the destination as it complements the traditional marketing mix to develop and implement the necessary support instruments to enhance and assist the whole tourist experience in a more assertive way.

Sensory experiences can only be physically lived in the destination itself. Based in comments of previous visitors we were able to analyze and identify conclusions of specific sensory features that are more noticed in the destination Cape Verde. Each one of the sensory elements may individually or in a group translate the identity of the destination. They therefore need to be identified so that they can be incorporated in the best way in the identity of Cape Verde promotion.

This chapter reports on a research focused on multisensory dimensions of tourist experiences. It identified the authors who previously studied senses in tourism, namely sight, hearing, smell, taste and touch. Sensory elements most used in the scientific literature were also addressed. Forty-four thousand words were extracted from online reviews in TripAdvisor across accommodation, restaurants and tourist attractions with regard to Cape Verde, a small island developing state, in all its nine islands, specifically: four islands of theSenses (Brava, Fogo, Santo Antão, São Nicolau), three islands of the Sun (Boa Vista, Maio, Sal), two islands of the Essence (Santiago, São Vicente).

The visual sense is clearly predominant throughout the islands of the archipelago, followed at a significant distance by gustatory and auditory senses, and with less stimuli being perceived by the olfactory and tactile senses. Results show visual sense with a focus on beach, sea, sand, water and green. However, both the auditory and olfactory senses of sea and water are not explicit in the tourist reviews, contrary to what was expected after performing the review of the literature. The same holds for the tactile sense provided by sea and sand. According to literature, food and beverage tend to pair gustatory and olfactory senses as was the case for meat, salad, wine and coffee in online reviews about Cape Verde. In turn, music, street and quietness played an important role as far as auditory sense is concerned but the visual sense associated with street was not found in the reviews.

Cold, water and wind are given relevance to their tactile sense but the auditory sense related with the latter is not expressed in the reviews. Curiously, animals are only matched with the tactile sense, leaving out the visual, auditory and olfactory senses elicited in the literature. Finally, fresh and air are underlined as olfactory sensory elements. Although the same happens with clean and fish, the former omits both visual and tactile senses whereas the latter somewhat surprisingly does not stress its gustatory sense. Interestingly, when compared with the gustatory sense, we find fish missing in taste, although included in smell. Moreover, meat/steak as well as wine and coffee match both gustatory and olfactory senses.

This research was limited to a SIDS, Cape Verde, and used online reviews from only TripAdvisor, this being the largest travel-related online review platform in the world. Therefore, future research could consider other islands as well as extract data from other review sites. Moreover, our analysis was mostly performed in Cape Verde as a whole, although also addressing more striking differences between the groups of islands. Nevertheless, it would be interesting to zoom in and focus on results by individual islands. In addition, future research could fine tune the sensory elements per sense and proceed with a more in-depth analysis of online reviews.

In summary:

♦ Tourist perceptions are created from stimuli being captured by human senses, thus making the study of the senses from a consumer perspective an important area of research.

♦ Online reviews are a proxy of tourist experience since the former elicit the testimonials of visitors expliciting the latter and being conductive to tourist satisfaction.

♦ Cape Verde NTO, local businesses and also the community can greatly benefit from the reading and analysis of the data available in the social media give better understanding of today's tourist.

♦ Sensory features were identified and analysed from a large number of visitor comments extracted from TripAdvisor with regard to accommodation, restaurants and tourist attractions in the nine islands of Cape Verde, a small island developing state.

♦ The visual sense was by far the most predominant one, followed by gustatory and auditory senses. Most notable visual sensory elements were beach, sea, sand, water and green.

♦ Whereas music and quietness were frequently mentioned as auditory sensory impressions, food & beverage (e.g. wine and coffee) often underlined and coupled together gustatory and olfactory senses. Water and animals showed associations with the tactile sense.

References

Agapito, D., Valle, P.O.D. & Mendes, J. (2012). Sensory marketing and tourist experiences. *Spatial and Organizational Dynamics Discussions Papers*, **10**, 7-19.

Agapito, D., Mendes, J. & Valle, P. (2013). Conceptualizing the sensory dimension of tourist experiences. *Journal of Destination Marketing & Management*, **2**(2), 62-73. doi.org/10.1016/j.jdmm.2013.03.001

Agapito, D., Valle, P. & Mendes, J. (2014). The sensory dimension of tourist experiences: Capturing meaningful sensory-informed themes in Southwest Portugal. *Tourism Management*, **42**, 224-237. doi.org/10.1016/j.tourman.2013.11.011

Agapito, D., Pinto, P. & Mendes, J. (2017). Tourists' memories, sensory impressions and loyalty: In loco and post-visit study in Southwest Portugal. *Tourism Management*, **58**, 108-118. doi.org/10.1016/j.tourman.2016.10.015

Almeida, A.M.M., Correia, A. & Pimpão, A. (2014). Segmentation by benefits sought: The case of rural tourism in Madeira. *Current Issues in Tourism*, **17**(9), 813-831. doi.org/10.1080/13683500.2013.768605

Ballantyne, R., Packer, J. & Sutherland, L. (2011). Visitors' memories of wildlife tourism: Implications for the design of powerful interpretive experiences. *Tourism Management*, **32**(4), 770–779. doi.org/10.1016/j.tourman.2010.06.012

Bitner, M. J. (1992). Servicescapes: The impact of physical surroundings on customers and employees. *The Journal of Marketing*, **57-71**. doi: 10.2307/1252042. https://www.jstor.org/stable/1252042

Briassoulis, H. (2003). Crete: Endowed by nature, privileged by geography, threatened by tourism. *Journal of Sustainable Tourism*, **11**(2-3), 97-115. doi.org/10.1080/09669580308667198

Canavan, B. (2014). Sustainable tourism: Development, decline and degrowth. Management issues from the Isle of Man. *Journal of Sustainable Tourism*, **22**(1), 127-147. doi.org/10.1080/09669582.2013.819876

Cashman, A., Cumberbatch, J. & Moore, W. (2012). The effects of climate change on tourism in small states: Evidence from the Barbados case. *Tourism Review*, **67**(3), 17-29. doi.org/10.1108/16605371211259803

Dann, G.M. & Jacobsen, J. K. (2002). Leading the tourist by the nose. In G. M. S. Dann (Ed.), *The Tourist as a Metaphor of the Social World* (pp. 209-236). New York: CABI Publishing.

Davis, L. & Thys-Şenocak, L. (2017). Heritage and scent: Research and exhibition of Istanbul's changing smellscapes. *International Journal of Heritage Studies*, **23**(8), 723-741. doi.org/10.1080/13527258.2017.1317646

Del Chiappa, G. & Presenza, A. (2013). The use of network analysis to assess relationships among stakeholders within a tourism destination:

An empirical investigation on Costa Smeralda-Gallura, Italy. *Tourism Analysis*, **18**(1), 1-13. doi.org/10.3727/108354213X13613720283520

Diţoiu, M. C. & Căruntu, A. L. (2014). Sensory experiences regarding five-dimensional brand destination. *Procedia-Social and Behavioral Sciences*, **109**, 301-306. doi.org/10.1016/j.sbspro.2013.12.461

Govers, R., Go, F. & Kumar, K. (2007). Virtual destination image: A new measurement approach. *Annals of Tourism Research*, **34**(4), 977–997. https://doi.org/10.1016/j.annals.2007.06.001

Gretzel, U. & D. R. Fesenmaier (2003). Experience-based internet marketing: An exploratory study of sensory experiences associated with pleasure travel to the Midwest United States. In *Proceedings of the International Conference on Information and Communication Technologies in Tourism*, edited by A. Frew, M. Hitz, and P. O'Connor. Wien-New York: Springer Verlag, pp. 49–57.

Gretzel, U. & Fesenmaier, D. (2010). Capturing sensory experiences through semi-structured elicitation questions. *The Tourism and Leisure Experience: Consumer and Managerial Perspectives*, 137-160.

Harrison, D. (Ed.). (2001). *Tourism and the Less Developed World: Issues and Case Studies*. CABI Publishing, UK.

Howes, D. & Marcoux, J.S. (2006). Introduction à la culture sensible. *Anthropologie et Sociétés*, **30**(3), 7-17. doi: 10.7202/014922a

Howes D. & Classen C. (2014). *Ways of Sensing: Understanding the Senses in Society*. 1st Edition, Routledge. doi.org/10.4324/9781315856032

Hultén, B., Broweus, N. & van Dijk, M. (2009). *Sensory Marketing*. New York: Palgrave Macmillan.

Hung, Y. C., Zheng, X., Carlson, J. & Giurge, L. M. (2017). The weight of the saddened soul: the bidirectionality between physical heaviness and sadness and its implications for sensory marketing. *Journal of Marketing Management*, **33**(11-12), 917-941. doi.org/10.1080/02672 57X.2017.1323775

INE (2013) Instituto Nacional de Estatística, Cape Verde. Retrieved February 2019 from http://ine.cv/.

INE (2016) Instituto Nacional de Estatística, Cape Verde.Retrieved February 2019 from http://ine.cv/.

Jafari, J. (1974). The socio-economic costs of tourism to developing countries. *Annals of Tourism Research*, **2**, (5), 237–245.

Jaworska, S. (2017). Metaphors we travel by: A corpus-assisted study of metaphors in promotional tourism discourse. *Metaphor and Symbol*, **32**(3), 161-177. doi.org/10.1080/10926488.2017.1338018

Kastenholz, E., Carneiro, M., Marques, C. & Lima, J. (2012). Understanding and managing the rural tourism experience—the case of a historical village in Portugal. *Tourism Management Perspectives*, **4**, 207–214. doi.org/10.1016/j.tmp.2012.08.009

Khadaroo, J. & Seetanah, B. (2007). Transport infrastructure and tourism development. *Annals of Tourism Research*, **34**(4), 1021-1032. doi.org/10.1016/j.annals.2007.05.010

Kilic, H. & Okumus, F. (2005). Factors influencing productivity in small island hotels: evidence from Northern Cyprus. *International Journal of Contemporary Hospitality Management*, **17**(4), 315-331. doi.org/10.1108/09596110510597589

Kim, D. & Perdue, R. (2013) The effects of cognitive, affective, and sensory attributes on hotel choice. *International Journal of Hospitality Management*, **35**, 246-257. doi.org/10.1016/j.ijhm.2013.05.012

Kim, Y. & Eves, A. (2012) Construction and validation of a scale to measure tourist motivation to consume local food. *Tourism Management*, **33**(6), 1458-1467. doi.org/10.1016/j.tourman.2012.01.015

Kim, Y., Eves, A. & Scarles, C. (2009). Building a model of local food consumption on trips and holidays: A grounded theory approach. *International Journal of Hospitality Management*, **28**(3), 423-431. doi.org/10.1016/j.ijhm.2008.11.005

Klint, L.M., Wong, E., Jiang, M., Delacy, T., Harrison, D. & Dominey-Howes, D. (2012). Climate change adaptation in the Pacific Island tourism sector: Analysing the policy environment in Vanuatu. *Current Issues in Tourism*, **15**(3), 247-274. doi.org/10.1080/13683500.2011.608841

Ko, D.W. & Stewart, W.P. (2002). A structural equation model of residents' attitudes for tourism development. *Tourism Management*, **23**(5), 521-530. doi.org/10.1016/S0261-5177(02)00006-7

Krishna, A. (Ed.) (2010). *Sensory Marketing: Research on the Sensuality of Products*. New York: Routledge.

Lee, W., Gretzel, U. & Law, R. (2010). Quasi-trial experiences through sensory information on destination web sites. *Journal of Travel Research*, **49**(3), 310-322. doi.org/10.1177/0047287509346991

Lindstrom, M. (2005). *Brand Sense: Build powerful brands through touch, taste, smell, sight and sound*. New York: Free Press.

Markwell, K. (2001). An intimate rendezvous with nature? Mediating the tourist-nature experience at three tourist sites in Borneo. *Tourist Studies*, **1**(1), 39–57. doi.org/10.1177/ 146879760100100103

Markwick, M. C. (2001). Tourism and the development of handicraft production in the Maltese islands. *Tourism Geographies*, **3**(1), 29-51.

Mateiro, B., Kastenholz, E. & Breda, Z. (2017). The sensory dimension of the tourist experience in mountain destinations: The case of Serra da Estrela Natural Park. *Revista Turismo & Desenvolvimento*, **1**(27/28), 2027-2038.

Mitchell, R.E. & Reid, D.G. (2001). Community integration: Island tourism in Peru. *Annals of Tourism Research*, **28**(1), 113-139. doi.org/10.1016/S0160-7383(00)00013-X.

Moro, S., Rita, P., Oliveira, C., Batista, F. & Ribeiro, R. (2018). Leveraging national tourist offices through data analytics. *International Journal of Culture, Tourism and Hospitality Research*, **12**(4), 420-426. doi.org/10.1108/IJCTHR-04-2018-0051

Moniz, A.I. (2012). A dynamic analysis of repeat visitors. *Tourism Economics*, **18**(3), 505-517. doi.org/10.5367/te.2012.0129

Nunkoo, R. & Gursoy, D. (2012). Residents' support for tourism: An identity perspective. *Annals of Tourism Research*, **39**(1), 243-268. https://doi.org/10.1016/j.annals.2011.05.006

Pan, S. & Ryan, C. (2009). Tourism sense making: The role of the senses and travel journalism. *Journal of Travel & Tourism Marketing*, **26**(7), 625–639. https://doi.org/10.1080/10548400903276897

Park (2011). Examining potential for cruise business in the American-affiliated pacific islands. *Asia Pacific Journal of Tourism Research*, **16**(1), 1-19. doi.org/10.1080/10941665.2011.539388

Pine, B.J. & Gilmore, J.H. (1998). Welcome to the experience economy. *Harvard Business Review*, **76**, 97-105.

Pollard, T., Steptoe, A. & Wardle, J. (1998). Motives underlying healthy eating: using the food choice questionnaire to explain variation in dietary intake. *Journal of Biosocial Science*, **30**(2), 165-179.

Rickly-Boyd, J.M. & Metro-Roland, M.M. (2010). Background to the fore: The prosaic in tourist places. *Annals of Tourism Research*, **37**, 1164–1180. doi.org/10.1016/j.annals.2010.06.001

Rivera, M., Croes, R. & Zhong, Y. (2016). Developing mobile services: A look at first-time and repeat visitors in a small island destination. *International Journal of Contemporary Hospitality Management*, **28**(12), 2721-2747. https://doi.org/10.1108/IJCHM-02-2015-0052

Santana-Gallego, M., Ledesma-Rodríguez, F. & Pérez-Rodríguez, J.V. (2011). Tourism and trade in small island regions: The case of the Canary islands. *Tourism Economics*, **17**(1), 107-125. doi.org/10.5367/te.2011.0029

Schmitt, B. (1999). Experiential marketing. *Journal of Marketing Management*, **15**(1-3), 53-67. https://doi.org/10.1362/026725799784870496

Seetanah, B. & Sannassee, R. V. (2015). Marketing promotion financing and tourism development: The case of Mauritius. *Journal of Hospitality Marketing & Management*, **24**(2), 202-215. doi.org/10.1080/19368623.2014.914359

Sharpley, R. (2003). Tourism, modernisation and development on the island of Cyprus: Challenges and policy responses. *Journal of Sustainable Tourism*, **11**(2-3), 246-265. doi.org/10.1080/09669580308667205

Small, J., Darcy, S. & Packer, T. (2012). The embodied tourist experiences of people with vision impairment: Management implications beyond the visual gaze. *Tourism Management*, **33**(4), 941–950. doi.org/10.1016/j. tourman.2011.09.015

Son, A. & Pearce, P. (2005). Multi-faceted image assessment: international students' views of Australia as a tourist destination. *Journal of Travel & Tourism Marketing*, **18**(4), 21–35. doi.org/10.1300/J073v18n04_02

Stăncioiu, A. F., Diţoiu, M. C., Teodorescu, N., Onişor, L. F. & Pârgaru, I. (2014). Sensory marketing strategies. Case study: Oltenia. *Theoretical & Applied Economics*, **21**(7).

Steptoe, A., Pollard, T.M. & Wardle, J. (1995). Development of a measure of the motives underlying the selection of food: the food choice questionnaire. *Appetite*, **25**, 267-284.

Tussyadiah, I. P. & Zach, F. J. (2012). The role of geo-based technology in place experiences. *Annals of Tourism Research*, **39**(2), 780–800. doi. org/10.1016/j.annals.2011.10.003

UN (2016). *Partnerships for Small Island Developing States*. United Nations, New York.

UNCED (1992). United Nations Conference on Environment and Development, United Nations, New York.

UNCED (2012). Earth Summit. United Nations conference, Rio de Janeiro, Brazil.

UNWTO (2012). Tourism: a development opportunity for Small Island States. UNWTO report, PR No: PR12038. media.unwto.org/press-release/2012-06-19/tourism-development-opportunity-small-island-states-finds-unwto-report

UNWTO (2014). Conference on Small Island Developing States, Apia Samoa.

Urry, J. (2002). *The Tourist Gaze* (2nd ed.). London: Sage.

Walls, A. R., Okumus, F., Wang, Y. R. & Kwun, D. J. W. (2011). An epistemological view of consumer experiences. *International Journal of Hospitality Management*, **30**(1), 10-21. doi.org/10.1016/j.ijhm.2010.03.008

Wu, K., Raab, C., Chang, W. & Krishen, A. (2016). Understanding Chinese tourists' food consumption in the United States. *Journal of Business Research*, **69**(10), 4706-4713. doi.org/10.1016/j.jbusres.2016.04.018

7 The eWOM effects on service performance in hospitality

Carimo Rassal, Antónia Correia and Francisco Serra

The objectives of this chapter are to:

☐ Explore the effects of electronic word of mouth (eWOM) on satisfaction in hospitality through the service performance scope;

☐ Gain further understanding as to which attributes are relevant to the guest's overall assessment of a hotel experience;

☐ Highlight findings that show the importance of, staff (language, assurance, responsiveness, reliability), rate promotions, hotel design and location, operational organization (facilities and services), room experience, food and beverage and price, in the overall assessment of the hotel's service performance.

Keywords: eWOM, TripAdvisor, service performance, tourist satisfaction, hospitality.

Introduction

Tourism remains one of the world's fastest growing sectors with bookings in 2017 reaching almost US $1.6 trillion and travel and tourism contributing 10.4% to global GDP (Deloitte, 2018). That equates to 4.6% growth compared to 2016, furthermore globally, almost 10% of all jobs are linked to the travel and tourism industry (World Travel & Tourism Council, 2018). Social media now has more influence over traveller decision making than ever before. In fact, more than 50% of travellers from the US, UK, Canada, and Australia said that content, promotions and deals on social media influences their travel plans (Expedia, 2018). Travel brands are adapting their marketing strategies in line with traveller behaviour, reporting that on average, 61% of their marketing budget is now spent on digital advertising (Phocuswire, 2018).

Consumer approaches to hotel online bookings have clearly changed dramatically. The democratization of the internet in the scope of the affordability of access cost-per-gigabyte of use grounded in the technological revolution of the smartphone has made it possible to redefine how, where and when the consumer buys throughout ecommerce platforms (Chung & Koo, 2015). The evolution of new distribution platforms in order to increase the engagement between the businesses and consumers is a reality. Moreover, the development of social media platforms such as Facebook, Twitter and Instagram brought an all-new meaning to interconnectivity between brands and consumers (Okazaki et al., 2017). According to Eurostat (2016), four out of ten Europeans look for online travel-related information, 55% of the trips of EU residents were booked online and 26% of holiday accommodation (including hotel rooms) were bought online. TripAdvisor is one of the industry's most heavily relied on sources for travel information with over 324 million monthly visitors recorded in 2017 (Salecycle, 2018).

The contribution of this chapter depends upon on the identification of the relationship between the overall assessment and a multitude of comments, categorized in thirteen dimensions that represent all the facets of the hospitality service. The aim is to understand what are the service values that have the most impact on the customer satisfaction considering the number of stars of the hotels. This research is unique by contributing to understanding how comments moderate the overall assessment. It is also unique since it makes it possible to depict the most important hospitality services dimensions in each type of hotel. Further, this research uses qualitative comments that were categorized to allow this research. Hence this is shaping the avenues of research by using simultaneously qualitative and quantitative analysis, thus making a unique and invaluable contribution to the hospitality development strategies.

Literature review

Word of Mouth and eWOM

In 1957, word of mouth (WOM) was defined by Brooks as a powerful source of product and service information dissemination, which when negative had a greater impact than when it was positive (Brooks, 1957). Initially, word of mouth was described by Katz and Lazarsfeld as an exchange of marketing information among consumers, who often alter their behaviour and attitudes toward products or services (Katz & Lazarsfeld, 1966). Dichter explained in 1966 that when a customer feels that the seller cares for him, such as a friend, he becomes more relaxed and accepts the recommendation more easily (Dichter, 1966). According to Arndt (1967) WOM, interpersonal influence are fundamental sources of information in the purchasing decision process, especially important in the hotel and tourism industry, due to the perishability and intangibility of its products. In 1968 Merton defined word-of-mouth as a process of personal influence, in which interpersonal communications have a major impact on the recipient's attitudes and behaviours (Merton, 1968). Day found that word of mouth as advertising is nine times more effective because there is a much higher degree of trust in the source and the flexibility of interpersonal communication (Day, 1971). In 1987 Mangold's review of the impact of word of mouth on professional services proved the emphatic influence of word of mouth on the purchase decision process (Mangold, 1987).

According to Murray, the high degree of influence of WOM is due to the fact that people sources are considered more viable (Murray, 1991). Dellarocas states that WOM is one of the oldest forms of transmitting information (Dellarocas, 2003). Since WOM is a process of interpersonal exchanges, they provide information related to the consumption of a product or service that unintentionally influences consumers (Brown, 2007). In 2008 Litvin defined WOM as a process of communication between consumers, independent of commercial influence (Litvin, 2008). More recently, Daugherty and Hoffman consider WOM to be one of the most influential factors in consumer behaviour (Daugherty & Hoffman, 2014).

The definition of WOM is divided into three perspectives: non-commercial, commercial and intermediate. For the non-commercial perspective, several researchers define WOM as an informal, personal, non-commercial communication process (Ardnt, 1967; Still, 1984; Bayus, 1985; Harrison-Walker, 2001; Grewal et al., 2003). The business perspective for Hartline and Jones (1998) and Gremler and Brown (1999) define WOM as the recommendation of a product or service with commercial intentions, as it is a marketing information exchange. Herr (1991) and Anderson (1998) state the intermediate perspective that defines WOM as informal communication, in which products are evaluated according to the experience of each consumer and may or may not include a recommendation that may be positive or negative. Gilly et al. (1998), argue that WOM communication is bi-directional and interactive, consisting of two groups: opinion leaders and opinion seekers. Opinion leader's express information that interferes with consumer choices, relating to products or services (Burt, 1999; Feick & Price, 1987; Lazarsfels et al., 1944; Wotts & Dudds, 2007). The opinion seekers pursue information in the public opinion in order to assist the evaluation process of products or services, taking into account their purchases (Feick et al., 1986; Flynn et al., 1996).

Electronic word of mouth (eWOM) was defined in Henni-Thura, as a process of information dissemination through the internet, that is, a word of mouth online (Hennin-Thurau et al., 2004). According to Rodgers and Wang (2011), eWOM consists of any degree or combination of positive, negative, or neutral comments, recommendations, or statements about companies, brands, products or services, discussed or shared between consumers in digital or electronic formats (Rodgers & Wang, 2011). The internet becomes a means for consumers to express themselves. According to Litvin et al. (2008), eWOM can be defined as all informal communications addressed to consumers through internet-based technologies related to the use or characteristics of goods or services and their suppliers. This type of communication can be exercised between supplier and consumer or between consumers. These same authors also mention that communication has two dimensions: the scope and the level of interactivity. The scope defines whether communication is done one-to-one (emails), one to many (TripAdvisor) or many to many (virtual communities). The level of interactivity defines synchronization, or the absence of it, for example, emails are asynchronous because a sender sends a message, but the receiver may not read and respond immediately. On the other hand, in the case of chat rooms, there is synchronization because the sender sends a message and it is received instantly by the receiver.

Another study by Sun et al. (2006) suggests that the main difference between WOM and eWOM is that the latter is more used for its speed, convenience and lack of personal communication. Schiffman and Kanuk (2000) also point out that the expectation of receiving information that may shorten decision-making time results in more satisfactory decision-making. eWOM has a growing importance in consumption and therefore should be taken into account by companies, namely the travel and tourism related companies. Most of the online reviews shared on the hotel websites or in other platforms work as a eWOM, and this is one of the best formats to promote and enhance the reputation of a hotel.

Online reviews

According to Sparks and Browning (2010), online reviews have a significant impact on consumer confidence. Reviews influence the choice (or not) of a particular brand, have an impact on the reputation of the brand / company, are a source of pre-purchase information and are, for consumers, a reliable source of information (Noone & McGuire, 2013). For Cantallops and Salvi (2014), there are factors that generate reviews that will later produce effects on the perception of consumers and companies. The factors that produce the most reviews are quality of service and satisfaction, failure and recovery, customer dissatisfaction and sense of belonging in the community. Swanson and Hsu (2009) argue that although a customer has had a satisfactory experience, he may not recommend the service to other consumers. However, eWOM contributes to the development of a company's reputation and trust (Riegelsberger et al., 2005). In spite of these considerations, Ye et al. (2008) consider it of utmost importance that the hotel directors take into account the reviews published on third party websites about their hotels.

There are advantages and disadvantages to take into account regarding the reviews. The advantages are to expose the weaknesses and strengths of the hotel, are a positive indirect marketing source (if the reviews are positive), they let us know the feedback of the clients and serve as a link between guests and hotels. On the other hand, some of the disadvantages are that the bad reviews can be seen by everyone, which leads to a greater vulnerability of the hotel and there is still an increase in the expectations of the clients, that is, the more information the clients have the greater is their critical level (higher expectation), which can sometimes lead to dissatisfaction with the service (Ladhari & Michaud, 2015). In analysing the advantages and disadvantages, eWOM is indeed an important source of information. There is only one setback, this information still lacks data processing that enable an empirical analysis whose output allows us to know the preferences and needs of guests. If this data processing is possible, and according to several authors there are already some models, then we will know almost immediately the real needs of the customers, which will allow us to exceed their expectations, which will lead to the main objective of involving and pleasing the guests.

Hospitality service dynamics and satisfaction

From the customer´s point of view, resort hotel services are intangible and heterogeneous (Ali et al., 2016); therefore, in a highly competitive and dynamic hospitality industry, service providers today are developing various strategies to ensure customer satisfaction (Geissler & Rucks, 2011; Wu & Liang, 2009). It is evident that customer satisfaction is closely linked to many other marketing concepts including service quality, customer relationship marketing, customer confidence, loyalty, distribution, price, and emotions (Ali & Zhou, 2013; Ryu et al., 2012). For example, in the hospitality industry, customer satisfaction can be ensured by developing an attractive physical environment or servicescape (Ali & Amin, 2014; Ryu et al., 2012), eliciting positive emotions (Kincaid et al., 2010; Lin & Liang, 2011), providing memorable service experiences (Hou et al., 2013), and ensuring great interaction with staff members and customers (Jani & Han, 2011; Ruiz et al., 2012). In this context, the influence of the service experience on customer satisfaction has received significant attention from researchers (Dölarslan, 2014; Olsson et al., 2012).

The core principle of the resort concept is the creation of an environment that will promote and enhance a feeling of well-being and enjoyment. Furthermore, Gee (2000) identified two characteristics of a resort hotel: (a) sufficient indoor amenities, including quality services, pleasant physical surroundings, convenient entertainment, service experience, emotions, satisfaction, and price acceptance and other facilities; and (b) a unique location in terms of climate, scenery, and recreational attractions. This definition of resort hotels is also supported by other scholars and practitioners (Ali & Amin, 2014; Meng et al., 2008). Moreover, the United Nations World Tourism Organization also stated that the importance of resort hotels in tourism and hospitality has been consistently growing (UNWTO, 2013); however, it is surprising that this sector has not gained much attention in research (Ali et al., 2013). For example, Line and Runyan (2012) reviewed 274 articles published in four top hospitality journals from 2008 to 2010 and suggested that resort hotels are an emergent research trend and continually growing in hospitality marketing research (Kim, 2014). This research may emphasize the encounter between hosts and guests as one of the major forms of generate satisfaction.

Conceptual model and research hypothesis

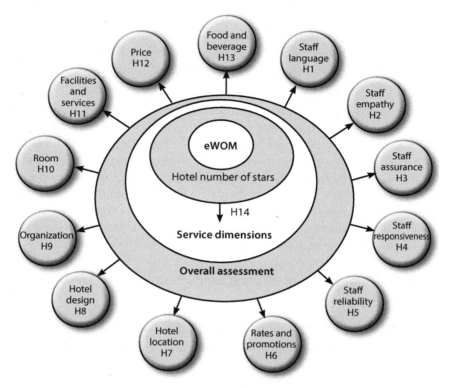

Figure 7.1: eWOM effects on overall assessment through service dimensions. Adapted from Verma (2010) and Cantallops & Salvi (2014).

In a service industry, while good technical and interpersonal skills are essential, the two alone cannot warrant customer satisfaction (Gu & Chi, 2009). The greater a customer's perception of a service firm's performance, as compared to their expectations of the firm the higher the customer will perceive the level of service quality (Rauch et al., 2015). In this scope, Kandampully (2007) stated that, reliability is defined as the dependability, consistency and accuracy with which the service is performed by the provider. Responsiveness refers to the willingness of the service personnel to assist customers in a timely, efficient manner and includes items such as helpfulness, friendliness and warmth of the service staff. Assurance is the degree to which the service personnel inspire trust and confidence among the customers of the firm. Empathy is related to the caring personal attention extended to customers, as well as the level of understanding personnel demonstrate relative to customer needs, while the tangibles component refers to appearance of the physical facilities, as well as the perceived quality of the materials, personnel and equipment utilized by the service provider. Nevertheless, advances in information technology and the introduction of new methods of communication have led to increasingly significant changes in consumer behavior. These changes have produced a shift in focus in companies' marketing strategies and business administration, especially in the hotel industry.

Purchase decision processes are nowadays composed of several variables that influence consumer choice for certain products and services (Kim et al, 2006). Customers might choose a hotel based on its location (for instance, close to an airport, tourist location, or downtown), brand name, various facilities (such as swimming pool, golf course, and spa and fitness center), service quality, price, loyalty program, atmosphere and design, and quality ratings by past guests. Any or all of these would enter into the customer choice mix (Verma, 2010). This research uses 13 service dimensions to depict the value of the overall assessment, by hotel stars:

♦ H1: Comments about **staff language** would influence overall assessment.
   According to Akan (1995) staff language is important in hotel guest/ staff interactions in order to process communications (Akbaba, 2006) about needs in an understandable (Getty and Getty, 2003) and efficient manner (Zhou et al., 2014).

♦ H2: Comments about **staff empathy** would influence overall assessment.
   Parasuraman et al. (1988) and later Albacete-Saez et al. (2007) tested staff empathy relevance to overall assessment of the guest's experience in a hotel and confirmed the dimensional relevance of this attribute in the nonphysical category.

♦ H3: Comments about **staff assurance** would influence overall assessment.
   According to Juwaheer (2004) staff assurance is associated with knowledgeable employees that can be trusted with the guest expectations in competent manner (Choi & Chu, 2001).

♦ H4: Comments about **staff responsiveness** would influence overall assessment.
   Staff training is in the core of the responsiveness capacity of the service delivery, and in this sense can influence the overall assessment about the hotel service (Choi & Chu, 2001).

- H5: Comments about **staff reliability** would influence overall assessment.

  Juwaheer (2004), refers to reliability as the ability to perform the service according to promises; in this scope consistency of performance is crucial to reliability (Akbaba, 2006).

- H6: Comments about **rates and promotions** would influence overall assessment.

  A cognitive estimation of the benefits in hospitality related products was hypothesized and produced a positive correlation towards hotel guests (Christou, 2011). Therefore, it can be tested in overall assessment.

- H7: Comments about **hotel location** would influence overall assessment.

  Location is consistently identified as the primary criterion in initial hotel selection, therefore is expected to influence the willingness to share about this attribute (Chan & Wong, 2006; Lockyer, 2005; McCleary et al., 1994; Knutson, 1988).

- H8: Comments about **hotel design** would influence overall assessment.

  As a factor of hotel service, hotel design influences the environmental quality assessment of service quality and consequently the overall assessment of the hotel (Juwaheer, 2004; Heide & Grønhaug, 2009; Naqshbandi & Munir, 2011; Wu & Ko, 2013).

- H9: Comments about **organization** would influence overall assessment.

  Akan (1995) notes that the organization attribute has been related with service quality effectiveness. Akbaba (2006) found a positive relationship between organization awareness and satisfaction in hotel service. In this perspective the relationship between organization and overall assessment can be hypothesised.

- H10: Comments about **room** would influence overall assessment.

  Saleh and Ryan (1991) identified clean rooms, comfortable beds, quiet stay, safety and security and location as the most important attributes, utilizing a measurement tool developed by Lewis (1984). We can therefore hypothesise the influence of room quality in overall assessment of the hotel experience.

- H11: Comments about **facilities and services** would influence overall assessment.

Wuest et al. (1996) define perceptions of hotel attributes as the degree to which travelers find various services and facilities important in promoting their satisfaction with hotel stays, which can thus can influence the overall assessment of the hotel.

♦ H12: Comments **about price** would influence overall assessment.
Generally associated as a service value attribute (Chang & Wildt, 1994), price can be dimensionally scoped in terms of value for money in the hotel guest experience, consequently it can influence the overall assessment.

♦ H13: Comments about **food and beverage** would influence overall assessment.
As an attribute that influences customer satisfaction in hotels in terms of value perception (Zhou et al., 2014), food and beverage quality, variety and diversity play an important role in customer loyalty (Sim et al., 2006) and therefore we should be exploring its influence on overall performance.

Furthermore, the overall assessment is likely to be related to hotel characteristics Yang et al. (2012), as such the following hypothesis was defined:

♦ H14: Comments about each of the **service dimensions** are conditioned by the **number of hotel stars.**
As stated by Martin-Fuentes (2016), the number of hotel stars influence service quality comments by each dimension of the guest experience in hospitality, as such it should be hypothesized.

Research design

Qualitative comments were coded in three-point Likert scales (1 for the negative comments, 2 for indifferent and 3 for positive comments). The overall assessment was kept as collected from the web site (this scale varies from 1 to 10) so as not to lose the variance of the variable. An Order Probit model by number of hotel stars was created to test the effects of each of the service dimensions on the final assessment. This model is the most appropriate to test the effects the conceptual model proposes, as the data is of the ordinal type (Ben-Akiva et al., 1997). It thus makes it possible to estimate relationships between an ordinal dependent variable and a set of independent variables. In ordered probit, an underlying score is estimated as a linear function of the independent variables and a set of cut points. The probability of observing outcome i corresponds to the probability that the estimated linear function, plus random error, is within the range of the cut points estimated for the outcome. The cut-off of the model was set for the last category that means totally satisfied. The variables were re-categorized accordingly with the number of nodes they presented in this original form. This means that a variable with only one category comprise only negative or positive comments. Stata 7 was used to estimate the model through a maximum likelihood function. The first step of the analysis is to examine the influence of the thirteen service dimensions comments over the overall assessment, depicting the effect of number of hotel stars over the verbalized comments. Data were split accordingly the number of stars of the hotels comprised on the sample and each of the models were adjusted to get a good fit.

Survey methods

The empirical study was carried out by means of a content analysis of hotels in Algarve through TripAdvisor. Comments were randomly collected at TripAdvisor within 4 to 5 star hotels. The central aim of this research was to assess how social contexts and hotel features ,as well as the dimensions of the hospitality service, may contribute to an overall assessment. The sample comprises 1134 observations, from which 1059 are related with 4 star hotels and 75 relates with 5 star hotels.

Findings

Table 7.1 summarizes the results of the Order Probit model estimated to measure the effects of service dimensions over the final assessment, by the number of stars of the hotels. All the variables with non-significant beta weights or collinearity were eliminated to improve each of the models estimated. As it illustrates, the results of the regression of the 13 variables accounted for 19.88% of the variance for 4 star hotels, and 23.26% for 5 star hotels; the likelihood-ratio test with 16 degrees of freedom for each of the models were -2491.381 (p<.05), -2433.356 (p<.05) and -143.369 (p<.05), respectively. All the variables retained show significant beta weights, most of them with mixed effects. Table 7.1 illustrates the results of the Order Probit models.

Discussion

A list of 13 hypotheses has proposed that staff language, staff empathy, staff assurance, staff responsiveness, staff reliability, rates and promotions, hotel location, hotel design, organization, room experience, facilities and services price, food and beverage comments, influence the respondent's overall assessment of hospitality services within different rates of hotels.

Table 7.1: Results of the order probit models

	4 star hotels				5 stars Hotels			
	Coef.	**Std. Err.**	**z**	**P>z**	**Coef.**	**Std. Err.**	**z**	**P>z**
Staff language	.306	.150	2.04	0.041	ns	ns	ns	ns
Staff empathy								
1	-.163	.217	7.49	0.000	-.401	.166	-2.41	0.016
2	.409	.074	5.53	0.000	.270	.779	3.47	0.001
Staff responsiveness								
1	ns	ns	ns	ns	-.257	.119	-2.15	0.032
2	ns	ns	ns	ns	.247	.815	3.04	0.002
Staff reliability								
1	ns	ns	ns	ns	-.410	.207	-1.98	0.048
2	ns	ns	ns	ns	.328	.112	2.91	0.004
Rates and promotions								
1	-.994	.239	4.15	0.000	ns	ns	ns	ns
2	.443	.199	2.22	0.026	ns	ns	ns	ns
Location	-.625	.225	2.78	0.005	ns	ns	ns	ns
Hotel design								
1	-.112	.158	7.10	0.000	ns	ns	ns	ns
2	.343	.073	4.68	0.000	ns	ns	ns	ns
Organization	-.559	.124	4.49	0.000	ns	ns	ns	ns
Room experience	-.853	.100	8.51	0.000	ns	ns	ns	ns
Facilities and Services	-.450	.107	4.21	0.000	-.187	.667	-2.81	0.005
Price	-.789	.162	4.86	0.000	-.155	.677	-2.30	0.022
Food and beverage								
1	-.590	.165	3.56	0.000	-.290	.858	-3.39	0.001
2	.357	.091	3.91	0.000	.518	.479	1.08	0.280
N	1059				75			
LR chi2(16)	533.17				43.85			
Log likelihood	-2433.356				-143.369			
Pseudo R2	0.1988				.2326			

Staff language was proved to influence guest's satisfaction in 4 star hotels (β=0.306, p<.05) but not significant for 5 star hotels, this might suggest that in 5 star hotels it is assumed that staff are able to communicate with some proficiency with their guests (Schuckert et al., 2015). As such H1 is partially accepted as a condition to ensure satisfaction.

Staff empathy was proved to be significant in both types of hotels with negative comments influencing negatively satisfaction and positive ones influencing positively. H2 is not rejected and these results suggest that hosts' empathy are critical to please hotel guests (Tussyadiah & Park, 2018), being this the best evidence that hotel service is a human to human relationship (Nieves & Quintana, 2018). H5 is partially accepted as staff reliability is not significant for 4 star hotels but it is significant for 5 star hotels (β=-0.410, p<.05 for negative comments and β=0.328, p<.05 for positive comments) these results suggest that guests are willing to trust their hosts at least at the high-ranking hotels (Wang, et al., 2014).

As expected H6 is also partially accepted as rates and promotions are valued only in 4 star hotels (β=-0.994, p<.05 for positive comments and β=0.443, p<.05 for positive ones) these results suggest that value for money is more emphasized in mid-price hotels than in high price hotels (Rhee & Yang, 2015). Location seems to influence negatively 4 star hotels (β=-0.625, p<.05) and it is not significant in 5 star hotels, suggesting that H7 is also partially accepted, this might suggest that 4 star hotels should be in conformity with guest's preferences (Liu, et al., 2014). Organization also influences negatively satisfaction with 4 star hotels (β=-0.625, p<.05) whereas in 5 star hotels is not significant; these results leads to partially accept H9, which is in accordance with Ali & Amin (2014), that proves that investing in improvements in facilities pays off in terms of the positiveness between physical environment and overall satisfaction.

In 4 star hotels, hypotheses with a mixed effect were H2, H6, H8 and H13. That means that staff empathy comments influence negatively (beta weight -.163, p<.05) or positively (beta weight .0409, p<.05) overall assessment depending on the direction of the comment. Rates and promotion are influencing negatively (beta weight -.994, p<.05) or positively (beta weight .443) overall assessment. Hotel design also plays a role on overall assessment (beta weight –112, p<.05) for negative comments and (.343) if the comment is positive. In the same vein appears food and beverage with a beta weight of -.590, p<.05 or .357, p<.05. When the comments rely mostly in negative comments the influence is negative for location (-,625, p<.05), for organization (-.559, p<.05), for room experience (-.853, p<.05), for facilities (-.450, p<.05) and for price (-.789) supporting H7, H9, H10, H11, and H13 even if the absence of positive comments may lead to redraft these cues of hospitality service in 4 star hotels. Staff language has a positive influence in overall assessment even when the comment is not so positive, bringing to the light the lack of care these customers put on this issue (beta weight .306, p<.05). For these hotels H3, H4 and H5 were not supported, suggesting that staff assurance, staff responsiveness, staff reliability is not perceived by customers lodging in 4 star hotels.

Looking at the size of beta weight caused by negative comments in 4 star hotels, it is possible to concluded that rates and promotions (-.994), room experience (-.853) and prices (-.590) are critical and need to be reassessed. On the other hand, positive comments influence satisfaction the most when related with rates and promotions (.443), staff empathy (.409) and food and beverage (.357). Overall the effects are more negative than positive suggesting that much more could be done to improve customers' experiences.

For 5 star hotels, H2, H4, H5 and H13 were supported with a mixed effect. Negative comments about staff empathy (-.401, p<.05), staff responsiveness (-.257, p<.05), staff reliability (-.410, p<.05) and food and beverage (-.290, p<.05) contribute to decreased customer satisfaction. Whereas positive comments about staff empathy (.270, p<.05), staff responsiveness (.247, p<.05), staff reliability (.328, p<.05) and food and beverage (.518, p<.05) are likely to contribute to a higher level of satisfaction. Facilities and services (-.187, p<.05) and price (-.155, p<.05) are negative comments and as such decrease the overall assessment, giving support for H11 and H12.

The hypotheses that were not supported were H1 (staff language) H3 (staff assurance), H6 (rates and promotions), H8 (hotel design), H9 (organization), H10 (room experience) and H11 (facilities and services), probably because of the sample size related with these kinds of hotels. Looking at the size of beta weight caused by negative comments in 5 star hotels, it is possible to conclude that staff reliability (-.410), staff empathy (-.401) and food and beverages (-.290) are critical and need to be addressed. On the other hand, positive comments are influence satisfaction the most when related with food and beverages (.518), staff reliability (.328) and staff empathy (.270). Suggesting that good service in 5 star hotels relies on interpersonal relations between hosts and guests.

Conclusion

eWOM plays each day a more relevant role in the purchase behaviour process in the hospitality industry. Particularly in hotel management operations, the dimensional assessment of each department is crucial in order to anticipate, fulfil and surpass guests' expectations and desires.

In the social digital era of the human communications, the need to share moments instantly drives the self-motivation to share continuously.

This chapter addresses the issue of decoding between how hotel operations perform in each department, clustered in the 13 attributes identified by hotel stars rating, and contributes to a deeper understanding about the overall assessment of satisfaction effects in the comments shared in TripAdvisor, oné of today's most influential platforms.

The identification of the relationship between the online comments and the overall assessment of the service performance segmented by hotel category (stars), contributes to the understanding of the most relevant service values in each facet of the hotel operation dynamic, therefore, it can be assumed to have a practical implication for hotel managers. Additionally, the underlying contribution of this research for the development of strategies within hotel experiences can be assessed by a more accurate matching between the design of the service experience and the perceived value of the service by hosts/guest.

The generalizability of this research may be challenged, as the study was conducted within the context of a Sun and Sea mature destination (Algarve, Portugal) and considered only the reviews written in the TripAdvisor platform. Nevertheless, this research may be replicated in other Sun and Sea destinations (mature or not) and other relevant platforms, in order to assess if a similar bundling of attributes occurs in hotels and/or other types of accommodation businesses within tourism.

References

Akan, P. (1995). Dimensions of service quality: A study in Istanbul. *Managing Service Quality: An International Journal*, **5**(6), 39-43.

Akbaba, A. (2006). Measuring service quality in the hotel industry: A study in a business hotel in Turkey. *International Journal of Hospitality Management*, **25**(2), 170-192.

Albacete-Saez, C. A., Fuentes-Fuentes, M. M., & Lloréns-Montes, F. J. (2007). Service quality measurement in rural accommodation. *Annals of Tourism Research*, **34**(1), 45-65.

Ali, F. & Amin, M. (2014). The influence of physical environment on emotions, customer satisfaction and behavioural intentions in Chinese resort hotel industry. *Journal for Global Business Advancement*, **7**(3), 249-266.

Ali, F. & Zhou, Y. (2013). An assessment of the perceived service quality: Comparison of Islamic and conventional banks at Pakistan. *International Journal of Innovation and Business Strategy*, **2**.

Ali, F., Amin, M. & Cobanoglu, C. (2016). An integrated model of service experience, emotions, satisfaction, and price acceptance: An empirical analysis in the Chinese hospitality industry. *Journal of Hospitality Marketing & Management*, **25**(4), 449-475.

Arndt, J. (1967). Role of product-related conversations in the diffusion of a new product. *Journal of Marketing Research*, **4**(3), 291-295.

Bayus, B.L., Carroll, V.P. & Rao, A.G. (1985) Harnessing the power of word-of-mouth. In V. Maha (ed.) *Innovation Diffusion Models of New Product Acceptance*. Cambridge, MA: Ballinger.

Ben-Akiva, M., McFadden, D., Abe, M., Böckenholt, U., Bolduc, D., Gopinath, D., ... & Steinberg, D. (1997). Modeling methods for discrete choice analysis. *Marketing Letters*, **8**(3), 273-286.

Brooks Jr, R. C. (1957). 'Word-of-mouth' advertising in selling new products. *Journal of Marketing*, **22**(2), 154-161.

Burt, R. S. (1999). The social capital of opinion leaders. *Annals of the American Academy of Political and Social Science*, **566**, 37.

Cantallops, A. S. & Salvi, F. (2014). New consumer behavior: A review of research on eWOM and hotels. *International Journal of Hospitality Management*, **36**, 41-51.

Chan, E. S. & Wong, S. C. (2006). Motivations for ISO 14001 in the hotel industry. *Tourism Management*, **27**(3), 481-492.

Chang, T. Z. & Wildt, A. R. (1994). Price, product information, and purchase intention: An empirical study. *Journal of the Academy of Marketing Science*, **22**(1), 16-27.

Christou, E. (2011). Exploring online sales promotions in the hospitality industry. *Journal of Hospitality Marketing & Management*, **20**(7), 814-829.

Choi, T. Y. & Chu, R. (2001). Determinants of hotel guests' satisfaction and repeat patronage in the Hong Kong hotel industry. *International Journal of Hospitality Management*, **20**(3), 277-297.

Chung, N. & Koo, C. (2015). The use of social media in travel information search. *Telematics and Informatics*, **32**(2), 215-229.

Daugherty, T. & Hoffman, E. (2014). eWOM and the importance of capturing consumer attention within social media. *Journal of Marketing Communications*, **20**(1-2), 82-102.

Day, G. S. (1971). Attitude change, media and word of mouth. *Journal of Advertising Research*.

Deloitte. (2018). *Travel and Hospitality Industry Outlook*. Retrieved 09/02/2019 from https://www2.deloitte.com/us/en/pages/consumer-business/articles/travel-hospitality-industry-outlook.html

Dellarocas, C. (2003). The digitization of word of mouth: Promise and challenges of online feedback mechanisms. *Management Science*, **49**(10), 1407-1424.

Dichter, E. (1966). How word-of-mouth advertising works. *Harvard Business Review*, **44**(6), 147-160.

Dölarslan, E. (2014). Assessing the effects of satisfaction and value on customer loyalty behaviors in service environments: High-speed railway in Turkey as a case study. *Management Research Review*, **37**(8), 706-727.

Eurostat. (2016). *Tourism Statistics*. Retrieved 10/02/2019 from ec.europa.eu/eurostat/web/main/news/themes-in-the-spotlight/tourism

Expedia. (2018). *Multi National Travel Trends in the Tourism Industry*. Retrieved 02/02/19 from https://info.advertising.expedia.com/multi-national-travel-trends-in-the-tourism-industry

Feick, L. F. & Price, L. L. (1987). The market maven: A diffuser of marketplace information. *Journal of Marketing*, **51**(1), 83-97.

Feick, L. F., Price, L. L. & Higie, R. A. (1986). *People who use people: The other side of opinion leadership.* ACR North American Advances.

Flynn, L. R., Goldsmith, R. E. & Eastman, J. K. (1996). Opinion leaders and opinion seekers: Two new measurement scales. *Journal of the Academy of Marketing Science*, **24**(2), 137.

Gee, C.Y. (2000) *Resort Development and Management,* Educational Institute of the American Hotel & Motel Association, Michigan.

Geissler, G. L. & Rucks, C. T. (2011). The critical influence of customer food perceptions on overall theme park evaluations. *Journal of Management and Marketing Research, **8**, 1.

Getty, J. M., & Getty, R. L. (2003). Lodging quality index (LQI): assessing customers' perceptions of quality delivery. *International Journal of Contemporary Hospitality Management*, **15**(2), 94-104.

Gilly, M. C., Graham, J. L., Wolfinbarger, M. F., & Yale, L. J. (1998). A dyadic study of interpersonal information search. *Journal of the Academy of Marketing Science*, **26**(2), 83-100.

Gremler, D. D., & Brown, S. W. (1999). The loyalty ripple effect: appreciating the full value of customers. *International Journal of Service Industry Management*, **10**(3), 271-293.

Grewal, R., Cline, T. W., & Davis, A. (2003). Early-entrant advantage, word-of-mouth communication, brand similarity, and the consumer decision-making process. *Journal of Consumer Psychology*, 13(3), 187–197.

Gu, Z., & Chi Sen Siu, R. (2009). Drivers of job satisfaction as related to work performance in Macao casino hotels: An investigation based on employee survey. *International Journal of Contemporary Hospitality Management*, **21**(5), 561-578.

Harrison-Walker, L. J. (2001). The measurement of word-of-mouth communication and an investigation of service quality and customer commitment as potential antecedents. *Journal of Service Research*, **4**(1), 60-75.

Hartline, M.D. & Jones, K.C. (1996) Employee performance cues in a hotel service environment: Influence on perceived service quality, value and word of mouth intentions. *Journal of Business Research*, **35**, 207–15.

Heide, M., & Grønhaug, K. (2009). Key factors in guests' perception of hotel atmosphere. *Cornell Hospitality Quarterly*, **50**(1), 29-43.

Hou, M., Wu, X., & Hu, Z., (2013). Personnel service, consumption emotion, and patronageintention in department stores. *International Business Research*, **6**(3), 6–21.

Jani, D. & Han, H. (2011). Investigating the key factors affecting behavioral intentions: Evidence from a full-service restaurant setting. *International Journal of Contemporary Hospitality Management*, **23**(7), 1000-1018.

Juwaheer, T. D.(2004). Exploring international tourists' perceptions of hotel operations by using a modified SERVQUAL approach–a case study of Mauritius. *Managing Service Quality: An International Journal*, **14**(5), 350-364.

Kandampully, J. (2007). *Services Management: The new paradigm in hospitality*. Upper Saddle River, NJ: Pearson Prentice Hall.

Katz, E. & Lazarsfeld, P. F. (1966). *Personal Influence: The Part Played by People in the Flow of Mass Communications*. Piscataway, NJ: Transaction Publishers.

Kim, J., Naylor, G., Sivadas, E. & Sugumaran, V. (2016). The unrealized value of incentivized eWOM recommendations. *Marketing Letters*, **27**(3), 411-421.

Kim, W. G., Ma, X., & Kim, D. J. (2006). Determinants of Chinese hotel customers' e-satisfaction and purchase intentions. *Tourism Management*, **27**(5), 890-900.

Kincaid, C., Baloglu, S., Mao, Z. & Busser, J. (2010). What really brings them back? The impact of tangible quality on affect and intention for casual dining restaurant patrons. *International Journal of Contemporary Hospitality Management*, **22**(2), 209-220.

Knutson, B. J. (1988). Frequent travelers: Making them happy and bringing them back. *Cornell Hotel and Restaurant Administration Quarterly*, **29**(1), 82-87.

Ladhari, R., & Michaud, M. (2015). eWOM effects on hotel booking intentions, attitudes, trust, and website perceptions. *International Journal of Hospitality Management*, **46**, 36-45.

Lazarsfeld, P. F., Berelson, B. & Gaudet, H. (1944). *The People's Choice. How the Voter Makes Up His Mind in a Presidential Campaign*. New York: Columbia University Press, .

Lin, J. & Liang, H. (2011). The influence of service environments on customer emotion and service outcomes. *Managing Service Quality,* **21**(4), 350–372.

Line, N. D., & Runyan, R. C. (2012). Hospitality marketing research: Recent trends and future directions. *International Journal of Hospitality Management,* **31**(2), 477-488.

Litvin, S. W., Goldsmith, R. E. & Pan, B. (2008). Electronic word-of-mouth in hospitality and tourism management. *Tourism Management,* **29**(3), 458-468.

Liu, W., Guillet, B. D., Xiao, Q. & Law, R. (2014). Globalization or localization of consumer preferences: The case of hotel room booking. *Tourism Management,* **41,** 148-157.

Lockyer, T. (2005). Understanding the dynamics of the hotel accommodation purchase decision. *International Journal of Contemporary Hospitality Management,* **17**(6), 481-492.

Mangold, W. G., Berl, R., Pol, L. & Abercrombie, C. L. (1987). An analysis of consumer reliance on personal and non-personal sources of professional service information. *Journal of Professional Services Marketing,* **2**(3), 9-29.

Martin-Fuentes, E. (2016). Are guests of the same opinion as the hotel star-rate classification system? *Journal of Hospitality and Tourism Management,* **29,** 126-134.

McCleary, K.W., Weaver, P.A., Lan, L., (1994). Gender-based differences in business travelers lodging preferences. *The Cornell Hotel and Restaurant Administration Quarterly,* **32**(2), 51–58.

Meng, F., Tepanon, Y. & Uysal, M. (2008). Measuring tourist satisfaction by attribute and motivation: The case of a nature-based resort. *Journal of Vacation Marketing,* **14**(1), 41-56.

Merton, R. K. (1968). *Social Theory and Social Structure,* Free Press.

Murray, K. B. (1991). A test of services marketing theory: Consumer information acquisition activities. *Journal of Marketing,* **55,** 10–25.

Naqshbandi, D. M., & Munir, R. (2011). Atmospheric elements and personality: Impact on hotel lobby impressions. *World Applied Sciences Journal,* **15**(6), 785-792.

Nieves, J., & Quintana, A. (2018). Human resource practices and innovation in the hotel industry: The mediating role of human capital. *Tourism and Hospitality Research,* **18**(1), 72-83.

Noone, B. M. & McGuire, K. A. (2013). Pricing in a social world: The influence of non-price information on hotel choice. *Journal of Revenue and Pricing Management,* **12**(5), 385-401.

Okazaki, S., Andreu, L. & Campo, S. (2017). Knowledge sharing among tourists via social media: a comparison between Facebook and TripAdvisor. *International Journal of Tourism Research*, **19**(1), 107-119.

Olsson, L. E., Friman, M., Pareigis, J., & Edvardsson, B. (2012). Measuring service experience: Applying the satisfaction with travel scale in public transport. *Journal of Retailing and Consumer Services, ***19**(4), 413-418.

Parasuraman, A., Zeithaml, V. A., & Berry, L. L. (1988). Servqual: A multiple-item scale for measuring consumer perc. *Journal of Retailing*, **64**(1), 12.

Phocuswire. (2018). *The Travel Marketer´s Guide to the US Digital Travel Landscape*. Retrieved 01/02/19 from https://www.phocuswire.com/Bing-Phocuswright-digital-travel-marketing-study

Rauch DA, Collins MD, Nale RD, et al. (2015) Mea- suring service quality in mid-scale hotels. *International Journal of Contemporary Hospitality Management, ***27,** 87–106.

Rhee, H. T., & Yang, S. B. (2015). Does hotel attribute importance differ by hotel? Focusing on hotel star-classifications and customers' overall ratings. *Computers in Human Behavior*, **50**, 576-587.

Riegelsberger, J., Sasse, M. A. & McCarthy, J. D. (2005). The mechanics of trust: A framework for research and design. *International Journal of Human-Computer Studies, ***62**(3), 381-422.

Rodgers, S., & Wang, Y. (2011). Electronic word of mouth and consumer generated content: From concept to application. In M.S. Eastin, N.M. Burns (eds.) *Handbook of Research on Digital Media and Advertising: User generated content consumption*, pp. 212-231. IGI Global.

Ruiz, D., Castro, B. & Diaz, I. (2012). Creating customer value through service experiences: An empirical study in the hotel industry. *Tourism and Hospitality Management, ***18**(1), 37–53.

Ryu, K., Lee, H., & Kim, W. (2012). The influence of the quality of the physical environment, food, and service on restaurant image, customer perceived value, customer satisfaction, and behavioral intentions. *International Journal of Contemporary Hospitality Management,* **24**(2), 200–223.

Salecycle.(2018). *Digital Trends in the Travel Industry: 12 Fascinating Stats*. Retrieved 02/03/19 from https://blog.salecycle.com/stats/digital-trends-travel-industry-12-fascinating-stats/

Saleh, F. & Ryan, C. (1991). Analysing service quality in the hospitality industry using the SERVQUAL model. *Service Industries Journal,* **11**(3), 324-345.

Schuckert, M., Liu, X. & Law, R. (2015). A segmentation of online reviews by language groups: How English and non-English speakers rate hotels differently. *International Journal of Hospitality Management,* **48,** 143-149.

Sim, J., Mak, B. & Jones, D. (2006). A model of customer satisfaction and retention for hotels. *Journal of Quality Assurance in Hospitality & Tourism*, **7**(3), 1-23.

Sparks, B. A. & Browning, V. (2010). Complaining in cyberspace: The motives and forms of hotel guests' complaints online. *Journal of Hospitality Marketing & Management*, **19**(7), 797-818.

Sun, T., Youn, S., Wu, G. & Kuntaraporn, M. (2006). Online word-of-mouth (or mouse): An exploration of its antecedents and consequences. *Journal of Computer-Mediated Communication*, **11**(4), 1104-1127.

Tussyadiah, I. P. & Park, S. (2018). When guests trust hosts for their words: Host description and trust in sharing economy. *Tourism Management*, **67**, 261-272.

UNTWO (2013). *Sustainable Tourism for Development: Guidebook: Enhancing Capacities for Sustainable Tourism for Development in Developing Countries*. United Nations World Tourism Organization.

Verma, R. (2010). Customer choice modeling in hospitality services: A review of past research and discussion of some new applications. *Cornell Hospitality Quarterly*, **51**(4), 470-478.

Wang, L., Law, R., Hung, K., & Guillet, B. D. (2014). Consumer trust in tourism and hospitality: A review of the literature. *Journal of Hospitality and Tourism Management*, **21**, 1-9.

Watts, D. J. & Dodds, P. S. (2007). Influentials, networks, and public opinion formation. *Journal of Consumer Research*, **34**(4), 441-458.

Wu, C. H. J., & Liang, R. D. (2009). Effect of experiential value on customer satisfaction with service encounters in luxury-hotel restaurants. *International Journal of Hospitality Management*, **28**(4), 586-593.

Wu, H. C., & Ko, Y. J. (2013). Assessment of service quality in the hotel industry. *Journal of Quality Assurance in Hospitality & Tourism*, **14**(3), 218-244.

Wuest, B. E., Tas, R. F., & Emenheiser, D. A. (1996). What do mature travelers perceive as important hotel/motel customer services?. *Hospitality Research Journal*, **20**(2), 77-93.

Yang, Y., Wong, K.K. & Wang, T. (2012). How do hotels choose their location? Evidence from hotels in Beijing. *International Journal of Hospitality Management*, **31**(3), 675-685.

Ye, Q., Gu, B., Chen, W. & Law, R. (2008). Measuring the value of managerial responses to online reviews – A natural experiment of two online travel agencies. *ICIS 2008 Proceedings*, 115.

Zhou, L., Ye, S., Pearce, P. L., & Wu, M. Y. (2014). Refreshing hotel satisfaction studies by reconfiguring customer review data. *International Journal of Hospitality Management*, **38**, 1-10.

Part II:
Motivations and Identity

8 Motivations to travel to Macau: a multi–group analysis

Ali Bavik, Antónia Correia and Metin Kozak

The objectives of this chapter are to:

☐ Bridge the gap in the literature around the tourism market of Macau through a motivation-based clustering analysis to depict what goes beyond gambling motivations;

☐ Assess empirical data collected through the development of a questionnaire survey that was conducted in Macau;

☐ Introduce two clusters derived from the study findings, namely gamblers and non-gamblers, with culture, value for money, socialization, relaxation, and nightlife found to be the main drivers of all tourist groups;

☐ Address both theoretical and practical implications of gambling tourism.

Keywords: tourist motivations, gambling tourism, culture tourism, market segmentation, Macau.

Introduction

The number of tourists visiting casino resorts has increased in recent years. Their visits are mostly driven by leisure purposes, where gambling is one of the many activities they could do during their stay (Zeng et al., 2014). They prefer traveling to destinations where gambling is legal, even if they do not spend all the time at the casinos (Shaffer & Korn, 2002). Macau has become a hot spot for gambling tourism nowadays, mostly due the legal and fashion status casinos have in Macau (Loi & Kim, 2010). This status was achieved in the last two decades, mostly by the huge increase of Chinese gamblers in Macau (Lam, 2005; Tao et al., 2011; Vong, 2007; Zeng et al., 2014); residents' support for this activity (Carmichael, 2000); and gambling tourism development (Beeton & Pinge, 2003). Other authors have developed essays to analyse the gambling tourism market (Morrison et al., 1996; Wong & Rosenbaum, 2012).

The extremely focused research on gambling tends to forget that for most of the tourists, gambling is not the only motivation they have. In fact, in Macau leisure gamblers spend less time in gambling compared to those who gamble on a regular base (Shaffer & Korn, 2002). Tourism literature offers a multitude of motives to travel, starting from the widely known push and pull motivations of Crompton (1979) to a context-specific motivation models (e.g., Cohen, 1979; Crompton, 1979; Dann, 1977; Dann, 1981; Fodness, 1994; Hsu & Huang, 2008; Iso-Ahola, 1982). Motivations to visit a particular destination have been explained by learning motives (Klenosky, 2002), socialization motives (Saayman & Saayman, 2012), adventure (Cha et al., 1995), relaxation (Turnbull & Uysal, 1995) and nightlife (Kozak, 2002). These are some of the motives that drive tourists to travel for leisure or other purposes. This study aims to bridge the gap of literature assessing tourists' motivations to visit Macau, where gambling seems to be only one of the motivations. A structural equation model was developed and tested, and the sample was divided in two groups – gamblers and non–gamblers – to depict how their motivations differ by means of a multi-group analysis.

Literature review

Motivation, particularly human motivation, has been one of the most popular topics in psychology (e.g., Murray, 1938). In general, motivation refers to the "factors that activate, direct, and sustain goal-directed behavior" (Nevid, 2012, p. 284). The goal here may be wanting, interest, need, or desire that drives someone in a certain way. The *need* refers to "a disequilibrium which stresses toward equilibrium" (Murray, 1938,

p. 67). Motivation involves the physiological and/or biological, social, emotional, and cognitive elements that trigger behavior (Gnoth, 1997). The arousal of these factors is called *motive*. It relates to the reason for an action trigger or strengthens the behavior (Crompton, 1979; Kim et al., 2007).

Inclusively conceptual and empirical studies indicate that two main types of motivations influence the direction and the strength of the behavior. The first one is *intrinsic* motivation, which arises from the intrinsic value of the outcome (enjoyment or interest) for an individual; and the second is *extrinsic* motivation, which arises from the desire to obtain some outcomes (reward) or to avoid negative consequences (Dann, 1977; Pearce & Caltabiano, 1983; Solomon et al., 2014; Uysal & Hagan, 1993). With these internal and external forces, motivation plays a major role in the decision-making process for consumers particularly for tourists (Mansfeld, 1992), and influence the choice of a visit to a certain tourism destination.

Iso-Ahola (1982, p. 257) defines tourist motivation as "a meaningful state of mind which adequately disposes an actor or a group of actors to travel". In the last five decades, significant effort has been devoted to examining tourist motivations, owing to tourism's considerable amount of economic contribution to destinations. The relevant literature shows that tourist motivations are complex in nature, a multi-dimensional phenomenon, and there have been a variety of approaches. Several authors proposed various scales, frameworks and classifications to explain motivations of tourists to travel (e.g., Cohen, 1979; Crompton, 1979; Dann, 1977; Dann, 1981; Fodness, 1994; Hsu & Huang, 2008; Iso-Ahola, 1982; Kim, Goh & Yuan, 2010; Ryan & Glendon, 1998).

Why do people travel? And, why do people go to certain places? Basically, these two questions have been paid considerable attention in the tourism literature. To answer these questions, some preliminary studies were conducted in the early 1970s. For example, Lundberg (1971) identifies and categorizes 18 motivational attributes into four groups, including educational and cultural motivations, escape and pleasurable motivations, ethnic motivations, and sundry motivations. Plog (1974) aimed to understand tourists' lifestyles, including attitudes, perceptions, needs, interests, opinions and activities, and he proposed a typology based on personality traits, motivations and activity preferences. The author classified on two traits: *psychocentric* (self-centered) and *allocentric* (other-centered). Based on the model, psychocentric tourists prefer familiar destinations whilst allocentrics are considered as adventurous.

A number of other studies attempted to advance the literature by better classifying and conceptualizing tourist motivations. For example; Iso-Ahola (model of tourism motivations, 1982), Beard and Raghep (leisure motivation scale, 1983), Pearce (travel career ladder, 1983, 1991, 2005), Gnoth (motivation and expectation formation process, 1997), Witt and Wright (expectancy model and recently, 1992), and Hsu, Chai, and Li (a tourist behavioral model, 2010). Despite the fact that these studies provided mindful insights and alternative explanations about travel motivations, Dann (1977) and Crompton's push and pull model (1979) is commonly accepted and used in the relevant literature (Baloglu & Uysal, 1996; Kim et al., 2007; Kim & Lee, 2002; e.g., Klenosky, 2002; Turnbull & Uysal, 1995; Uysal & Jurowski, 1994).

The most common classification used in the literature for tourist motivations results from the evidence of these studies, which indicate that the motivations behind the choice of travel destinations are generally driven by two factors, namely *push* and *pull*. To date, the conceptualization of push and pull factors are broadly accepted for use in tourism research and marketing (Baloglu & Uysal, 1996; Cha et al., 1995; Kim et al., 2007; Kim & Lee, 2002; Turnbull & Uysal, 1995; Uysal & Jurowski, 1994). The term 'push motive' is generally understood as the internal motive that drives an individual to go away from their natural environment (Dann, 1977). For instance, the need for a change of scenery and/or escape from routine life. Heckhausen, Dixion, and Baltes (1989) emphasize the emotional aspects of motives. Accordingly, Yoon and Uysal (2005) suggest that push factors represent emotional and internal desires, including self-actualization, rest, leisure or social interaction.

Therefore, people considered to be motivated to travel for prestige and socialization purposes as well (Crompton, 1979; Heckhausen et al., 1989). Reversely, the term 'pull factors' refer to characteristics of the destination that triggers an individual desire for travel (Crompton, 1979; Kim et al., 2007; Uysal & Hagan, 1993; Uysal & Jurowski, 1994; Yoon & Uysal, 2005). Some examples of pull factors would be natural landscapes, special events at a destination, and specific activities (Baloglu & Uysal, 1996; Cha et al., 1995; Uysal & Jurowski, 1994). Literature shows that several studies adopted the dichotomy of push-pull factors broadly in tourism research to identify tourists' motives. While doing this, an overwhelming majority of studies prefer quantitative (e.g., Baloglu & Uysal, 1996; Kozak, 2002; Turnbull & Uysal, 1995; Uysal & Jurowski, 1994; Yuan & McDonald, 1990) whilst only a few studies utilize qualitative approach (Crompton, 1979; Klenosky, 2002).

The conceptualization of gambling

Gambling generally refers to "a reallocation of wealth, on the basis of deliberate risk, involving gain to one party and loss to another, usually without the introduction of productive work on either side. The determining process always involves an element of chance and maybe only chance" (Halliday & Fuller, 1974, p. 12). Researchers have thus far focused on finding out why people gamble and what factors motivate them to gamble. The temptation driving gambling is sourced from the expectancy of potentially winning a better outcome by risking a small bet. Gambling is a complex behavior. Findings regarding the motivation associated with people's gambling behavior have been inconclusive in the literature. According to Freud (1945), gambling is an instinctive, impulsive and irrational behavior. Similarly, some researchers suggest that gamblers are mainly motivated by false hopes or beliefs (see Rogers, 1998; Walker, 1992). For example, Raylu and Oei (2004) identified five categories of false beliefs of gambling motivations. These are, illusion of control (the belief that the individual has control over gambling outcomes), predictive control (the belief that individual can predict gambling outcomes), interpretive bias (the belief that the individual's skill and luck can influence the outcome), gambling expectancy (the individual's personal feelings and emotions), and perceived inability to stop/control gambling (self-fulfilling prophecy on outcome).

Studies that focus on exploring the driving force of gambling in the literature have predominantly drawn their theoretical views from the self-determination theory (Deci & Ryan, 1985). While there are studies that provided gambling motivational categories (see Custer & Milt, 1985; Neighbors et al., 2002), in general, the magnitude of motivations for gambling can be categorized into internal, external, or amotivational in nature.

Intrinsic motivation is a non-monetary type of reward. Here the act of gambling stimulates individuals' sense of satisfaction such as a sense of accomplishment, excitement, learning, and fun (Chantal et al., 1994; Neighbors et al., 2002; Tarras et al., 2000).

Extrinsic elements boost gambling behavior through external, introjected, and identified regulations. In external regulation, the primary motivation of an individual is to win the game or money (Blaszczynski & Nower, 2002; Walker, 1992). In *introjected* regulation, an individual has a desire for potential secondary reward (e.g., becoming rich), and in *identified* regulations, an individual gambles for personally valuable gain (desire to be popular in the eyes of other people).

Finally, in *amotivation*, an individual has no desire or willingness to gamble for the potential outcomes (no gambling).

Prior studies also suggest that, although individuals' gambling behavior is commonly motivated by internal or external forces (Chantal et al., 1994), it can be subject to the effects of individual characteristics or contextual factors (Beattie et al., 1999; Raylu & Oei, 2004; Scull & Woolcock, 2005; Ye, 2009). In terms of individual characteristics, gambling motivation may vary in terms of gender differences (Chen et al., 1993; Gray, 2004; Tarras et al., 2000). Specifically, Blaszczynski, Huynh, Dumlao, and Farrell (1998) found that compulsive gambling behavior is stronger among males (4.3%) than females (1.6%). Not only until recently have researchers begun to address contextual factors, such as culture, as a factor that governs individuals' gambling motivation in various countries and cultures. Among these studies, several studies yielded findings which showed that Chinese gamblers had a greater tendency to higher gambling, risk-taking and compulsive gambling, compared to gamblers in other cultures (Blaszczynski et al., 1998; Chen et al., 1993; Clarke et al., 2006; Lau & Ranyard, 2005; Loo et al., 2008; Ye, 2009). Related research demonstrates that compare to Western gamblers, Chinese gamblers demonstrated higher risk-taking, compulsive gambling (Ye, 2009). Chinese gamblers were generally risk-takers (Lau & Ranyard, 2005; Tao et al., 2011) because, unlike Western gamblers, Chinese gamblers also have greater beliefs for luck and (Papineau, 2001), a stronger illusion of control (Loo et al., 2008).

Tourism in Macau

Macau is a Special Administrative District (SAR) and a former Portuguese colony located in the southeast of mainland China. Macau is (29.2 km2), and according to Macau the Statistics and Census Service (DSEC) (2016), the population in Macau is approximately 644,900. In terms of tourism, Macau took its first steps right after it became a Special Administrative Region in 1999 and was given some economic and social privileges. However, the significant development of tourism started at the beginning of the millennium, notably, after the liberalization of the gaming industry in 2002. A destination like Macau, where the primary economic influence contributed by gambling, such activities as visiting historical and cultural sites are not only a secondary attraction for tourists, but also became one of the most significant factors in attracting tourists after Macau was inscribed on the UNESCO World Heritage list in 2005.

These developments have changed Macau dramatically in the last two decades, and Macau has become one of the well-recognized gambling destinations. It is known as the 'Monte Carlo of the Orient'. Tourism has been growing massively and it has become the main source of income of Macau. In 2015, Macau generated 31,303 million US$ in international tourism receipts, which is equivalent to 7.5% of the total income (UNWTO, 2016). In terms of tourists arrival, Macau hosted a total of 30,950,336 million visitors, predominantly from mainland China between 2015-2016 (DSEC, 2016). As one of the major components in tourism, gambling continues to play a major role in the Macau economy. Currently, there are 38 casinos in Macau. In 2016, the Macau gambling industry generated 80 percent of the local economy, whilst it generated 34 percent of the global gambling revenues.

Methodology

The study is based on a questionnaire survey developed by benefiting from the related literature. With a structure of 25 motivation items, the form employs a 5-point Likert scale ranging from '5-definitely agree' to '1-definitely disagree'. In the questionnaire, all the items were originally developed in English. In order to ensure reliability and validity, the questionnaire items were translated into Chinese using the back-translation method (Brislin, 1986). The faculty members of the Hong Kong Polytechnic University and those in the Institute for Tourism Studies who were fluent in both languages further tested the cross-linguistic comparability of the questionnaire.

The target population of this study was international tourists who visited Macau. Considering the purpose of the study and the nature of the respondents, a non-probability sampling technique was used in the study. Specifically, data was collected through judgmental sampling. The data was collected between September and December 2014. Data collection was conducted in Chinese (Mandarin).

The questionnaires were conducted through a self-administrated manner and distributed and monitored by field surveyors. To increase the response rate, the field surveyors were instructed to approach every other traveler found at designated locations including airport, ferry terminal, hotels, casinos, and bus stations. 1,200 questionnaires were distributed to potential respondents who were agreed to participate in filling out the questionnaire. Of these, 992 questionnaires were found to be useful, which represents an 82.6% response rate. The proportion of male respondents (52.1%) is a little more than females (47.9%). The sample is mainly dominated by young people (67.2%), with a much less propor-tion attained to elderly people (i.e., seniors) (2.6%). The respondents are predominantly Chinese (94.4%). All income groups are almost equally represented while the income group of 50,000 Euro and less is the high-est (30.1%).

Model

The research model was assessed through Structural Equation Model-ling (SEM), using AMOS 22.0 software. SEM is conducted to measure the six motivations constructs which it is not feasible to measure directly, and the relations within these constructs called path analysis. The maxi-mum likelihood estimation method of SEM was applied to the analy-sis, as it is robust to minor variations of normality (Hellier et al., 2003; Marôco, 2010; Van Rijn et al., 2011), and for estimating a set of model parameters that maximize the likelihood of observing the true value of the population, with normal distribution (Hair et al., 2011; Marôco, 2010; Reinartz et al., 2009). Normality tests were performed for each of the 24 items; all of them show a skewness and kurtosis that ensure normality.

A three-step approach was employed (Anderson & Gerbing, 1988). The first is the measurement model, i.e., it starts with conventional assump-tions about items and their relationships to the dependent factor and sources of error (Marôco, 2010), through Confirmatory Factor Analysis (CFA). To test measurement model reliability, Convergent and Discrimi-nant Validity was first conducted and then other statistical tools, such as correlation analysis, were used for data analysis. The second stage was to perform structural equation modeling to validate the structural rela-tionships between the latent constructs in the research model (Jarvenpaa et al., 1999; Ng et al., 2011). The third step was to perform a multi-group analysis that will demonstrate if there are different motivations between gamblers and non-gamblers.

Findings

Motivations to travel were labeled Prestige motivations, Relaxa-tion, Culture, Nightlife, Value for money and Sports. This structure of motivations was depicted with an Exploratory Factor Analysis and then confirmed by Confirmatory Factor Analysis. Cronbach's alpha for these factors exceeds 0.7, indicating a good degree of internal consist-ency. Prestige motivation refers to the social effect their holidays bring to their relationship with their peers. Relaxation motivation refers to doing nothing, emotional and psychological refreshment. Cultural motivation comprises self-development, local food, culture, and new experiences.

Nightlife motivation comprises music, social relations, and entertainment. Sports motivation comprises activity and nature. Value for money refers to reputation, shopping and tourism prices (Table 8.1).

Table 8.1: Exploratory factor analysis results

Variables and Items I came to Macau...	Mean	Std. Deviation	Factor Loadings	% Variance	Cronbach Alpha
1: Prestige				7.5	0.81
... to spend time with people I care deeply about.	3.79	1.37	0.79		
... because my friends/relatives have been there before.	4.03	1.32	0.71		
... because my friends/relatives have not been before.	3.90	1.35	0.67		
... because I have been there before.	3.99	1.30	0.69		
2: Relaxation				7.5	0.84
... to relax.	4.36	1.18	0.82		
... to be emotionally and physically refreshed.	4.09	1.10	0.87		
... to get away from home.	4.08	1.16	0.59		
... to do nothing at all.	3.87	1.21	0.53		
3: Cultural motivations				5.3	0.80
... to increase my knowledge of new places.	4.22	1.26			
... to visit historical and cultural sites.	4.20	1.06	0.74		
... because it has a different culture.	4.31	1.14	0.59		
... for local food.	4.32	1.15	0.71		
4: Nightlife				6.1	0.81
... to seek adventure.	4.10	1.23	0.67		
... to meet people of opposite sex.	3.92	1.41	0.74		
... to have fun.	4.46	1.32	0.64		
... because it has good nightlife & entertainment.	4.22	1.28	0.65		
5: Sports				25.7	0.92
... to be active.	4.37	1.19	0.66		
... to engage in sports.	4.12	1.27	0.87		
... to get close to nature.	4.16	1.26	0.86		
... to enjoy good weather.	4.25	1.16	0.80		
... to meet local people.	4.14	1.27	0.77		
6: Value for money				3.7	0.72
... because it offers good shopping opportunities.	4.36	1.18	0.55		
... because it offers good value for money.	4.11	1.21	0.75		
... because it is a well-publicized destination.	4.08	1.17	0.63		

Notes: KMO (Kaiser-Meyer-Olkin Test of Sampling Adequacy) → .828

Bartlett's Test of Sphericity → 3846.927 $p < 0.001$

The CFA of the measurement model specifies the relationship of each observed variable with the latent construct. The sample was randomly divided into two (496 each). The results showed a good overall fit for both, suggesting that the CFA structure is feasible for any sample of data, which ensures the generalizability of the results. This is confirmed by CFA estimate values, indicated in Table 8.2.

Table 8.2: Confirmatory factor analysis results

Items. I came to Macau...		Standardized Re-gression Weights	S.E.	C.R.	P
... to spend time with people I care deeply about.	Prestige	0.80			
... because my friends/relatives have been there before.	Prestige	0.73	0.04	21.04	***
... because my friends/relatives have not been before.	Prestige	0.68	0.04	19.75	***
... because I have been there before.	Prestige	0.68	0.04	19.71	***
... to relax.	Relaxation	0.86			
... to be emotionally and physically refreshed.	Relaxation	0.90	0.03	31.96	***
... to get away from home.	Relaxation	0.66	0.03	22.47	***
... to do nothing at all.	Relaxation	0.58	0.04	19.13	***
... to increase my knowledge of new places.	Cultural	0.77			
... to visit historical and cultural sites.	Cultural	0.63	0.04	18.00	***
... because it has a different culture.	Cultural	0.72	0.04	20.45	***
... for local food.	Cultural	0.72	0.04	20.29	***
... to seek adventure.	Nightlife	0.70			
... to meet people of opposite sex.	Nightlife	0.74	0.06	19.25	***
... to have fun.	Nightlife	0.72	0.06	18.84	***
... because it has good nightlife and entertainment.	Nightlife	0.70	0.06	18.48	***
... to be active.	Sports	0.75			
... to engage in sports.	Sports	0.89	0.04	28.99	***
... to get close to nature.	Sports	0.90	0.04	29.30	***
... to enjoy good weather.	Sports	0.83	0.04	26.82	***

... to meet local people.	Sports	0.81	0.05	26.10	***
... because it offers good shopping opportunities.	Value for money	0.84			
... because it offers good value for money.	Value for money	0.77	0.09	11.13	***
... because it is a well-publicized destination.	Value for money	0.66	0.08	9.60	***

Model	X2	DF	P	X2/DF
Default model	834.728	235	0	3.552
	RMR	GFI	AGFI	CFI
Default model	0.06	0.93	0.911	0.945

Results show that prestige motivation is explained by the tourists who want to be with the people they care about (0.8) and because their friends and relatives have been there before (0.73). Relaxation motivations are the true essence of their trip (0.86) where they expect to be emotionally and physically refreshed (0.90). Cultural motivations refer to their self-development (I came to Macau to increase my knowledge of new places, 0.77), and because Macau has a different culture (0.72) and Local Food (0.72). Nightlife refers to socialize (I came to Macau to meet people of opposite sex, 0.74) or only to have fun (0.72). Sports motivations are explained by the desire to engage in sports (0.89) or to be close to nature (0.90).

Furthermore, average variance extracted (AVE), i.e., the degree to which the measurement items are explained by the construct and are dissimilar, above 0.5 is adequate for convergent-discriminant validity. In this sense, Table 8.3 shows the results of Convergent and Discriminant Validity.

Table 8.3: Discriminant validity

	CR	AVE	MSV	ASV	Cultural	Prestige	Relaxation	Nightlife
Cultural	0.80	0.51	0.17	0.14	0.71			
Prestige	0.81	0.52	0.11	0.06	0.33	0.72		
Relaxation	0.84	0.58	0.17	0.13	0.41	0.24	0.76	
Nightlife	0.81	0.51	0.16	0.07	0.36	0.19	0.40	0.71
Sport	0.92	0.70	0.15	0.07	0.39	0.26	0.39	
Value for money	0.80	0.58	0.16	0.06	0.40	0.22	0.32	

For the analysis of construct reliability, component reliability (CR) above 0.7 for all constructs is considered indicative of a reliable instrument (Udo et al., 2010), which means good internal consistency and reliability, as indicated by Marôco (2010). In this sense, it can be concluded that the results in Table 8.3 show signs of high reliability for all constructs. In the present analysis, the goodness of fit measures was considered, in order to be able to summarize the overall fit of the model. Despite the overall fit indices, with x^2/df ratio = 3.552 (p = 0.000), being on the recommended interval (between 2.0 and 5.0 for some authors' suggestions) (Marôco, 2010). Moreover, several fit-indices are considered acceptable: goodness-of-fit index (GFI) = 0.93; adjust GFI (AGFI) = 0.911; comparative fit index (CFI) = 0.945, as these values are greater than 0.9 (Anderson & Gerbing, 1988). However, for root-mean-square residual index (RMSR) and for root-mean-square error of approximation index (RMSEA), the values should be less than 0.1 to be acceptable (Anderson & Gerbing, 1988), (RMSR = 0.06, RMSEA = 0.051). As the CFA presents good fits, without validity concerns and with all the items willing to contribute to the latent construct above 0.7, and further as all the factors were proved to be freely correlated among themselves, the structural model could be tested. The estimation of the complete model with the path coefficients and significant levels is given in Figure 8.1.

All the coefficients are significant at a 1% significance level. The x^2/df ratio = 3.493 (p = 0.000) is in the recommended interval. The other relationships seem to indicate a good overall model fit (GFI = 0.925; AGFI=0.91, CFI= 0.939, RMSR= 0.068, RMSEA = 0.051), these indicators of the model fit summary indicate an adequate and incremental fit for the structural model. Results indicate that the model fits the data well (see Figure 8.1).

The results in Figure 8.1 show a significant statistical relationship between motivations and prestige (path coefficient=0.401; p <.001). This implies that tourists are driven by the prestige the trip to Macau may provide. There is also a significant relationship between relaxation and motivations (path coefficient=0.609; p <.001) showing that Macau is also a destination where rebalancing drives tourists. With similar effect is value for money (path coefficient=0.506; p<.001). The most important motivations are Nightlife (path coefficient=0.656; p<.001), culture (path coefficient=0.634, p<.001) and sports (path coefficient=0.633; p<.001). All of them being responsible for more spending when the motivations increase (path coefficient=0.185, p<.001). These findings suggest that Nightlife is a key driver for Macau, but it is not the only motivation.

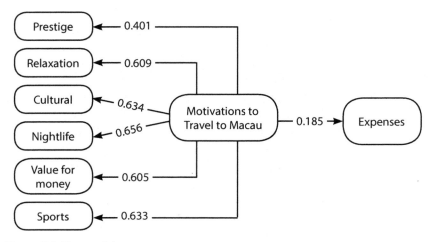

Figure 8.1: The model.

Multi-group analysis

Finally, variables correlations were tested for invariance among two different groups of residents. Multi-group analysis, as displayed in Table 8.4, highlights how gamblers and non-gamblers perceived their trip to Macau. The table includes only those paths that were proved to be different within the market segments. According to the analysis, cultural motivations are more intense within gambler-tourists, which may suggest that gambling is part of Macau culture. Furthermore, nightlife is not the main priority although gamblers are more motivated for nightlife than non-gamblers, gamblers also show more intense motivations that means that gambling is a sports activity. Gamblers also spend more.

Table 8.4: Multi-group analysis

Variables			Non-Gamblers		Gamblers		
		Estimate	P	Estimate	P	z-score	
Cultural	<---	Motives	0.55	0.000	0.67	0.000	2.378**
Nightlife	<---	Motives	0.54	0.000	0.65	0.000	1.773*
Sports	<---	Motives	0.73	0.000	0.82	0.000	1.746*
Expenses	<---	Motives	0.67	0.000	0.75	0.000	2.482**

Notes: *** p-value < 0.01; ** p-value < 0.05; * p-value < 0.10

Conclusion

This study was designed to understand which factors better explain the motivations that drive tourists' intention of traveling to Macau. Further, we also investigated if motivations influence the level of tourist spending and explored if these two groups of analysis vary, based on gamblers and non-gamblers. The results of the study supported the notion, with six motivational factors accounting for tourists' traveling intention, namely cultural, sports, nightlife, relaxation, value for money, and prestige. Culture, sports, and nightlife were found to be the main drivers of tourists in general.

Another interesting result yielded from our data demonstrated that gamblers and non-gambler tourists did not differ in terms of their motivation in coming to Macau. Regardless of tourists' gambling motivation, culture remained the most important driver of tourism expenditure in Macau. The empirical results of this study provide reasonable evidence that tourist motivation is closely linked with destination's image. Macau has established a strong and salient image of cultural attractions and international sports events. Hence, Macau has several historical places and many are in the World Heritage list. Every year popular events and festivals held in Macau, and these include the Grand Prix, the International Fireworks Display Contest, and Macau Arts Festival. Finally, and most importantly, there is a variation between gamblers and non-gamblers. Despite the fact that the majority come for gambling and the existence of differences in motivation groups, gamblers also value other motivations. Gamblers also spend more.

Tourist motivations play a major role for marketers and managers. Bearing in mind the importance of the topic, several researchers identified various push and pull factors that motivates tourists for travel to certain destinations. There are several motivational factors available, so understanding tourist behaviors and the motivation behind is significantly important for marketers and managers where tourism is the primary economic influence, so that they can develop segmental strategies to meet all of the tourist expectations.

From the practical point of view, these results open paths to new forms of promoting Macau. First, as happens in sun and sand destinations, the key focus should be gambling and casinos. However, other products such as culture, sports, nightlife activities, special events, and cuisine, should be added to marketing campaigns. Perhaps it is to develop a gambling destination of a second generation, the one that needs to combine more alternatives to gambling. Therefore, promoting and focusing on cultural tourism may be a way of increasing tourist expenditure at Macau, which may provide direct benefits for the local economy.

The findings in this study are subject to at least two limitations. First, the scope of this study was limited in terms of tourist profile. In particular, this study focused on travel motivation profiles of tourists. Future studies may reveal tourist demographic and socio-economic profiles which may potentially reveal some differences between gamblers and non-gamblers tourists. Alternatively, future studies may focus on the relationship between travel patterns and behavioral and/or emotional characters. Second, cross-sectional research was used in order to understand tourist motivations, which makes it difficult to draw strong conclusions. Hence, because of the expected difficulty of identifying the different tourist profile, almost 1000 samples were collected. However, even with relatively large sample size, caution must be applied given the highly dynamic tourist flow in Macau. Future studies are encouraged to investigate the role of alternative tourist motivations in facilitating or hindering tourists' intention to visit and the amount of expenses incurred during their traveling.

References

Anderson, J.C. & Gerbing, D.W. (1988). Structural equation modeling in practice: A review and recommended two-step approach. *Psychological bulletin,* **103**(3), 411.

Baloglu, S. & Uysal, M. (1996). Market segments of push and pull motivations: A canonical correlation approach. *International Journal of Contemporary Hospitality Management,* **8**(3), 32-38.

Beard, J.G. & Ragheb, M.G. (1983). Measuring leisure motivation. *Journal of Leisure Research,* **15**(3), 219.

Beattie, L., Blaszczynski, A., Maccallum, F. & Joukhador, J. (1999). *Gambling Problems in a Multicultural Society.* Paper presented at the Developing Strategic Alliances: Proceedings of the 9th National Associations of Gambling Studies Conference National Association of Gambling Studies, Gold Coast, Queensland.

Beeton, S. & Pinge, I. (2003). Casting the holiday dice: Demarketing gambling to encourage local tourism. *Current Issues in Tourism,* **6**(4), 309-322.

Blaszczynski, A., Huynh, S., Dumlao, V. & Farrell, E. (1998). Problem gambling within a Chinese speaking community. *Journal of gambling studies,* **14**(4), 359-380.

Blaszczynski, A. & Nower, L. (2002). A pathways model of problem and pathological gambling. *Addiction,* **97**(5), 487-499.

Brislin, R. (1986). The wording and translation of research instruments. *Field Methods in Cross Cultural Research. Beverly Hills, California: Sage Publications*, 159-163.

Carmichael, B.A. (2000). A matrix model for resident attitudes and behaviours in a rapidly changing tourist area. *Tourism Management*, **21**(6), 601-611.

Cha, S., Mccleary, K.W. & Uysal, M. (1995). Travel motivations of Japanese overseas travelers: A factor-cluster segmentation approach. *Journal of Travel Research*, **34**(1), 33-39. doi:doi:10.1177/004728759503400104

Chantal, Y., Vallerand, R. & Vallieres, E. (1994). On the construction and validation of the Gambling Motivation Scale (GMS). *Society and leisure*, **17**, 189-212.

Chen, C.-N., Wong, J., Lee, N., Chan-Ho, M.-W., Lau, J. T.-F. & Fung, M. (1993). The Shatin community mental health survey in Hong Kong: II. Major findings. *Archives of general psychiatry*, **50**(2), 125-133.

Clarke, D., Abbott, M., Tse, S., Townsend, S., Kingi, P. & Manaia, W. (2006). Gender, age, ethnic and occupational associations with pathological gambling in a New Zealand urban sample. *Journal of Gambling Studies*, **30**(2), 503–51.

Cohen, E. (1979). A phenomenology of tourist experiences. *Sociology*, **13**(2), 179-201.

Crompton, J. L. (1979). Motivations for pleasure vacation. *Annals of Tourism Research*, **6**(4), 408-424. dx.doi.org/10.1016/0160-7383(79)90004-5

Custer, R. & Milt, H. (1985). *When Luck Runs Out: Help for compulsive gamblers and their families*: Facts on File.

Dann, G. M. (1977). Anomie, ego-enhancement and tourism. *Annals of Tourism Research*, **4**(4), 184-194.

Dann, G. M. (1981). Tourist motivation an appraisal. *Annals of Tourism Research*, **8**(2), 187-219.

Deci, E.L. & Ryan, R.M. (1985). The general causality orientations scale: Self-determination in personality. *Journal of research in personality*, **19**(2), 109-134.

DSEC (Statistics-and-Census-Service). (2016). Macau in Figures. Retrieved 10/03/2017 from http://www.dsec.gov.mo/Statistic. aspx?NodeGuid= ba1a4eab-213a-48a3-8fbb-962d15dc6f87

Fodness, D. (1994). Measuring tourist motivation. *Annals of Tourism Research*, **21**(3), 555-581. doi:dx.doi.org/10.1016/0160-7383(94)90120-1

Freud, S. (1945). Dostoevsky and parricide (1928). *The International journal of psycho-analysis*, **26**, 1.

Gnoth, J. (1997). Tourism motivation and expectation formation. *Annals of Tourism Research*, **24**(2), 283-304.

Gray, P.B. (2004). Evolutionary and cross-cultural perspectives on gambling. *Journal of Gambling Studies,* **20**(4), 347-371.

Hair, J.F., Ringle, C.M. & Sarstedt, M. (2011). PLS-SEM: Indeed a silver bullet. *Journal of Marketing theory and Practice,* **19**(2), 139-152.

Halliday, J. & Fuller, P. (1974). *The Psychology of Gambling:* London.

Heckhausen, J., Dixon, R.A. & Baltes, P.B. (1989). Gains and losses in development throughout adulthood as perceived by different adult age groups. *Developmental Psychology,* **25**(1), 109.

Hellier, P.K., Geursen, G.M., Carr, R.A. & Rickard, J.A. (2003). Customer repurchase intention: A general structural equation model. *European Journal of Marketing,* **37**(11/12), 1762-1800.

Hsu, C.H. & Huang, S. (2008). Travel motivation: A critical review of the concept's development. *Tourism Management: Analysis, behaviour and strategy,* 14-27.

Hsu, C.H., Cai, L.A. & Li, M. (2010). Expectation, motivation, and attitude. **A tourist behavioral model.** *Journal of Travel Research,* **49**(3), 282-296.

Iso-Ahola, S. E. (1982). Toward a social psychological theory of tourism motivation: A rejoinder. *Annals of Tourism Research,* **9**(2), 256-262. doi:dx.doi.org/10.1016/0160-7383(82)90049-4

Jarvenpaa, S.L., Tractinsky, N. & Saarinen, L. (1999). Consumer trust in an Internet store: A cross-cultural validation. *Journal of Computer-Mediated Communication,* **5**(2), JCMC526.

Kim, K., Oh, I.K. & Jogaratnam, G. (2007). College student travel: A revised model of push motives. *Journal of Vacation Marketing,* **13**(1), 73-85.

Kim, K., Noh, J. & Jogaratnam, G. (2007). Multi-destination segmentation based on push and pull motives: Pleasure trips of students at a US university. *Journal of Travel & Tourism Marketing,* **21**(2-3), 19-32.

Kim, S.-S. & Lee, C.-K. (2002). Push and pull relationships. *Annals of Tourism Research,* **29**(1), 257-260. doi:dx.doi.org/10.1016/S0160-7383 (01)00043-3

Kim, Y.H., Goh, B.K. & Yuan, J. (2010). Development of a multi-dimensional scale for measuring food tourist motivations. *Journal of Quality Assurance in Hospitality & Tourism,* **11**(1), 56-71.

Klenosky, D. B. (2002). The 'pull' of tourism destinations: A means-end investigation. *Journal of Travel Research,* **40**(4), 396-403.

Kozak, M. (2002). Comparative analysis of tourist motivations by nationality and destinations. *Tourism Management,* **23**(3), 221-232.

Lam, D. (2005). Slot or table? A Chinese perspective. *UNLV Gaming Research & Review Journal,* **9**(2), 69.

Lau, L.-Y. & Ranyard, R. (2005). Chinese and English probabilistic thinking and risk taking in gambling. *Journal of Cross-Cultural Psychology,* **36**(5), 621-627.

Loi, K.-I. & Kim, W.G. (2010). Macao's casino industry: Reinventing Las Vegas in Asia. *Cornell Hospitality Quarterly,* **51**(2), 268-283.

Loo, J.M., Raylu, N. & Oei, T.P.S. (2008). Gambling among the Chinese: A comprehensive review. *Clinical Psychology Review,* **28**(7), 1152-1166.

Lundberg, D.E. (1971). Why tourists travel. *Cornell Hotel and Restaurant Administration Quarterly,* **12**(4), 64-70.

Mansfeld, Y. (1992). From motivation to actual travel. *Annals of Tourism Research,* **19**(3), 399-419.

Marôco, J. (2010). *Análise de equações estruturais: Fundamentos teóricos, software & aplicações*: ReportNumber, Lda.

Morrison, A.M., Braunlich, C.G., Cai, L.A. & O'Leary, J.T. (1996). A profile of the casino resort vacationer. *Journal of Travel Research,* **35**(2), 55-61.

Murray, H. A. (1938). *Explorations in Personality*. New York: Oxford University Press

Neighbors, C., Lostutter, T. W., Cronce, J. M. & Larimer, M. E. (2002). Exploring college student gambling motivation. *Journal of gambling studies, 18*(4), 361-370.

Nevid, J. (2012). *Psychology: Concepts and applications*: Nelson Education.

Ng, S.I., Sambasivan, M. & Zubaidah, S. (2011). Antecedents and outcomes of flight attendants' job satisfaction. *Journal of Air Transport Management,* **17**(5), 309-313.

Papineau, E. (2001). Pathological gambling in the Chinese community, an anthropological viewpoint. *Loisir et Société,* **24**(2), 557-582.

Pearce, P. L. & Caltabiano, M. L. (1983). Inferring travel motivation from travelers' experiences. *Journal of Travel Research,* **22**(2), 16-20.

Pearce, P.L. (2005). *Tourist Behaviour: Themes and Conceptual Schemes.* Bristol: Channel View Publications.

Pearce, P.L. & Stringer, P.F. (1991). Psychology and tourism. *Annals of Tourism Research,* **18**(1), 136-154.

Plog, F. (1974). *The Study of Prehistoric Change*: Academic Press.

Raylu, N. & Oei, T.P. (2004). The gambling related cognitions scale (GRCS): Development, confirmatory factor validation and psychometric properties. *Addiction,* **99**(6), 757-769.

Reinartz, W., Haenlein, M. & Henseler, J. (2009). An empirical comparison of the efficacy of covariance-based and variance-based SEM. *International Journal of Research in Marketing,* **26**(4), 332-344.

Rogers, P. (1998). The cognitive psychology of lottery gambling: A theoretical review. *Journal of gambling studies,* **14**(2), 111-134.

Ryan, C. & Glendon, I. (1998). Application of leisure motivation scale to tourism. *Annals of Tourism Research,* **25**(1), 169-184.

Saayman, M. & Saayman, A. (2012). Determinants of spending: An evaluation of three major sporting events. *International Journal of Tourism Research,* **14**(2), 124-138.

Scull, S. & Woolcock, G. (2005). Problem gambling in non-English speaking background communities in Queensland, Australia: A qualitative exploration. *International Gambling Studies,* **5**(1), 29-44.

Shaffer, H.J. & Korn, D.A. (2002). Gambling and related mental disorders: A public health analysis. *Annual Review of Public Health,* **23**(1), 171-212.

Solomon, M.R., Dahl, D.W., White, K., Zaichkowsky, J.L. & Polegato, R. (2014). *Consumer Behavior: Buying, having, and being*: Prentice Hall Upper Saddle River, NJ.

Tao, V.Y., Wu, A.M., Cheung, S.F. & Tong, K.K. (2011). Development of an indigenous inventory GMAB (Gambling Motives, Attitudes and Behaviors) for Chinese gamblers: An exploratory study. *Journal of gambling studies,* **27**(1), 99-113.

Tarras, J., Singh, A. & Moufakkir, O. (2000). The profile and motivations of elderly women gamblers. *UNLV Gaming Research & Review Journal,* **5**(1), 3.

Turnbull, D.R. & Uysal, M. (1995). An exploratory study of German visitors to the Caribbean: Push and pull motivations. *Journal of Travel & Tourism Marketing,* **4**(2), 85-92.

Udo, G. J., Bagchi, K. K. & Kirs, P. J. (2010). An assessment of customers'e-service quality perception, satisfaction and intention. *International Journal of Information Management,* **30**(6), 481-492.

UNWTO. (2016). Tourism Highlights. Retrieved from 10. 03. 2017 from http://www2.unwto.org/

Uysal, M. & Hagan, L. A. R. (1993). Motivation of pleasure travel and tourism. *Encyclopedia of hospitality and tourism,* *21,* 798-810.

Uysal, M. & Jurowski, C. (1994). Testing the push and pull factors. *Annals of Tourism Research,* **21**(4), 844-846. doi:dx.doi.org/10.1016/0160-7383(94)90091-4

Van Rijn, H., Kononowicz, T.W., Meck, W.H., Ng, K.K. & Penney, T.B. (2011). Contingent negative variation and its relation to time estimation: a theoretical evaluation. *Frontiers in Integrative Neuroscience, 5,* 91.

Vong, F. (2007). The psychology of risk-taking in gambling among Chinese visitors to Macau. *International Gambling Studies,* **7**(1), 29-42.

Walker, M. B. (1992). *The Psychology of Gambling*: Pergamon Press.

Witt, C.A. & Wright, P.L. (1992). Tourist motivation: Life after Maslow, In: Johnson P and Thomas B (eds), *Choice and Demand in Tourism*. London: Mansell, pp. 33-56.

Wong, I. A. & Rosenbaum, M. S. (2012). Beyond hardcore gambling: Understanding why mainland Chinese visit casinos in Macau. *Journal of Hospitality & Tourism Research,* **36**(1), 32-51.

Ye, L. (2009). A Comparison of gambling motivation factors between Chinese and western casino players. UNLV Theses, Dissertations, Professional Papers, and Capstones.

Yoon, Y. & Uysal, M. (2005). An examination of the effects of motivation and satisfaction on destination loyalty: a structural model. *Tourism Management,* **26**(1), 45-56.

Yuan, S. & McDonald, C. (1990). Motivational determinates of international pleasure time. *Journal of Travel Research,* **29**(1), 42-44.

Zeng, Z., Prentice, C. & King, B. E. (2014). To gamble or not? Perceptions of Macau among Mainland Chinese and Hong Kong visitors. *International Journal of Tourism Research,* **16**(2), 105-112.

9 Being outbound Chinese tourists: An identity perspective

Carol Zhang

The objectives of this chapter are to:

☐ Introduce identity theory and tourism;

☐ Provide an overview of research and government measures in dealing with uncivilised behaviours;

☐ Explore the way in which Chinese tourists reflect on the recent negative identity of the country;

☐ Draw out the dominant themes that underpin the reflections of Chinese tourists on the projected negative identities;

☐ Offer recommendations to the government and industry providers to deal with the increasing negative perception on Chinese tourists.

Keywords: Identity, China, Chinese, perceptions, tourism.

Introduction

The term 'Chinese outbound tourist' was almost non-existent until the initiation of the Open Door Policy in 1978. At present, Chinese tourists are among the fastest-growing segments of global tourism. With the increasing disposable income, the beneficial exchange rate of Chinese *yuan*, growing direct flights and ease of visa applications, the number of Mainland Chinese outbound tourists increased from 3.74 million in 1993 to 130.51 million in 2017. In addition, Chinese tourists spent 115.29 billion US dollars in 2017, which ranked Chinese tourists as the first and most profitable outbound tourists in the market (CTA & Ctrip, 2018; UNWTO, 2003). As a fast-growing market, Chinese tourists are different from other tourists due to their unique culture. Chinese tourist behaviour has become the most popular topics among all China-related tourism research (Bao et al., 2018). To understand Chinese tourist behaviour, existing studies have focused on demystifying culturally-embedded travel motivation and behaviours to examine the way in which tourism providers can understand and engage in the growing market (e.g. Hsu & Hsu, 2016; Pearce et al., 2013). With academic research primarily addressing the economic benefits of this group of tourists, the social impacts of such growth have received relatively less attention.

When searching for the words 'Chinese tourist' in the Internet, although a few articles continue to address the beneficial elements of this profitable market, the majority of news articles describe this group of tourists as 'uncivilised', 'stupid' and even 'the world's worst tourists' (e.g. Ejinsight, 2018; Pile, 2017). Such uncivilised or negative behaviours have been represented as salient characteristics to define Chinese tourists and even China as a country. Given the intensified projected identity of Chinese tourists, such a topic has received relatively less attention, especially in the English literature. Only a few studies concerning the perceptions of host countries on Chinese tourists have implicitly touched the topic (e.g. Chen et al., 2018). On the contrary, academic studies in the Chinese language have increasingly focused on improving the projected perceptions (e.g. Chen, 2016; Guo & Zhang, 2008). With the fast-growing number of Chinese tourists, understanding how individuals reflect on these imposed identities is urgent. This chapter introduces a national-based social identity to understand the reflective process. Social identity is particularly useful for understanding intergroup interaction in defining the self (Tajefl, 1982). As any form of socially constructed identity inevitable involved in the continuous interaction with 'us' and 'others' (Sarup, 1996), the interactive nature of social identity is useful to understand individuals' behaviour towards 'us' and 'others' (Tajfel,

1979). Without such an understanding, the interaction between tourists and host communities remains incomplete.

Drawing on the social identity, this chapter employs a constructivism–interpretivism research paradigm to highlight the interactive nature of identity formation (Jennings, 2005). Data used in this chapter came from multiple resources, including semi-structured in-depth interviews, administrative documents and other literature, to provide an overview about the reflections of Chinese tourists on their projected negative image. Twenty frequent Chinese outbound tourists, comprising diverse professional backgrounds, geographic locations, annual incomes, genders and ages, were interviewed. On average, the semi-structured interviews took 45 minutes. All of the informants have had at least five outbound international travel experiences.

Identity and tourist behaviour

Identity concept is strongly associated with unity, which establishes the limits of a subject and allows it to be distinguished from any other; identity, by its definition, identifies who we are as a group and who I am as an individual that belongs to that group (Schlesinger, 1987). The basic idea of any form of identity is that individuals have a fundamental need to belong to different social groups. Social identity as the emotional and evaluative consequences of belonging to groups links self-concept with group normative values (Tajfel, 1982). As a specific type of social identity, national-based social identity is conceptualised as a powerful means of locating individuals in the world through a prism of collective personality and its distinctive culture (Smith, 1991). Hence, nationality is traditionally used as a key indication to understand tourist behaviours and values (e.g. Chen et al., 2018; Hsu & Huang, 2016).

An often neglected aspect of identity construction is the idea of *otherness*. Sarup (1996) stated that identity is always related to what one is not – the other. To maintain a separate identity, one has to define oneself against the other. Other scholars extended the idea of otherness and argued that perception with others, and the response associated with such perception also plays a vital role in identity construction in a global context (Alexander et al., 2005). By taking the idea of otherness into consideration, identity is not just related to self-concept but an interactive term which involves negotiations between 'us' and different 'others'.

In fact, social identity theory aims to understand intergroup relation (Tajfel, 1982) and indicates that negotiations between intragroup (us) and intergroup (others) make identity unique. Brown (2000) agreed with such conceptualisation and argued that group differentiation is the essence of social identity. It is the process of having a positive self-concept attached to group superiority over others, and explains intergroup and intragroup behaviours. To understand one's social identity, scholars have often proposed three interlinked elements: cognitive, evaluative and emotional components (Ellemers et al., 1999; Hornsey, 2008; Tajfel, 1982). Cognitive component indicates any sense of belonging that involves the awareness of group memberships and its associated characteristics (Ellemers et al., 1999). The cognitive understanding of the group is socially constructed and negotiated between 'us' and 'others'. When the social identity is formed, boundaries between social groups are created to define members' uniqueness in relation to that of non-members. Hence, cultural values are often utilised as symbolic boundaries to categorise different groups (Anderson, 1991).

Based on the understanding of cognitive characteristics of 'us', the evaluative component further highlights essential group values to define membership (Tajfel, 1982). To maintain a positive social identity, the sense of superiority is often addressed; positive evaluations of 'us' over 'others' enhance self-esteem (Ellemers et al., 1999). The last component, namely, social identity, highlights the emotional investment of the other two processes: cognitive and evaluation (Tajfel, 1982). Although nations are imagined as community (Anderson, 1991), the emotional commitment of the social group enhances the social cohesion and motivates individuals to continuously improve the group status (Smith, 1991).

Identity and tourism are not new juxtapositions. Indeed, recent studies have considered tourism an appealing way of enforcing social cohesion (e.g. Gielling & Ong, 2016). Bossen (2000) noted that tourism reinforces national identity through the process of making homogeneity out of existing heterogeneity, which creates a sense of common descent among groups. In this sense, visiting national heritage and archaeological sites can be regarded as an emotional journey for domestic tourists to seek cultural affinity and identity with their homeland (e.g. Pretes, 2003). Through the utilisation of the national heritage attractions in demonstrating the uniqueness of a nation, the tourism industry has constructed the 'commonly seen world' (Hollinshead, 2009). Heritage-related studies primarily concern common ancestry and their relation to national identity construction.

Another group of research has addressed the usefulness of social identity in understanding collective behaviour and social differentiation. Many of these studies have focused on how belonging to a social group influences a host country's collective behaviour in welcoming tourists (e.g. Chen et al. 2018; Palmer et al., 2013; van Rekom & Go, 2006). Chen, Hsu and Li (2018) specifically paid attention on the negative encounters of Chinese tourists with the host community. By adopting the social identity theory, their study found out that Hong Kong residents share two intertwined mentalities: a sense of superiority and a feeling of deprivation towards incoming Mainland Chinese tourists. Although the study provides insights into how host communities reflect on dominant tourists in the region, the tourists' side of the story seems relatively underdeveloped. To understand host–tourist interactions, studies conducted from the perspective of tourists primarily focused on tourist experiences (e.g. Luo et al., 2015; Pizam et al., 2000) rather than the tourists' overall feelings and reflections on any direct and indirect interaction. The majority of host–tourist research has typically focused on a specific destination (e.g. Chen et al. 2018; Pizam et al., 2000). As a result, the current research examined the reflections of Chinese tourists on the negative identities projected by host communities on them.

Uncivilised and pro-civilised behaviours of Chinese outbound tourists

The projected negative identities of Chinese tourists have drawn attention since the early 2000s. In 2006, the Central Committee on Spiritual Civilization and the China National Tourism Administration (CNTA) jointly promulgated the '*Guide to Civilized Behaviours of Outbound Chinese Tourists*' to establish a good international image of Chinese citizens (China.com.cn, 2006). The guide aims at providing proper behavioural guidance to outbound Chinese tourists in reaction to well-reported problems, including littering, queue jumping, talking loudly, breaking regulations, inscribing heritage attractions and disrespecting local customs. To solve this issue, many academic studies (especially in Chinese) have examined the reasons behind such uncivilised behaviours. For them, cultural differences, lack of public spirit, lack of civic education, absence of effective legislation and mentality of behaving negatively during holidays have been listed as primary reasons (e.g. Chen, 2016; Liu, 2007). Others have started to worry about the consequences of the dramatised globally recognised image of Chinese tourists and its impact on the image of China and Chinese people in general. Guo and Zhang (2008) argued that the economic status of China has not made it a strong country in the global stage and the widespread negative image of such behaviours prevents China in doing so.

Moreover, the uncivilised behaviours of a few Chinese outbound tourists have stimulated social conflicts. For example, the massive increase of

Mainland Chinese tourists in Hong Kong and their associated negative behaviours indirectly cause numerous social–political crises. A derogatory phrase '强国人' (*people from powerful country*) has become popular in Hong Kong to symbolise uncivilised behaviours and arrogant attitudes of Mainland Chinese tourists. Extreme local nationalists have utilised the well-reported negative images of Chinese tourists to differentiate Hong Kong from Mainland China; anti-Chinese tourist movements accentuate the social crisis in the region (Sun, 2015). The widely expressed uncivilised behaviour of Chinese tourists is not purely a tourism issue but a social one. Improving education and enacting effective legislation are considered effective measures to promote pro-civilised outbound travel behaviours (e.g. Xu & Pan, 2016).

In 2013, the Central Government enacted the Tourism Law, in which respecting local customs when traveling abroad is required by the law (Gov.cn, 2013). In 2015, uncivilised tourist behaviour blacklist was announced by the CNTA to name and shame inappropriate behaviours (Xinhua, 2016). The CNTA encourages Chinese citizens to take photos or video of any negative behaviour they spot and pass it on to authorities. The rationale behind the online blacklist is to embarrass unruly tourists among Chinese citizens and warn other tourists to behave appropriately especially during international trips. The comic presented below summarises this argument:

Figure 9.1: Uncivilised tourist behaviour blacklist (Zhou & Fan, 2017).

As shown in the comic, a blacklist is issued to warn Chinese citizens to behave appropriately during travels. Chinese tourists should be aware of the consequences of their inappropriate behaviours on themselves and on the country. 'We need to follow the rule during vacation' is presented as an appropriate mentality in Figure 9.1 to protect the image of China in a global context. Importantly, people on the blacklist are prohibited to take any outbound trips. Maintaining a positive social image of the group during international trips is deemed more important than domestic travel. This finding indicates that threats to positive group esteem are often magnified by outgroup perception (Ellemers et al., 1999). With government anxiety over tourist behaviours and the efforts of associating individual behaviours to Chinese identity, understanding how individual travellers reflect on the current situation is thus interesting.

Reflections of individual tourists on projected uncivilised behaviours

This section mainly contains data gathered from semi-structured interviews and provides an overview of the reflections of Chinese frequent travellers on the negative image projected on them by others. Two subsections cover their understanding of belonging to the outbound Chinese groups and the emotional reflections towards belonging.

Being a civilised Chinese tourist

When asked to describe the group of Chinese outbound tourists and themselves as Chinese tourists, all respondents are aware of the dramatic growth of outbound travels and the associated uncivilised behaviours. For them, they denounce the uncivilised behaviours displayed by their fellow citizens. At the same time, as the projected negative images identify Chinese tourists as a group and also individuals belonging to the group (Schlesinger, 1987), respondents unconsciously attribute the negative behaviours to cultural reasons. The responses below illustrate this argument in detail:

> Some Chinese tourists are very rude and littering everywhere. When I travel, I try to avoid going to famous places where they hate Chinese tourists. In some small villages in Eastern Europe, for example, they are still nice to me and are curious about China. I think that when a lot of less educated Chinese tourists come through package tours, their attitudes will change. Those tourists will litter everywhere like what they did in China (Peter, 50, doctor).

> The concept of queuing is relatively new to the elderly, because in China, we used to gather around and have a little random chat when waiting for services. Also, people in villages often are sitting on the floor for gathering. It's just cultural differences (Liz, 22, HR assistant).

> A lot of people complain about package tours, and I do think they are very loud. But, I think they talk loudly because Chinese people

like '热闹' *(a warm, friendly but noisy environment)*. When I travel with my friends, I feel that if I talk loudly about something, it shows my enthusiasm and I can warm up the conversation (Tom, 27, lawyer).

As shown in the responses presented above, the respondents are highly aware of the specific uncivilised behaviours projected on the group. The awareness of inappropriate behaviours conducted by intragroup members did not motivate them to show any intention to leave the group. Instead, a few respondents utilise culturally specific examples to explain the reasons behind uncivilised behaviours, including talking loudly in public, queue jumping and sitting on floors. Although Peter denounced how uncivilised Chinese tourists change their travel behaviours, the phrase 'like what they did in China' explains that cultural differences are the main reason behind such behaviours. To protect self-esteem, individuals show more empathy towards negative intragroup behaviours projected by others (Ellemers et al., 1999).

Individuals typically prefer a positive image than a negative one (Tajfel, 1979); maintaining positive group images in host communities helps to achieve this. For example, Cathy (32, administrator) illustrated that "of course I hate those uncivilised behaviours. Not all Chinese behave this way. As a Chinese, I often become more careful when I travel aboard. I need to let them know how Chinese behave". Through an evaluative process, an unchangeable social identity motivated respondents to behave appropriately abroad (Tajfel, 1982). The interlink between self-esteem and group esteem confirms the recent efforts of the government in linking China's global image with individual traveller behaviours (Guo & Zhang, 2008).

Although protecting the national image of China in host communities is commonly mentioned by individuals, the sense of having harmonious intergroup and intragroup interactions during travelling influences such initiatives, as shown in several responses:

When I realised that Western people do not talk loudly in public, not even in little home-feeling pubs, I started to talk in a much lower volume. I do not want people to point at me (Jack, 45, lecturer).

When we visited a Church, my mom still has her phone on maximum volume and speaks very loudly. I apologise for her behaviour, but I couldn't bring myself to stop her consistently; her hearing is not very good now and it is not very serious. I want to have a peaceful and enjoyable moment with her during travels (Renee, 33, businessman).

> To protect the image of China and avoid unnecessary conflicts with local people, we always supervise one another during international trips. It is not worth getting in trouble in unfamiliar places (Anna, 31, salesperson).

Chinese tourists consistently justify their 'inappropriate behaviours' to protect the 'image of China'. Monitoring self and intragroup behaviours is utilised to achieve the objective. As expressed by respondents, having a peaceful and harmonious travelling experience is also strongly associated with such behaviours. The sense of harmony is deeply rooted in Chinese culture and guides tourist behaviour (Hsu & Huang, 2016). Here, harmonious interactions with host communities ensure positive image and personal safety. To maintain a harmonious travel experience with fellow travellers, inappropriate behaviours have become tolerable. This finding thus explains why nearly all respondents show unwillingness to stop or report other Chinese travellers in international destinations. For instance, once stated, "I am not a police and I want to avoid conflicts with others". Individuals' desire for a harmonious travel experience plays a paradoxical role in encouraging civilised behaviours. The emotional judgement towards intergroup and intragroup interactions influences decisions on behaviour modification. Hence, the next section explains in-depth emotional responses of individuals towards the projected negative behaviours.

Emotional responses and civilised behaviours

The CNTA's initiative of using a blacklist to name and shame inappropriate behaviours (Xinhua, 2016) shows the role that emotional responses play in tourist behaviours. Emotional attachments to a nation motivate individuals to fight for its positive status (Smith, 1991). Here, most respondents used the word 'ashamed' and 'embarrassed' to express their feeling towards uncivilised behaviours displayed by fellow citizens. The following responses show this argument in detail:

> I know the blacklist. I feel cheerful. We all know how we, Chinese, care about self-image among our family and friends. Shame from people who know you is serious here. It might solve the problem (John, 32, analyst).

> Shame on them. They destroy the image of our nation. When I travel, some other Asian tourists behave badly. Local people always think they are Chinese. We need to behave well to leave a good impression to people (Laurence, 40, photographer).

Chinese love shopping and we do shop a lot. It is cheaper compared with the price in China. After knowing that we are treated as rich and stupid for blind shopping, I became very angry and shop niche brand in less quantity (Renee, 33, businessman).

I used to stand really close to the people in front of me for queuing up. After some people pointed at me, I feel embarrassed in front of other people. They must think I am less educated. Now, I try to keep a lot distance from people. Some Westerners jump the queue as I have a great gap (Sharon, 38, accountant).

Given a strong emotional commitment to being Chinese, individuals' emotions in reaction to others show modification of behaviours. The idea of otherness shows the interactive nature of social identity (Alexander et al., 2005; Sarup, 1996). Feeling ashamed in front of others, especially outgroup, magnifies emotional responses and encourages civilised behaviours. The responses also confirm that the damages in the social group status have consequences to those who belong to the same social group (Tajfel, 1982). Anticipated embarrassment plays an important role here. Like Sharon's response, 'they must think I am less educated' indicates the strong self-consciousness of travel behaviours abroad. Although Sharon noticed that other travellers also behave negatively, anticipated embarrassment encourages her to continuously behave appropriately.

Enjoyment is part of the fundamental nature of tourism; tourism providers often try to find out the best possible way to make tourists feel comfortable. The continuous negotiation mentioned above between self and others' view potentially put extra stress for outbound Chinese tourists. As mentioned before, the blacklist issued by the CNTA further confirmed the importance of monitoring tourist behaviours abroad. The following responses thus show how the widely disseminated negative identity of Chinese tourists makes an individual behaves meticulously:

We went Spain. My daughter booked an apartment hotel for us. Before checking out, she read the instruction saying that we need to keep tidy. They also translated that in Chinese. When my daughter went out to buy breakfast, I cleaned the room. I even mopped the floor and washed all the towels. When my daughter returned, she felt so bad. She said she want me to enjoy the trip and not be a house keeper. Even at home, I hired people to clean my house. But I feel I must do this; they know we are Chinese. I need let them know we do not leave a mess (Joyce, 63, retiree).

I know some Westerners think that Chinese are cheap and take little advantages. But I only drink hot water. I always prepare some coin to ask them to fill my hot water bottle. Some of my friends pretend to purchase hot tea to achieve such mission. We never do this inside China (Chris, 27, project manager).

Both responses show that individuals often became more careful when traveling abroad. Modifications of behaviour in foreign countries have become a common norm among individuals. Innovative strategies are utilised to maintain a positive self-image and avoid any anticipated embarrassment from others. Moreover, some extreme 'civilised' behaviour patterns can potentially damage the fundamental nature of tourism: the enjoyment.

Conclusion

The increasingly negative perception of the way Chinese tourists behave in uncivilised ways has intensified conflicts between Chinese tourists and host communities they visit. As the projected uncivilised behaviours have become salient group characteristics to define Chinese, this chapter adopts a national-based social identity theory to explain individual reflections on it. Identity construction often involves interactions between 'us' and 'others' (Sarup, 1996; Tajfel, 1979). By acknowledging the interactive nature of social identity, the chapter contributes to the rich understanding of the reflections of tourists on the projected identities and associated behaviours. The chapter also introduces the current academic and government approaches in handling the negative perceptions on Chinese tourists. A blacklist has been employed since 2015 by CNTA to name and shame unruly tourist behaviours (Xinhua, 2016). With the intensified host–tourist relation and potential danger of damaging the national image of China, studying this area is timely.

Specifically, 20 semi-structured in-depth interviews were conducted to gather information from frequent Chinese outbound travellers. The study confirms that the government's call for protecting China's national image abroad did work at the individual level. In addition, the study found that the unchangeable sense of belonging to China did motivate individuals to display more civilised behaviours (Tajfel, 1982). The desire of maintaining harmonious interactions with intergroup and intragroup members moderates the strength of behaving appropriately. In addition, as all respondents are aware of the widespread image of Chinese tourists, the anticipated feeling of embarrassments and the potential association of them with those negative images motivate individuals to modify their behaviours during travel. The feeling of embarrassment is often magnified by outgroup perception (Ellemers et al., 1999). Associated behaviour justification based on the magnification is deemed to be strong as the negative perception of others threatens the status of China in a global context. Protecting one's own social identity for a positive self-esteem is thus achieved by behaving appropriately (Tajfel, 1982). The study therefore recognised the interactive nature of identity formation and its potential role in behaviour changes to contribute to the complex relation between host and tourist.

As tourists' behaviour depends on the interactions with intergroup and intragroup members, destination conflicts are not the exclusive purview of those who lived in destinations. The current chapter shows that Chinese outbound tourists reflect on the constructed group identity by the host communities and other Chinese tourists' behaviours. Clearly, several Chinese tourists are aware of the need to behave appropriately in a host community and willing to contribute to a harmonious destination environment. Clear instructions should be provided for Chinese tourists. Importantly, service providers in a destination should understand the uniqueness of being Chinese tourists in a contemporary tourism context. Therefore, more tailor-made services can be provided to enhance satisfaction and release the anxiety of behaving inappropriately. Although the study confirms the government's efforts in stimulating the feeling of embarrassment to encourage civilised behaviours, the fact that many tourists are unwilling to intervene or report any uncivilised behaviour needs attention. The key point here is when focusing on understanding a group of tourists, the tourism industry needs to be aware of their identities as projected by others and their reflections towards it. In summary, the highlights of the chapter are listed below:

♦ Understanding the interactive nature of national-based social identity in tourism context.

♦ Providing insights into the interlink between identity and tourism.

♦ Contributing to understand the complexity of host–tourist relationship.

♦ Providing an overview of Chinese uncivilised tourism behaviours.

♦ Examining the reflections of Chinese tourists on the negative image magnified by host communities.

References

Alexander, M.G., Levin, S. & Henry, P.J. (2005). Image theory, social identity, and social dominance: Structural characteristics and individual motives underlying international images. *Political Psychology*, **26**(1), 27-45.

Anderson, B.R.O. (1991). *Imagined Communities: reflections on the origin and spread of nationalism*. London: Verso.

Bao, J., Chen, G. & Jin, X. (2018). China tourism research: A review of publications from four top international journals, *Journal of China Tourism Research*, **14**(1), 1-19.

Bossen, C. (2000). Festival Mania, tourism and nation building in Fiji: The case of the Hibiscus Festival, 1956-1970. *The Contemporary Pacific*, **12**(1), 123–154

Brown, R. (2000). Social identity theory: Past achievements, current problems, and future challenges. *European Journal of Social Psychology*, **30**, 745-778.

Chen, N., Hsu, C.H. & Li, X.R. (2018). Feeling superior or deprived? Attitudes and underlying mentalities of residents towards Mainland Chinese tourists. *Tourism Management*, **66**, 94-107.

Chen, J. (2016). An analysis of uncivilised behaviours of Chinese outbound tourists and the governance measures. *Chinese and Foreign Entrepreneurs*, **33**, 258-259. (in Chinese)

CTA & Ctrip. (2018). *China Tourism Academy and Ctrip jointly released the 2017 Outbound Tourism Big Data Report*. Available at: http://mp.weixin. qq.com/s/hVxO3ZRcO5YmdebH9XO5iA. (Accessed: June 6, 2018).

China.com.cn. (2006). *Guide to Civilized Behaviours of Outbound Chinese Tourists*.Available at: http://www.china.com.cn/policy/txt/2006-10/02/content_7212276.htm. (Accessed: May 31, 2018).

Ellemers, N., Kortekaas, P. & Ouwerkerk, J.W. (1999). Self-categorization, commitment to the group and social self-esteem as related but distinct aspects of social identity. *European Journal of Social Psychology*, **29**, 371-389.

Ejinsight (2018). *Beijing to blame for bad behavior of some Chinese tourists*. Available at: http://www.ejinsight.com/20180220-beijing-to-blame-for-bad-behavior-of-some-chinese-tourists/(Accessed: June 6, 2018).

Gieling, J. & Ong, C.-E. (2016). Warfare tourism experiences and national identity: The case of Airborne Museum 'Hartenstein' in Oosterbeek, The Netherlands. *Tourism Management*, **57**, 45-55.

Guo, L. & Zhang, S. (2008). A study on outbound tourism ethics of Chinese citizens and 'soft power' upgrade. *Tourism Tribune*, **23**(12), 18-22. (in Chinese)

Gov.cn (2013). *Tourism Law* Available at: http://www.gov.cn/flfg/2013-04/25/content_2390945.htm. (Accessed: June 16, 2018).

Hornsey, M.J. (2008). Social identity theory and self-categorization theory: A historical review. *Social and Personality Psychology Compass*, **2**(1), 204-222.

Hollinshead, K. (1999). Surveillance of the worlds of tourism: Foucault and the eye-of-power. *Tourism Management*, **20**, 7-23.

Hollinshead, K. (2009). The 'worldmaking' prodigy of tourism: The reach and power of tourism in the dynamics of change and transformation. *Tourism Analysis*, **14**(1), 139-152.

Hsu, C.H.C. & Huang, S. (2016). Reconfiguring Chinese cultural values and their tourism implications. *Tourism Management*, **54**, 230-242.

Jennings, G.R. (2005). Interviewing: A focus on qualitative techniques. In B.W. Ritchie, P. Burns & C. Palmer (Eds.), *Tourism research methods: Integrating theory with practice* (pp. 99-117). UK: CABI.

Liu, L. (2007). The cultural analysis of the uncivilized behaviors and the cognition of the management strategy. *Journal of Guilin Institute of Tourism*, **18**(5), 662-665. (in Chinese)

Luo, X. , Brown, G. & Huang, S. (2015). Host perceptions of backpackers: Examining the influence of intergroup contact, *Tourism Management*, **50**, 292-305

Palmer, A., Koening-Lewis, N. & Jones, L. (2013). The effects of residents' social identity and involvement on their advocacy of incoming tourism. *Tourism Management*, **38** (2), 142-151.

Pizam, A., Uriely, N. & Reichel, A. (2000). The intensity of tourist–host social relationship and its effects on satisfaction and change of attitudes: The case of working tourists in Israel. *Tourism Management*, **21** (4), 395-406

Pearce, P. L., Wu, M. & Osmond, A. (2013). Puzzles in understanding Chinese Tourist Behaviour: Towards a Triple-C Gaze, *Tourism Recreation Research*, **38**(2), 145-157.

Pretes, M. (2003). Tourism and nationalism. *Annals of Tourism Research*, **30**(1), 125–142

Pile, T. (2017). Who are the world's worst tourists? Six nations that stand out - you may be surprised. *South China Morning Post*. Available at: www.scmp.com/magazines/post-magazine/travel/article/2102308/who-are-worlds-worst-tourists-six-nations-stand-out (Accessed: February 24, 2018).

Tajfel, H. (1979). Individuals and groups in social psychology. *British Journal of Social Psychology*, **18**, 183-190.

Tajfel, H. (1982). Social psychology of intergroup relations. *Annual Review of Psychology*, **33**(1), 1-39.

Sarup, M. (1996). *Identity, Culture and the Postmodern World*. Edinburgh: Edinburgh University Press.

Schlesinger, P. (1987). On national identity: Some conceptions and misconceptions criticized. *Social Science Information*, **26**(2), 219–264

Smith, A. D. (1991). *National Identity*. University of Nevada Press.

Sun, N. (2015). Hong Kong tourism hit by anti-mainland China sentiment as tour groups stay away. *South China Morning Post*, 22 December.

van Rekom, J. & Go, F. (2006). Being discovered: a blessing to local identities? *Annals of Tourism Research*, **33**(3), 767-784

United Nations World Tourism Organisation(2003). *China outbound tourism*. Madrid, Spain: UNTWO.

Xu H. & Pan, H. (2016). A study on promotion of Chinese outbound tourists' moral quality from the perspective of civic morality. *Journal of Hangzhou Dianzi University (Social Sciences)*, **12**(2), 24-28. (in Chinese)

Xinhua (2016). *CNTA and shame on tourists on black list*. Available at: http://www.xinhuanet.com/fortune/2016-08/21/c_129244977.htm(Accessed: June 24, 2018).

Zhou, W. & Fan, S. (2017). *Stereotypes of Chinese tourists*. Chinese Youth.. Available at: http://news.cyol.com/yuanchuang/2017-07/19/content_16314234.htm. (Accessed: June 24, 2018).

Part III:
Narratives and Storytelling

10 Managing the co-creation of narratives in the heritage sector: The Surgeons' Hall Museum, Edinburgh

Ellis Urquhart and Anna Leask

The objectives of this chapter are to:

☐ Link together theoretical approaches to storytelling and narrative creation with the co-creation of heritage experiences;

☐ Identify and discuss management practices and associated opportunities for narrative co-creation;

☐ Present the case of Surgeons' Hall Museum as a site which considers narrative and storytelling as a critical management challenge;

☐ Propose that co-created narratives could lead to more engaging, individualised and memorable heritage visitor experiences;

☐ Present lessons for heritage management, including a need for narrative co-creation to be a considered within strategic heritage planning and operational decision-making.

Keywords: storytelling, narratives, co-creation, heritage, experiences, management.

Introduction

It is widely accepted in the academic literature that tourism and leisure are experientially driven industries (Tung & Ritchie, 2011). However, the role of the customer in the creation of memorable experiences has faced significant debate. From an experiential perspective, Frochot and Batat (2013) argued that the customer has become an economic actor who is actively involved in the consumption experience. Conversely, the business acts to facilitate and assist the customer in the production and achievement of their own experience. Increasingly in tourism, the concept of co-creation has proliferated in the experiential literature; however it has only recently been applied to the heritage sector. This is interesting, due to the unique nature of heritage tourism products, that often seek to establish a personal, emotive and symbolic connection with visitors (McIntosh, 1999). In addition, work in heritage management highlights the value of strong narratives in the creation of memorable visitor experiences (Magee & Gilmore, 2015; Moscardo, 2010). However, little research has explored how these can be co-created within the heritage experience, and subsequently how these can be fostered by heritage marketers and managers. The overall aim of this chapter is to reframe the academic understanding of heritage narratives within experience co-creation theory. Furthermore, the chapter aims to question how managers can encourage the co-creation of narratives in the heritage sector.

Following an evaluation of the existing literature in both narrative creation in heritage and experience co-creation, the chapter introduces the case of Surgeons' Hall Museum (SHM) in Edinburgh, UK. A brief background provides the necessary context before data is presented from an in-depth qualitative interview with a member of the interpretation team. The chapter concludes with the implications for managers with regards to managing the co-creation of narratives in the heritage sector.

Experience co-creation

The concept of co-creation has become firmly embedded in business and management disciplines. Drawing on wider paradigm shifts in service marketing, co-creation argues that the service experience (and its subsequent value) is developed incrementally through dialogue, interaction and personalisation between several actors within the service setting. Thus, the customer becomes an active co-creator of their own experience rather than it being predetermined by the service provider (Prahalad & Ramaswamy, 2004; Vargo & Lusch, 2004). Increasingly, as the conceptual discussions surrounding co-creation have advanced, so have the questions over how it is managed. While the literature stresses the autonomy of customers in the co-creation of experience, a number of authors highlight the importance of management practices that can support this process (Jaakkola et al., 2015; Payne et al., 2008).

Increasingly, co-creation has been applied to experiential contexts such as tourism, hospitality and events. Early work by Binkhorst and Den Dekker (2009) suggested viewing tourism experiences from a network perspective. The authors argued that tourists sat at the heart of a complex network of various actors, each with various relationships and connections. Conversely, it is the co-creative opportunities, engagements and interactions that exist between each of the actors which can generate value in the tourism experience. Similarly, a number of scholars have argued that with increased co-creative opportunities comes greater visitor attention and memorability after the experience (Campos et al., 2016; Zatori et al., 2018). Finally, from a commercial perspective, there is an argument to suggest that the successful co-creation of tourism experiences leads to increased visitor satisfaction and increased loyalty (Mathis et al., 2016).

While the popularity of co-creation is evident throughout tourism research, its application to the heritage sector has been slower. This is interesting as the heritage sector, being driven to generate quality visitor experiences, is particularly well-placed to consider co-creation as a worthwhile management strategy. Minkiewicz, Evans and Bridson (2014) argued that heritage organisations face significant competition both from within the tourism industry and from associated leisure providers. As such, heritage sites are increasingly adopting innovative ways to attract and retain audience groups. The authors further identified active visitor involvement in heritage experiences as being a significant driver for co-creation. Thyne and Hede (2016), however did highlight the balance between visitor empowerment and management control as a challenge for heritage sites, due to the fragile nature of their core resources. As a means to provide co-creative opportunities without compromising the heritage resource, new innovative technologies have been suggested as a way to enhance content and diversify the presentation (Jung & Tom Dieck, 2017). While a number of the studies above question the tools that can be used in co-creation, few studies have linked these to the co-creation of narratives and storytelling – which can be seen as a critical part of the heritage product (Chronis, 2005).

Narrative creation and storytelling in heritage

Storytelling has long played a significant part in consumer research and continues to interest researchers from a variety of disciplines. Adaval and Wyerjr (1998) argued that stories provide the basis for: understanding new experiences; making judgements about people, objects and events; and developing personal attitudes and beliefs. Grounded in tourism research, Moscardo (2010) advocated the importance of stories and themes in the construction of tourism experiences, however the author was critical of the lack of conceptual development in this area. Tung and Ritchie (2011) highlighted the strong link between storytelling and memorability in tourism experiences. The authors suggest that as tourists construct stories and then share these with their social groups, they crystallise the story into memory, which can then be recovered and remembered later. This was supported by Servidio and Ruffolo (2016), who note that in viewing tourism as an emotional and highly personal activity, the creation of narrative can have a profound effect on the memorability of tourism experiences.

Furthermore, Moscardo (2017b) explored the link between storytelling and mindfulness in tourism experiences, and argued that powerful stories can act as a mechanism to support mindful visitor behaviour that deepened engagement with the presented subject matter. The value of a memorable tourism experience for businesses is well documented in the literature. A number of authors have cited increased competitiveness (Ritchie & Crouch, 2003), increased sales (Woodside, 2010), and increased visit and revisit intentions (Kim & Youn, 2017) as potential outcomes of memorable tourism experiences.

The role of stories and narratives are especially significant in the heritage sector. In addition to offering unique experiential products, heritage sites are often driven by an underlying story that is hoped to be communicated with visitors. Through the use of interpretation, heritage sites can engage a range of audiences and foster participation in the heritage product, in addition to supporting conservation objectives and sustainability (Moscardo, 2014). Similarly, as highlighted by Mitsche et al. (2013), stories have the power to enhance and enliven existing material heritage resources for a wide range of visitors. Focussing on the visitor dimension, Chronis (2012) argued that heritage tourists have an active role as 'story-builders' within their own experience and suggested that they progressed through a three-stage narrative construction process. The author concluded that museum visitors took part in narrative enrichment (or an engagement with resources), followed by a period of narrative imagination (developing the story by their own imagination) and concluded with narrative closure (personally connecting with the story). Dimache, Wondirad and Agyeiwaah (2017) took this idea further by highlighting the inherent fluidity in heritage narratives and the subtle relationship between official and individual narratives which influence the visitor experience.

Much of the discussion surrounding narrative creation in heritage relates to management practices. As identified by Black (2012), contemporary heritage management encourages visitors to generate their own personal interpretations of heritage products and to co-create their own narratives both during and after the on-site experience. From a design perspective, Counts (2009) suggested that museums should consider the plot which visitor can follow to provide markers through which they can construct their own narrative. Similarly, Palombini (2017) applied various storytelling elements from narrative theory (the user, the characters and the environment) to cultural heritage and argued that such an approach could enhance visitor engagement with heritage products in the digital age. Increasingly, the use of mobile and smartphone applications and virtual platforms can be seen as valuable tools to support heritage narrative creation.

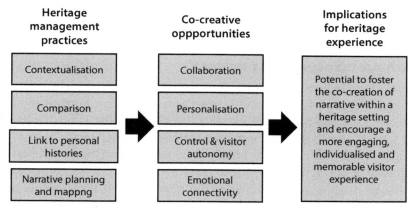

Figure 10.1: Heritage management practices and opportunities for the co-creation of narrative. Source: Authors

It is therefore clear that for experiences to be as memorable to visitors as possible, there needs to be strong links to a developing narrative. However, the means by which narratives form and how these can be fostered by heritage managers are more elusive. To explore these questions further, the case of SHM seeks to identify the management practices that contribute to narrative creation in a heritage setting and applies these to the concept of experiential co-creation. In drawing together the previous discussion, Figure 10.1 illustrates the connections between heritage management practices, co-creative opportunities and their potential implications for the heritage experience based on existing heritage management literature and provides a structure for the following sections.

The Case of Surgeons' Hall Museum, Edinburgh

Background

Surgeons' Hall Museum in Edinburgh is an award-winning anatomical museum owned by The Royal College of Surgeons of Edinburgh. Open to the public since 1832, SHM is one of Scotland's oldest museums and houses an extensive collection of surgical tools, dental equipment and pathology specimens. In 2009, the artefacts at SHM were named as a Nationally Significant Collection by the Scottish Government and have since been awarded a £4.4 million investment by the Heritage Lottery Fund. The Lister Project aimed to redevelop the visitor experience at the two museums based at SHM – The History of Surgery and the Wohl Pathology Museum. Updated interpretation, multimedia, interactive touch-points and presentations have since been launched across the site which reopened to the public in 2015 following a year's renovation. Visitors can view a reconstructed dissection in the Anatomy Theatre through the use of an introductory presentation that is projected onto a model cadaver. In addition, visitors can learn about the surgical procedures, instruments and stories associated with the collection.

Heritage management practices

As discussed above, SHM has recently undergone a significant redevelopment to its interpretative provision. As such, a number of new exhibits were developed throughout the site with the aim of enhancing their storytelling and the subsequent visitor experience. To provide insight into the management practices associated with the co-creation of narrative at SHM, the following extracts were drawn from an in-depth interview with a participant from the interpretation team. While this case is solely focussed on SHM, the following discussion draws parallels with the wider heritage sector and employs theory from both co-creation and heritage management fields.

The first quote below, discusses the design of interpretative media that provides contextualisation in the visitor experience:

> "So something fairly dry, like the history of the College in term of documentation and such like, I thought well let's put it on a timeline, that you swipe through, you put a bit of context there about other scientific things that were happening outside the college, a bit of social context about, Michelangelo starting the Sistine Chapel about the same time that this place was founded."

> (SHM Manager, June 2016)

This correlates with existing arguments that suggest interpretation that links with wider social context can significantly aid in visitor comprehension and understanding of the subject matter (Black, 2012; Prentice & Andersen, 2007). However, it could be further argued that effective contextualisation in heritage interpretation can contribute to the co-creation of narrative. The act of contextualising brings historical content that is external to the visitor, into their own frame of reference. The heritage manager provides contextual cues linked to social history which the visitor then individually negotiates in relation to their own knowledge, background and history. This process could be argued as a means of associating meaning or significance to an otherwise generic detail (such as a date or time frame). The narrative is therefore co-created based on the input from the exhibition curators, and the interpretation of individual visitors.

In a similar discussion, the participant highlighted the notion of comparison in exhibition design and management:

"So, in my head I thought, I'm thinking we've got to somehow give visitors a chance to explore that notion of comparison between what they're looking at and what it should look like. And the only way I could think of, was using the technology, and it is quite a modern bit of kit…quite fancy, and it's all bells and whistles and things…it works really well in that context, but there was a learning outcome behind it…"

(SHM Manager, June 2016)

The notion of comparison is a critical part of narrative creation by making content more relatable to visitors. This is particularly relevant to heritage sites that feature a specialist collection, such as in the SHM case, or in sites that cannot present tangible items that are immediately recognisable. As discussed in the quote above, the participant refers to the use of technology to facilitate comparison in the sites' presentation. This echoes the work of Gilbert and Stocklmayer (2001) and Poria, Biran, and Reichel (2009), who advocate the use of interactive technologies to support visitor comparison to support the understanding of complex subjects. In relating this to narrative co-creation, the ability for visitors to compare (and arguably contrast) content allows them to actively generate their own interpretation of what they are observing. Rather than being presented with one 'singular truth', visitors can explore content in greater depth and through comparison, evaluate the significance of the content to themselves as individuals (Latham, 2015). The ability to compare content in a heritage setting provides visitors with a level of control over what they are viewing and subsequently, it could be argued, creates opportunities to co-create their own narrative of the site and its content.

In addition to comparison, the participant raised the concept of personal histories in visitor experiences:

"…so that people at least get a feel for, oh right, I just want to know what that speciality is – there's a quick definition, or I'll go straight to the common operations and I'll want to look at a video clip of a hip replacement because my granny had a hip replacement."

(SHM Manager, June 2016)

In reference to the use of touchscreens to provide additional interpretative content, the participant highlights the role of personal histories in heritage experiences. This is particularly relevant in the context of SHM and its surgical/medical content that, as an emotive subject area, will resonate with individuals, families and groups. Emotional attachment has been a well-documented component of memorable experiences (Holbrook & Hirschman, 1982; Lugosi & Walls, 2013; Shaw & Ivens, 2002) and from a heritage management perspective, it could be argued that providing links to personal histories would allow visitors to generate emotional connections with the content they are engaging with. Beyond the content, Uzzell and Ballantyne (1998), argued that heritage sites should consider both 'cold' and 'hot' interpretation to present their stories. Where cold interpretation communicates factual information, its hot counterpart aims to elicit emotive and personal responses from visitors. Broader still, McIntyre (2009) argued that the environment in museums and galleries can go some way to prompt emotional responses. The author suggests there are hot, cool and cold spaces in heritage sites that vary between intense engagement and quiet reflection to allow for a deeper visitor engagement with the subject matter. Establishing links to personal histories and emotive interpretation provides a means for visitors to construct their own unique narrative based on their own heritage and history.

The final quote from the participant reflects on a critical heritage management practice - narrative planning and mapping:

"… in very basic terms that influences your thinking from the outset…What's the key part of that story. We've been around five hundred years, surgery has advanced massively in five hundred years, so what are the key bits of that that we want visitors to take away with them? What are the key bits that we think that visitors will be interested in?"

(SHM Manager, June 2016)

As discussed above, the participant highlights a need to be selective with the messages that the site chooses to convey. By identifying key messages that are most acceptable and applicable for the target audience, the site guards against visitors becoming overloaded with information. Furthermore, visitors are supported through the key parts of the sites' story and guided toward key messages. This balance of free information and management-led guidance can be viewed through a co-creative lens. While visitors need the freedom to develop their own interpretations of the narrative, the heritage manager continues to play a significant role in supporting the visitor on their journey. This in part agrees with the work of Moscardo (2017a), who suggested visitors' free-choice was integral to a co-created tourism experience. Conversely, it is also argued that visitors need adequate support in the process of co-creation to guard against fatigue or overload (Etgar, 2008; Voase, 2009). This reaffirms the need for heritage narratives to be co-created as a result of the relationship between visitor and heritage manager.

Co-creative opportunities

In co-creating the narrative rather than it being pre-determined, both actors (visitors and heritage managers) engage in collaboration. As a central tenet in co-creation research, collaborative engagement between the service provider and user is critical to the co-creative process (Ordanini & Pasini, 2008). In a heritage context, the negotiation of a shared narrative goes some way to integrate collaboration into the visitor experience. As such, there is great potential for heritage managers to not only *provide* the narrative, but to co-create one *with* visitors. In addition, collaboration in developing co-created heritage narratives can expand beyond the business-visitor relationship. External stakeholders (such as local communities, heritage trusts or scientific communities) may all be able to contribute to the generation of a heritage site's narrative. It is therefore necessary to consider the wider network of actors who can contribute to the co-creation of heritage narratives.

A further opportunity that arises from the management practices is personalisation. As discussed by Minkiewicz et al. (2014), the potential for visitors to personalise their heritage experience is vital for successful co-creation. This is complex in the context of narrative creation. Undoubtedly, heritage sites will have a core story which they will seek to convey to the visiting public, however to integrate opportunities for personalisation, the site must provide the space for visitors to tailor the story to their own needs and wants. The practices at SHM illustrate areas in which visitors can actively personalise the story they engage with throughout the museum. Through interactive technology, exhibition design and varied content, visitors can begin to craft the narrative to their own needs and wants. This however does need to be treated sensitively, as the core story of the site must remain authentic and truthful to its origins.

The third opportunity posed by the management practices discussed at SHM relates to control. The various management practices identified provide visitors an opportunity for control, not only over the narrative they receive, but the level and depth of content that they engage with. It is therefore important for heritage managers to consider integrating opportunities for visitors to exercise degrees of control over the narrative creation and their subsequent experience. These may range from small opportunities (such as providing a variety of interpretative texts that examine different facets of the story) to significant degrees of control (such as offering a range of visitor routes, specialised tours/trails or themed content that is selected by the visitor) depending on the nature of the heritage site. However, the issue of control can also pose a challenge for heritage management in that it requires curators, designers and developers to relinquish control of a prescribed narrative and to trust visitors to interpret the heritage story in their own way.

Finally, a significant opportunity for co-creation in heritage narratives is emotional connectivity. As discussed throughout this chapter, the heritage sector, in its very nature, is well-placed to build emotional connections with visitors. Often presenting historically significant, social or cultural content, the sector offers many opportunities for making emotional connections with different audiences. From a co-creative perspective, the ability to link narratives and stories to individual visitors' emotions can be argued as a means to achieve greater attention and memorability in the experience. Through the integration of personal stories and emotive content, there are opportunities for visitors to engage deeply with the heritage experience and construct their own narrative that is influenced by their individual emotions, feelings and values.

Implications for heritage experiences

In considering the implications of these practices and opportunities for the heritage experience, the final part of Figure 10.1 proposes that a co-created heritage narrative has the potential to encourage a more engaging, individualised and memorable visitor experience. At its most basic level, it could be argued that a co-created narrative (versus a prescriptive one) makes the visitor experience more engaging. As stated by Minkiewicz et al. (2014, p. 45):

"Heritage organisations should also facilitate emotional and cognitive engagement in the experience through creating stories, enabling customers to tell their own stories, and challenging their views and knowledge base."

Collaboratively negotiating the heritage narrative allows visitors to become immersed in the story of the site, whilst simultaneously enhancing the story with their own lived experiences. The interplay between the heritage management resources (interpretation and storytellers) and the knowledge, motivations and cultural capital of the visitor has significant potential to accelerate visitor engagement (Taheri et al., 2014). This in turn could arguably lead to more enriching and memorable experiences. As identified at the start of this chapter, the heritage sector is not immune from competition both within the tourism industry and from associated leisure operators. As such it has become increasingly important for heritage managers to explore ways to make their products unique and yet accessible to diverse audiences. The management practices and co-creative opportunities which they support provide an avenue for greater individualisation in the heritage narrative that visitors engage with. Co-creating the narrative is an ideal way to individualise the content of heritage attractions and therefore make the experience more unique, based on various visitors' needs and wants. Furthermore, narratives that encourage emotional connectivity and are personally relatable to visitors could arguably generate a more memorable experience. The co-creation of narrative would foster deeper-level engagement with the heritage product which, in turn, would aid in solidifying the experience to memory.

Lessons for heritage marketing and management

Based on the discussion throughout this chapter, several lessons have been identified for heritage marketers and managers:

Integrate a co-creative ethos into heritage management practices

As argued by Ramaswamy and Ozcan (2014), for co-creation to be a completely successful business approach, it must be woven into the fabric of the organisation. This requires a co-creative ethos to be integrated into not only the strategic direction of heritage sites, but also into the day-to-day running of the organisation. In the context of narrative and storytelling, managers should approach exhibition development and interpretation design with co-creation at the heart of their planning. As echoed by Moscardo (2010), it is critical for heritage managers to consider a balanced approach to narrative creation by providing sufficient detail to identify core messages but equally, provide suitable opportunities for visitors to freely interpret and construct their own narratives.

Encourage stakeholder participation

As discussed at the start of the chapter, co-creation occurs as a result of dialogue, interaction and engagement between multiple actors (such as visitors and managers) within an experiential setting. However, there are wider stakeholders involved in heritage tourism which can be engaged in narrative co-creation. Front-line staff are particularly well-placed to support narratives by facilitating engaging dialogue and sharing their own stories (Weiler & Walker, 2014; Zátori, 2016). Furthermore, wider stakeholders (such as heritage trusts, funding bodies, conservationists, academics and local communities) can contribute to evolving heritage narratives. For example, it may be beneficial to encourage locals to contribute their own stories to repositories linked to a site's content to strengthen the link between heritage narratives and local communities.

Explore innovative curatorial practice to foster the co-creation of narrative

In addition to adopting a co-creative approach toward narrative and storytelling, managers should also consider how they present the story. The vast array of interpretative techniques and curatorial practices that are available to heritage managers go a long way towards supporting the co-creation of narrative. Examples such as multi-sensory interpretation and augmented or virtual reality have the value of fostering customisation and personalisation within exhibitions and can be seen as viable ways to provide co-creative opportunities (Tussyadiah & Fesenmaier, 2009). Furthermore, heritage professionals could consider inviting visitors to have input into exhibition design and development. To extend the co-creative ethos beyond the boundaries of the on-site experience, it may be beneficial to involve visitors as collaborators in the development of interpretation and other co-creative opportunities.

Enhance evaluation tools and techniques

While the need for audience evaluation and visitor research is widely acknowledged in the heritage management literature, there is a need to integrate this with a co-creative ethos. Enhanced evaluation tools should aim to benchmark existing co-creative activities in addition to identifying further areas for development. While satisfaction studies are prominent in heritage evaluation, it may be necessary to incorporate alternative methods of internal and external evaluation (such as: mystery shoppers, focus groups, photo elicitation, experimentation, visitor tracking, or diary techniques) to gain insight into the success or failure of co-creative opportunities and evaluate their associated impact on the visitor experience. The findings of such evaluation should subsequently feed into strategic planning for exhibition design and associated marketing campaigns.

Conclusion

This chapter sought to explore the management practices associated with the creation of heritage narratives and to identify the co-creative opportunities that emerged. As an industry that is reliant on the generation of enriching, valuable and memorable visitor experiences, tourism and leisure is particularly well-placed to capitalise on co-creative management practices. Furthermore, the centrality of narratives and storytelling to tourism activity makes it the perfect vehicle to explore co-creation in various contexts. In the SHM case, four management practices were identified that contributed to narrative creation: contextualisation, comparison, link to personal histories, and narrative planning and mapping. In viewing these from a co-creative perspective, four opportunities were subsequently presented: collaboration, personalisation, control, and emotional connectivity. The combination of heritage management practices that capitalised on these opportunities provides the potential to foster the co-creation of narrative and encourage a more engaging, individualised and memorable visitor experience.

At a theoretical level, the co-creation of experience challenges many of the premises of experiential consumption. Not least that experiences, from this perspective, cannot be pre-determined and therefore cannot be 'consumed' as a commodity. Many of the foundational premises of co-creation challenge the very notion that experiences can be consumed at all. In contrast, this perspective would argue that the service provider (in this case the heritage manager) can only facilitate the visitor in their co-creative activities and as such, they provide the space for the experience rather than the experience itself. While such an approach may have its criticisms for applications to practice, co-creation continues to pose significant opportunities for experiential research in tourism. As visitor expectations continue to evolve and become more complex, it has become necessary for scholars to apply theory which advocates individuality, flexibility and subjectivity. As such, co-creation is in prime position to extend knowledge in experiential consumption as a burgeoning area of research. Further research could extend these propositions by capturing the visitor perspective toward narrative creation to identify commonalities and discords. Furthermore, future study could empirically question the implications of co-created narratives on the heritage experience and link this to visitor satisfaction, perceptions of experience quality and/or commercial outcomes.

In summary:

♦ Heritage managers should continue to view narratives and story-telling as critical to the visitor experience.

♦ The sector could benefit from further adopting concepts in the experiential co-creation literature to complement existing management practices.

♦ Co-creative opportunities should be considered as a viable management strategy for heritage marketers and managers while developing exhibitions and interpretation.

♦ Successful narrative co-creation could lead to a more engaging, individualised and memorable visitor experience, but would benefit from further scholarly work.

References

Adaval, R. & Wyerjr, R. (1998). The role of narratives in consumer information processing. *Journal of Consumer Psychology*, **7**(3), 207–245.

Binkhorst, E. & Den Dekker, T. (2009). Agenda for co-creation tourism experience research. *Journal of Hospitality Marketing & Management*, **18**(2-3), 311–327.

Black, G. (2012). *Transforming Museums in the Twenty-first Century*. Oxon: Routledge.

Campos, A.C., Mendes, J., do Valle, P.O. & Scott, N. (2016). Co-creation experiences: Attention and memorability. *Journal of Travel & Tourism Marketing*, **33**(9), 1309–1336.

Chronis, A. (2005). Our Byzantine heritage: Consumption of the past and its experiential benefits. *Journal of Consumer Marketing*, **22**(4), 213–222.

Chronis, A. (2012). Tourists as story-builders: Narrative construction at a heritage museum. *Journal of Travel & Tourism Marketing*, **29**(5), 444–459.

Counts, C.M. (2009). Spectacular design in museum exhibitions. *Curator: The Museum Journal*, **52**(3), 273–288.

Dimache, A., Wondirad, A. & Agyeiwaah, E. (2017). One museum, two stories: Place identity at the Hong Kong Museum of History. *Tourism Management*, **63**(1), 287–301.

Etgar, M. (2008). A descriptive model of the consumer co-production process. *Journal of the Academy of Marketing Science*, **36**(1), 97–108.

Frochot, I. & Batat, W. (2013). *Marketing and Designing the Tourist Experi-*

ence. Oxford: Goodfellow Publishers Limited.

Gilbert, J. & Stocklmayer, S. (2001). The design of interactive exhibits to promote the making of meaning. *Museum Management and Curatorship*, **19**(1), 41–50.

Holbrook, M. B. & Hirschman, E. C. (1982). The experiential aspects of consumption: Consumer fantasies, feelings, and fun. *Journal of Consumer Research*, **9**(2), 132–140.

Jaakkola, E., Helkkula, A. & Aarikka-Stenroos, L. (2015). Service experience co-creation: Conceptualization, implications, and future research directions. *Journal of Service Management*, **26**(2), 182–205.

Jung, T.H. & Tom Dieck, M.C. (2017). Augmented reality, virtual reality and 3D printing for the co-creation of value for the visitor experience at cultural heritage places. *Journal of Place Management and Development*, **10**(2), 140–151.

Kim, J.-H. & Youn, H. (2017). How to design and deliver stories about tourism destinations. *Journal of Travel Research*, **56**(6), 808–820.

Latham, K. F. (2015). What is 'the real thing' in the museum? An interpretative phenomenological study. *Museum Management and Curatorship*, **30**(1), 2–20.

Lugosi, P. & Walls, A.R. (2013). Researching destination experiences: Themes, perspectives and challenges. *Journal of Destination Marketing & Management*, **2**(2), 51–58.

Magee, R. & Gilmore, A. (2015). Heritage site management: From dark tourism to transformative service experience? *The Service Industries Journal*, **35**(15-16), 898–917.

Mathis, E.F., Kim, H., Uysal, M., Sirgy, J.M. & Prebensen, N.K. (2016). The effect of co-creation experience on outcome variable. *Annals of Tourism Research*, **57**(1), 62–75.

McIntosh, A. . (1999). Into the tourist's mind: Understanding the value of the heritage experience. *Journal of Travel & Tourism Marketing*, **8**(1), 41–64.

McIntyre, C. (2009). Museum and art gallery experience space characteristics: An entertaining show or a contemplative bathe? *International Journal of Tourism Research*, **11**(2), 155–170.

Minkiewicz, J., Evans, J. & Bridson, K. (2014). How do consumers co-create their experiences? An exploration in the heritage sector. *Journal of Marketing Management*, **30**(1-2), 30–59.

Mitsche, N., Vogt, F., Knox, D., Cooper, I., Lombardi, P. & Ciaffi, D. (2013). Intangibles: Enhancing access to cities' cultural heritage through interpretation. *International Journal of Culture, Tourism and Hospitality Research*, **7**(1), 68–77.

Moscardo, G. (2010). The shaping of tourist experience: The importance of stories and themes. In M. Morgan, P. Lugosi & J. R. B. Ritchie (Eds.), *The Tourism and Leisure Experience: Consumer and managerial perspectives* (pp. 43–58). Bristol: Channel View Publications.

Moscardo, G. (2014). Interpretation and tourism: Holy grail or emperor's robes? *International Journal of Culture, Tourism and Hospitality Research,* **8**(4), 462–476.

Moscardo, G. (2017a). Critical reflections on the role of interpretation in visitor management. In J. Albrecht (Ed.), *Visitor Management in Tourism Destinations* (pp. 170–190). Wallingford: CAB International.

Moscardo, G. (2017b). Exploring mindfulness and stories in tourist experiences. *International Journal of Culture, Tourism and Hospitality Research,* **11**(2), 111–124.

Ordanini, A. & Pasini, P. (2008). Service co-production and value co-creation: The case for a service-oriented architecture (SOA). *European Management Journal,* **26**(5), 289–297.

Palombini, A. (2017). Storytelling and telling history. Towards a grammar of narratives for cultural heritage dissemination in the digital era. *Journal of Cultural Heritage,* **24**(1), 134–139.

Payne, A., Storbacka, K. & Frow, P. (2008). Managing the co-creation of value. *Journal of the Academy of Marketing Science,* **36**(1), 83–96.

Poria, Y., Biran, A. & Reichel, A. (2009). Visitors' preferences for interpretation at heritage sites. *Journal of Travel Research,* **48**(1), 92–105.

Prahalad, C.K. & Ramaswamy, V. (2004). *The Future of Competition: Co-creating unique value with customers.* Boston: Harvard Business Press.

Prentice, R. & Andersen, V. (2007). Interpreting heritage essentialisms: Familiarity and felt history. *Tourism Management,* **28**(3), 661–676.

Ramaswamy, V. & Ozcan, K. (2014). *The Co-creation Paradigm.* Stanford: Stanford University Press.

Ritchie, J.R.B. & Crouch, G. (2003). *The Competitive Destination: A sustainable tourism perspective.* Wallingford: CAB International.

Servidio, R. & Ruffolo, I. (2016). Exploring the relationship between emotions and memorable tourism experiences through narratives. *Tourism Management Perspectives,* **20**, 151–160.

Shaw, C. & Ivens, J. (2002). *Building Great Customer Experiences.* New York: Palgrave Macmillan.

Taheri, B., Jafari, A. & O'Gorman, K. (2014). Keeping your audience: Presenting a visitor engagement scale. *Tourism Management,* **42**(1), 321–329.

Thyne, M. & Hede, A.M. (2016). Approaches to managing co-production for the co-creation of value in a museum setting: When authenticity matters. *Journal of Marketing Management,* **32**(15-16), 1478–1493.

Tung, V.W.S. & Ritchie, J.R.B. (2011). Exploring the essence of memorable tourism experiences. *Annals of Tourism Research*, **38**(4), 1367–1386.

Tussyadiah, I. & Fesenmaier, D. (2009). Mediating tourist experiences. *Annals of Tourism Research*, **36**(1), 24–40.

Uzzell, D. & Ballantyne, R. (1998). Heritage that hurts: Interpretation in a postmodern world. In D. Uzzell & R. Ballantyne (Eds.), *Contemporary Issues in Heritage and Environmental Interpretation: Problems and prospects* (pp. 152–171). London: The Stationary Office.

Vargo, S. L. & Lusch, R. F. (2004). Evolving to a new dominant logic for marketing. *Journal of Marketing*, **68**(1), 1–17.

Voase, R. (2009). Rediscovering the imagination: Meeting the needs of the 'new' visitor. In A. Fyall, B. Garrod, A. Leask & S. Wanhill (Eds.), *Managing Visitor Attractions: New directions* 2nd ed., (pp. 148–165). Oxford: Butterworth-Heinemann Ltd.

Weiler, B. & Walker, K. (2014). Enhancing the visitor experience: Reconceptualising the tour guide's communicative role. *Journal of Hospitality and Tourism Management*, **21**(1), 90–99.

Woodside, A.G. (2010). Brand-consumer storytelling theory and research: Introduction to a psychology & marketing special issue. *Psychology and Marketing*, **27**(6), 531–540.

Zátori, A. (2016). Exploring the value co-creation process on guided tours (the "AIM-model") and the experience-centric management approach. *International Journal of Culture, Tourism and Hospitality Research*, **10**(4), 377–395.

Zatori, A., Smith, M. K. & Puczko, L. (2018). Experience-involvement, memorability and authenticity: The service provider's effect on tourist experience. *Tourism Management*, **67**(1), 111–126.

11 Storytelling tourist experiences in the websites of world heritage historical centers

Catarina Frias, Carla Silva, Maria João Amante and Cláudia Seabra

The objectives of this chapter are to:

☐ To relate the concepts of world heritage sites, tourist experience and storytelling;

☐ To identify the dimensions of the pre-tourist storytelling experiences in world heritage historical centers in Portugal, based on the information provided in their official websites;

☐ To discuss the findings with world heritage historical centers management entities.

Keywords: Storytelling; tourist experience; Portuguese heritage historic centers

Introduction

Heritage tourism has been pointed out as one of the earliest forms of tourism (Timothy, 2011). It is defined as a wide category that includes eco-tourism and cultural tourism, focusing on conserving natural and cultural heritage, and with a market segment that includes visits to historic sites (Pedersen, 2002). In heritage tourism, consumers seek heritage experiences (Richards, 1996). Heritage products and experiences are designed and promoted with the main purpose of satisfying contemporary consumption (Su et al., 2018).

Tourism is a process that encourages people to learn (Maitland, 2010), especially through the awareness raising and sensory experiences achieved by a storytelling tourist experience. In fact, tourism industry is the activity of selling experiences (Kim, 2010), and stories are important elements of the tourists' experiences (Moscardo, 2009). Current travel experiences are all about consuming and producing narratives (Noy, 2004), and narratives in tourism are important factors in the process of contemplating, experiencing, remembering and spreading travel and tourism experiences (Tivers & Rakic, 2012).

Storytelling has the power to familiarize people with what is being told (Lee & Shin, 2014), and strengthens the connections between tourists and places. Consequently, it contributes to give greater value to the product (Mora & Livat, 2013). Also, in tourism, storytelling has the power to transform the past into the present (Chronis, 2012), which is particularly important when it involves the World Heritage Sites that are unique and exceptional testimonies of culture and history. Storytelling has the power to influence millions of people. A great storytelling leads to influence and power (Lund et al., 2017). Therefore, stories about the place can give a tourism destination a unique competitive advantage and simultaneously provide a more meaningful tourist experience (Mossberg, 2008).

Tourists engage in storytelling even before they arrive at their destinations. In the planning phase of their trip they look for information about the destinations they want to visit. When a story that involves a certain destination affects its visitors, it makes tourists Feel that these stories are authentic information. They will then, rapidly and deeply, process the information and build a certain kind of bond with that place, memorize its most relevant points of interest and will try their best to visit it (Overend, 2012). Within this context, the present study aims to analyse the pre-tourist storytelling experiences in different World Heritage Historical Centers in Portugal, based on the information promoted in their official websites.

To achieve this, the chapter is organized in four sections and respective final conclusions. First, we present a literature review on the concepts of storytelling, tourism experience and World Heritage Sites, with a brief description of the study's settings (Évora, Guimarães and Oporto' Historic Centers). Next, we present an overview of the methodological approach used. The third section is devoted to the results and their discussions. The final section draws the implications of the study, its limitations and point out orientations for future research.

Literature review

Heritage sites

Heritage tourism is not new. In fact, it is one of the most ancient forms of tourism (Timothy, 2011). But the number of tourists at heritage sites is still growing worldwide (Gilmore et al., 2007) largely because of the UNESCO classification awarded to some tourist sites. The UNESCO certification of tourist destinations, especially as World Heritage Sites, is sought after since it grants the place a universal recognition and is an important attractiveness factor for tourists (Li, Wu & Cai, 2008; Lanford, 2009). In fact, the UNESCO certification makes the site much more visible, in terms of national and international tourism, and acts as a significant incentive to make it more attractive and to increase the amount of money invested in its preservation (Drost, 1996; Arezki et al., 2009). Additionally, this prestige, achieved through international recognition, increases the opportunities for promotion and quality standards of those sites (Leask, 2006).

The literature on World Heritage Sites focuses on three main issues: (1) the connections between the stakeholders' power and the UNESCO classification process (Smith, 2006); (2) the effect the UNESCO heritage certification has on the site, and on its development and preservation (Wang, 2007; Winter, 2007); and (3) the reasons why the UNESCO classification is granted and how the advantages and disadvantages of this classification are perceived by the stakeholders (e.g. Ashworth & van der Aa, 2006; Hazen 2008; Li et al., 2008).

From a consumer behavior perspective, the issues of satisfaction and motivation regarding heritage tourism and the comparison between heritage tourist places and other tourist sites are also addressed in literature (Chandler, 2004; Chandler & Costello, 2002; Huh & Uysal, 2003; Kerstetter et al., 2001; Poria et al, 2004, 2006; Ryans & Higgins, 2006).

The tourist's perception of World Heritage Sites is conceptualized based on studies conducted within the sphere of human geography and the geography of heritage, that consider that the perception of a place affects visitation patterns as well as site experiences (Poria et al., 2011). According to Strauss and Lord (2001), "History is a popular theme for recreational travel" (2001, p.199) which emphasizes that history is part of the tourism experience desired by the heritage tourists.

Tourist experiences

Experiences have always been the core of the entertainment activity (Loureiro, 2014), and are more and more requested by tourists who are looking for appealing, unique and memorable leisure and tourism activities. Consumption experiences are multidimensional and include hedonic dimensions, such as feelings, fantasies, and fun (Holbrook & Hirschman, 1982). Much of the literature on consumption experiences has studied hedonic purposes that occur during and after the consumption of, for example, heritage products (Brakus et al., 2009).

Following the Theory of Information Processing (Bettman et al., 1986; Gabbott & Hogg, 1994) that considers the consumer's behaviour decision process as a series of rational steps (Chen, 1997), the tourist experience can also be regarded as having three main stages (Seabra et al., 2014, p. i) the pre-experience when tourists prepare and plan the trip; ii) the tourist experience itself, the moment when tourists are at their destination and purchase the products that are part of their trip; and iii) the post-experience phase when tourists return home and evaluate the trip. Within the concept of consumption experience, the product experience can be direct, when there is a physical contact between the consumer and the product (Hoch & Ha, 1986), or indirect, when a certain product is presented virtually or in advertisement (Hoch & Ha, 1986; Kempf & Smith, 1998). One way or another, it must stimulate the multisensory connections for consumers to Feel, learn, be and do (Mehmetoglu & Engen, 2011).

According to Schmitt (1999), tourist experiences can be classified into five categories: (1) Act; (2) Feel; (3) Relate; (4) Sense; (5) Think. The 'Act' dimension is about creating physical experiences aimed at the physical development of the consumer and showing him alternative ways of doing something, by experiencing alternative lifestyles and interactions. The 'Feel' dimension is related to the creation of Feelings and emotions, such as joy, happiness and pride. The 'Relate' dimension encompasses aspects of the remaining dimensions and is essentially related to the social and cultural identity of the 'I'. The 'Sense' dimension refers to the use of our Senses in order to create sensory experiences that will help add value to the products. And the 'Think' dimension is about involving the consumers' intelligence in order to create a cognitive experience that will engage them creatively as it will generate thought, surprise and provocation/teasing. The sensing, the feeling and the thinking are conceptualized as individual experiences. By contrast, the acting and relating are regarded as shared experiences (Loureiro, 2014).

Storytelling in pre-experience

Stories are the basis of human identity (Gubrium & Holstein, 2008). Therefore, telling stories is an essential part of human nature (Fisher, 1984). Also, stories have the power to involve people, immersing them in a fantasy world that provides them with escape sensations (Lund et al., 2017; McCabe & Foster, 2006). Additionally, stories come with many touch points to the listeners' lives, creating an emotional connection between tourists and destinations (Woodside, 2010).

Storytelling is about sharing the imaginary, the symbols and myths of a certain culture and community (Cyrulnik, 2009). Storytelling can be used as a powerful tool to interpret and share historical heritage contents (De Cave & Zaralli, 2016). Local stories often aim to record local memories before they are lost (Kerr, 2006) which is quite important to cultural and historical heritage destinations. Storytelling should involve educational information to raise awareness about social culture and about the history of destinations (Choi, 2016).

The World Heritage Sites, as well as other destinations, provide information on their websites. Online contents have become one of the most important sources of information about tourism destination (Buhalis & Foerste, 2015). Online stories and contents influence tourists and their behavior (Lund et al., 2017). Tourism and marketing literature emphasizes the importance of providing and promoting understandable, meaningful, and memorable information (McLellan, 2006). Official websites are designed to provide information to tourists in an effective way. This strategy aims to create some sort of connection between tourists and their destinations even before a possible visit.

Using different motivating aspects of the destinations and their stories, websites aim to establish an effective communication between tourists and destinations by telling stories in an emotional way using verbs, objects, experiences, places and characters (Yavuz et al., 2016). Symbols are effective contents for tourists since "the more the story is able communicate a metaphoric, symbolic story, the more power the story will have to engage others" (Pera et al., 2016, p. 52).

Methodology

The methodology used is based on content analysis. Content analysis is a qualitative research technique used to "examine artefacts of social communication ... based on explicit rules called 'selection criteria' (Berg, 1998, pp. 223-224), that allows a reliable, systematic and replicable examination of communication symbols (Kolbe & Burnett, 1991; Riffe et al., 1998), using a pre-design code sheet listing the specific symbols of tourists' experiences based on the literature review about tourism experiences, heritage tourism and storytelling. In line with this, and in order to analyze the pre-tourist experiences in World Heritage Historical Portuguese Centers based on the information promoted in their official sites, we used the contents of seven official websites with touristic information about the Historical Center of Guimarães; six official websites about the Historical Center of Oporto and six official websites with touristic information concerning the Historical Center of Évora.

The information collected was submitted to content analysis procedures. The next step was the coding process. The registration unit chosen was the topic itself and frequency was chosen as the enumeration rule. The categorization mode used was the topic (Mucchielli, 1972), and the categories were selected *a posteriori* after a first reading of the answers (Bardin, 1977). The contents of the websites were analyzed using Nvivo software, version 11.

The classification of the communication contents in tourist experience categories was based on Schmitt's tourist experience model (1999) that established five categories: Act, Feel, Relate, Sense and Think. However, after a first analysis, and taking into account these categories alone, we felt the need to deepen the investigation. Thus, the five categories were integrated into a larger dimension, the experience, to which two more dimensions were added: communication and information.

In the communication dimension, the following categories were considered: direct speech and quotes, sources and repetitions. The communication dimension aims to answer the question what linguistic resources are used to attract the attention of the 'tourist'/user of the sites as they look for tourist information? This assumes that, in communicative terms, the image available on the websites is much more important in terms of truthfulness and accuracy (sources, repetitions...) and not so much in terms of style, since this aspect will be assessed when dealing with the 'Experience' dimension. In response to this dimension, categories like direct speech and quotes will emerge, categories that will help distinguish between first-person speech and direct reference to the interlocutor. The sources, that confirm what is said and whose function is to support what was declared and reproduced, do not have to be identified. The repetitions identify situations in which the information is reproduced *ipsis verbis* on at least two different locations/websites even though the identity of the original source has yet to be revealed.

In the experience dimension, we took into account the five categories defined by Schmitt (1999) – Act, Feel, Relate, Sense and Think – and we added 'Storytelling' and 'Authenticity'. Different types of categories and subcategories were considered. In this dimension, we tried to identify the kind of feelings, sensations, etc. that are transmitted to the 'interlocutor'. In this case, the evaluation is mostly done through the use of different figures of speech.

Finally, the information dimension contains an analysis of the texts in informative terms, in other words, we want to know the type of 'clarification' that any user will obtain when he reads the contents available on the websites, categorized into different information categories: (1) architectural and artistic, (2) cultural and educational, (3) economic, (4) geographical, (5) historical and (6) touristic.

The study's settings

For a relatively small country, Portugal offers plenty of places classified by UNESCO as World Heritage Sites. Portuguese heritage is also present all over the world, with more than 25 World Heritage properties of Portuguese influence over four continents. Portugal has currently 15 World Heritage Sites. Among them, we have to point out the Historical Centers of Oporto, Guimarães and Évora.

Located in the North Coast of Portugal, the city of Oporto is one of the oldest cities in Europe. There has been an increasing visibility of the city both at a national and at an international level, a visibility that has been favored by the international awards that Oporto has received lately. In fact, it was considered as the European Best Destination in 2017. The Historic Center of Oporto grew on rugged lands, crossed by narrow streets and has a privileged view over the Douro River (Direção-Geral do Património Cultural, 2018; UNESCO, 2018)b. It was classified by UNESCO in 1996 as a World Heritage Site (Oporto City Council, 2018). The classified area covers part of the inner city and the route of the ancient medieval city walls – called the Fernandina Wall. It also includes adjacent areas with identical characteristics that were valued following later achievements (Moreira & Cordeiro, 2016). It is a picturesque area with monuments of different architectural styles, in which the merchants and the inhabitants of the historic center play a crucial part (Direção-Geral do Património Cultural, 2018; UNESCO, 2018; Porto Vivo, 2013). Regarding the tourist offer, the Historic Center of Oporto is quite varied, with different typologies of accommodations, monuments of great historical and cultural value, and unique landscapes. It is a place of market, consumption and urban life. In fact, it is the part of the territory that best translates Oporto's identity and history (Branco, 2006).

Figure 11.1: Historic centre of Oporto. Source: Municipality of Oporto

Another historic center in Portugal is Guimarães. It is known as "the birthplace of the Portuguese Nation" and therefore is a strong national symbol. This city in the North of the Portuguese territory is connected to a strong national and cultural identity (Remoaldo et al., 2016). According to UNESCO, the Historical Center of Guimarães conserves its historical integrity. It is very well preserved and manages to show the evolution of a medieval city into a contemporary one (União das Cidades Capitais de Língua Portuguesa, 2018). Despite its small area (only 5.3% of the total area of the town), Guimarães Historical Center concentrates a great number of services and people, being an important historical and cultural center but also a key social place in the city (Câmara Municipal de Évora , 2005).

Évora, the last Historical Center, is located in the South of Portugal, in the Alentejo region. It is regarded as a museum-city dating back to the Roman times. The Historical Center of Évora was recognized as a UNESCO World Heritage Site in 1986 (UNESCO, 2018a; VisitEvora, 2018) and includes the urban area within the city walls. The Historical Center of Évora covers a large area, in comparison to other Portuguese centers. The existing monuments with their religious and military architecture, offer a great patrimonial value. According to UNESCO, the city has endured many modern interventions and adaptations, especially in the 19th century, however they didn't affect its morphology and authenticity.

Figure 11.2: Historic centre of Guimarães. Source: www.guimaraesturismo.com

Figure 11.3: Historic Centre of Évora. Source: Municipality of Évora

Findings

The results clearly reflect the way in which the World Heritage Sites analyzed present the contents that will be responsible for the creation of a pre-experience state in the tourist who wants to visit the Portuguese World Heritage Historical Centers of Évora, OPorto and Guimarães. In a first analysis, and considering the different dimensions on a more general level, it is evident that the only contents that seemed to have an influence on the Information dimension were those related to the monuments of the cities of Oporto and Évora. Guimarães (general aspects and monuments), Oporto general aspects and Évora general aspects have a greater number of occurrences that we can relate to the Experience dimension (see Table 11.1). The data reveal that special attention is given to the message that they intend to send to the potential tourist to make him want to visit the country. More technical descriptions are used only to give information about the monuments.

Table 11.1: Relationship between sources and dimensions

Sources		Dimensions		
		Communication	Experience	Information
Guimarães	General aspect	7	32	22
	Monuments	6	76	68
Oporto	General aspect	5	39	23
	Monuments	37	77	137
Évora	General aspect	7	49	82
	Monuments	23	78	174

As for the Communication categories analyzed, we have to stress the number of repetitions that we could find in the sources providing information about Oporto monuments. This is a clear evidence that the same source is used in more than one website, albeit without official references/sources (Table 11.2). Direct speech and quotations are the most commonly used communication resources, however they don't seem to have a meaningful expression. It is in situations in which a direct request is made to the tourists that this kind of resources is used. An example of such a situation is the following statement: "stay a few more days, experience all there is to experience and, when intuition tells you it is time to leave, embrace the discovery of everything that is beyond its walls and that contributes so much to give it significance" (http:// www.visitalentejo.pt, one of the sources used in an Évora's website).

Table 11.2: Relationship between sources and the Communication dimension

	Sources	Communication		
		Direct Speech and Quotations	Sources	Repetitions
Guimarães	General aspect	5	---	3
	Monuments	6	---	---
Oporto	General aspect	5	2	---
	Monuments	13	---	28
Évora	General aspect	8	1	---
	Monuments	23	---	---

When assessing the Experience dimension, it will be convenient to analyze the results according to the different available sources, in other words, the three historical centers in analysis, Oporto, Évora and Guimarães have to be considered. In the end, it is how each of the sources will pass on the content and message that will allow us to draw conclusions about whether or not they were able to provide tourists with the right information to stimulate their interest and give them a pre-experience feeling, and whether or not this achievement has an impact on the number of visitors.

We can conclude that Guimarães favors the 'Feel' dimension. It is in the treatment of the historical center that people can find more references to authenticity and evidence shows that storytelling has also a meaningful expression, especially in the description of monuments (Table 11.3).

Table 11.3: Relationship between sources and categories

		Experiences						
	Sources	Act	Feel	Relate	Sense	Think	Authenticity	Storytelling
Guimarães	General aspect	8	16	15	4	5	11	---
	Monuments	16	43	4	1	6	7	21
Oporto	General aspect	20	11	8	9	2	2	5
	Monuments	25	20	10	22	1	10	15
Évora	General aspect	15	17	14	8	2	10	1
	Monuments	39	19	11	11	12	3	27

As far as Oporto is concerned, the 'Act' dimension is clearly valued. This perspective is chosen to clearly encourage the tourist's action and participation as he is directly invited to visit the city: "Visiting Oporto implies that you have to find enough time to go through publics places, to Feel indoor spaces, listen to the surrounding sounds and let your sight enjoy the whole picture as well as every single detail. Oporto makes you wish you could come back". This invitation is found in http://www.turismodeportugal.pt and is related to Oporto's general aspect source.

'Feel' and 'Sense' dimensions are also valued in the content analysis carried out about Oporto (Table 11.3) and are essentially connected with national pride: "Oporto is one of the rare European cities that still retains its medieval harbor structure", in http:// www.turismodeportugal.pt and to the direct appeal directed to the tourist's senses. This last conclusion is supported by the analysis conducted and the results are displayed in the subcategories presented in Table 11.5.

Évora, in turn, uses essentially 'storytelling' activities. "The old stone column that signals the whipping of Saint Manços by a Roman Praetor still remains", in http://conteudos.evora.net/turismo/pt-pt/relative related to Évora's monuments source. The 'Act' dimension is obviously valued as well, and is evident in the online promotion slogan "learning, discovering and, undoubtedly, wishing we could come back for more", found in http://conteudos.evora.net/turismo/pt-pt/.

The 'Feel' dimension also gets some recognition, but it is in Évora that the 'Think' dimension gets the highest recognition and the greater amount of references. "Roman heritages of extraordinary beauty that are testimony of the past", a comment found in http://www.visitevora.net/posto-turismo-praca-giraldo-evora. The 'Relate' dimension is also highly valued, as is clear in comments such as "The urban landscape of Évora is the only one that can allow us to understand the influence exerted by Portuguese architecture in Brazil, in places like Salvador da Bahia", in http://conteudos.evora.net/turismo/pt-pt/ (see Table 11.3).

The 'Information' dimension, the most objective of all the dimensions, is clearly the one which gets the highest number of references and the numbers are quite expressive. The references that follow are the kind which appear the most and it is in the description of the Oporto monuments that they find their greatest expression: architectural and artistic references: "This tower, 15 meters high, is visible from the stairs of the Caminho Novo and is a precious relic of the 14th century wall", in http://www.visitporto.travel; historical references: "Portugal was born in the north. It was in Oporto and in the country's northern region that the Portuguese were born as a people and a nation. Here we learned how valuable is the difference but also the complementarity of cultures", in https://www.visitportugal.com/pt; and geographical references: "Oporto, the capital of the region, has a privileged location as an Atlantic city over the estuary of an immense Iberian river: The Douro River", in http://www.turismodeportugal.pt, are in that same order, the kind of references which appear the most and it is in the description of the Oporto monuments that they find their greatest expression.

With these results, it is clearly perceptible that it is in the contents that have to do with the city's monuments that the 'Information' dimension has a greater expression. It should also be noted that Guimarães is the city that provides less tourist information to the tourists who visit the websites we had the opportunity to analyze (see Table 11.4).

Table 11.4: Relationship between sources and information

Sources		Information					
		Architectural and Artistic	Cultural and Educational	Economic	Geographical	Historical	Touristic
Guimarães	General aspect	33	11	5	12	20	6
	Monuments	66	27	9	47	65	19
Oporto	General aspect	37	7	7	27	15	23
	Monuments	197	66	33	133	140	53
Évora	General aspect	62	19	19	15	43	25
	Monuments	101	41	21	41	91	28

Table 11.5 was based on the analysis of the results gathered in Table 11.3 in which the categories of the 'experience' dimension are identified. It was built to better understand the communication strategy used by the websites of the three historical centers and to understand the kind of relationship they intend to maintain with the potential tourists that visit them in a pre-experience stage. In this table, it is possible to understand, according to what has been mentioned before, that Guimarães values the 'Feel' dimension above all others. This prevalence of this dimension is related to the city's Sense of pride, which is clearly demonstrated in comments like: "in the face of the facts described, no wonder that Guimarães is considered by the Portuguese as the birthplace of nationality! What a unique and special city!", in http://www. guimaraesturismo.com/.

As far as Oporto is concerned, it is in the interaction established with the visitors of the website that the 'Act' dimension finds its maximum expression: 'after seeing from the river the silhouette of the old houses and of the churches towers, we are ready to be amazed by the golden interior of St. Francis Church' in https://www.visitportugal.com/ pt/pt/ destinos/porto-e-norte. When we analyze the Oporto *monuments* dimension, there are many references to the *city lifestyle*, like: "used as a space of cultural animation, where the Hard Club is currently located" in http://www.visitporto.travel.

An important role is once more given to the pride people Feel for the city and the Sense dimension focuses mainly on the vision. This dimension is much stronger in this city than in all the others that are part of the study and the many references to the Palate dimension are quite evident in quotes like "Chocolate paired with Port wine is one of the most irresistible combinations" in http://www.visitporto.travel (Table 11.5).

As a way to attract visitors, the Oporto monuments dimension clearly values the 'I' subcategory. The tourists' pre-experience is encouraged and these possible visitors get involved in the city life, even before they take the decision of travelling, thanks to all the references made to the city's cultural identity, as part of the 'Relate' dimension.

Évora, which essentially appeals to 'Storytelling' and 'Act' dimensions to promote itself online, has in the interaction with the visitor its main strategy and in terms of occurrences is clearly different from the other historical centers. The 'Lifestyle' dimension is also very much valued in Évora. The 'Feel' dimension finds, once again, its expression thanks to the close relationship it has built up with the 'Pride' experience. This city has, however, something new to offer: the importance given to the 'Teasing/Challenge' subcategory (part of the 'Think' dimension) "Queen of the square in which it is located, its peaceful exterior spaces invite us to enter and just be", in http://www.visitevora.net/posto-turismo-praca-giraldo-evora/ (Table 11.5).

Table 11.5: Relation between sources and subcategories

Sources		Act		Feel		Relate		Sense					Think		
		Lifestyle	Interaction	Joy	Proud	Cultural Identity	Social Identity	Hearing	Smell	Taste	Touch	Sight	Thoughts	Challenge	Surprise
Guimarães	General	1	5	---	15	1	1	---	---	---	---	1	---	3	2
Guimarães	Monuments	3	13	---	42	4	---	---	---	1	---	---	---	3	3
OPorto	General	3	8	---	8	---	---	1	---	1	---	4	1	1	---
OPorto	Monuments	13	14	1	16	8	1	2	---	6	---	10	---	1	---
Évora	General	1	7	---	17	---	---	---	---	1	---	1	1	1	---
Évora	Monuments	10	30	2	16	3	2	---	---	2	---	4	---	11	1

Conclusion

Stories people associate to a certain destination can be successfully used in theme development and to promote a campaign (Yavuz et al., 2016). Stories link people and attach people to spaces, creating shared experiences. Offering compelling experiences is the key to building attractive tourism offerings. This study aims to analyze the pre-tourist storytelling experiences in World Heritage Historical Centers in Guimarães, Oporto and Évora, through the content analysis of the information provided by their official websites.

Since heritage resources are important attraction factors for tourists (Su, et al., 2018), the World Heritage Sites information promoted online is one of the most important aspects of destination marketing and communication. Thus, in the tourist destination management perspective, it is important to be able to communicate with tourists in meaningful ways, not only during their visits but also before that experience takes place, by identifying the characterisitics of the place and people, facts, activities and events in a narrative way, thus creating and plotting potential experiences as real storytelling tourist experiences.

The results indicate that websites are important pre-experience storytellers and that Oporto and Évora are the cities whose information strategy is the most complete and educational, providing their visitors with rich architectural, artistic and geographical information. On the other hand, Guimarães stimulates tourists' pre-experience relies mostly on the 'Feel' dimension, a dimension which shows how proud its inhabitants are of their nationality, and that helps strengthen the role played by the city to increase this national feeling, since it is recognized as the birthplace of the Portuguese nation. Finally, the sensorial dimension of the storytelling pre-experience is more stimulated in Oporto websites. Generally, results show that not all the dimensions are present in the websites' contents. Evidence show that 'Sense' and 'Think' dimensions are often undervalued.

Based on the results of this study, it is possible to draw some implications that can be quite useful to the managers and organizations that are responsible for World Heritage Sites. First, they should understand the importance of the storytelling in the creation of the tourist pre-experience. In the planning phase, most tourists look for information online, specifically in official websites (Buhalis & Foerste, 2015). The expectations that tourists build in this phase will influence their choices and behavior (Lund et al., 2017). Second, managers must take into account the crucial role that experiential marketing plays in the creation of memorable experiences in tourists. Tourists are emotional consumers who look for pleasurable experiences based on five sensory dimensions: Sense, Feel, Think, Act and Relate (Schmitt, 1999).

Through stories, the destination can create desirable meanings regarding its attributes. Storytelling adds value to the destinations, because through it historical and cultural heritages can be promoted.

Despite the theoretical and practical implications of these findings, the study has some limitations that must be considered, but it could also represent an opportunity for further research. First of all, the study might have omitted other existing and relevant dimensions of storytelling experiences and information. Second, the research focuses only on Portuguese World Heritage Sites, which can be limiting if we want to generalize the results. In order to overcome such limitation, additional research is suggested: we could compare these results with World Heritage Histo ric Centers from other countries, for instance. In this case, a content analysis methodology is suggested to replicate the study using the same procedures and classification scheme. Then, the study analysed only part of the whole tourist experience, focusing on the pre-tourist experience stage. Based on Moscardo's (2010) concept, storytelling is mainly a post-consumption activity. Consumers tell stories to others to provide memories of the experience as well as their significance in terms of identity. That way, it could be interesting in future research, to analyse the stories told by tourists in different social media platforms like travel blogs and others, and cross-check that information with the results of this study.

Acknowledgements:

This work is financed by national funds through FCT - Fundação para a Ciência e Tecnologia, I.P., under the projects UID/Multi/04016/2016, UID/ECO/00124/2013 and by POR Lisboa under the project LISBOA-01-0145-FEDER-007722. Furthermore we would like to thank the Instituto Politécnico de Viseu, CI&DETS and Caixa Geral de Depósitos for their support and funding under the project PROJ/CI&DETS/CGD/0015.

References

Arezki, R., Cherif, R. & Piotrowski, J. M. (2009). Tourism specialization and economic development: Evidence from the UNESCO World Heritage List. *International Monetary Fund, 9,* 17132,26.

Ashworth, G.J. & van der Aa, B.J. (2006). Strategy and policy for the world heritage convention: goals, practices and future solutions. In A. Leask & A. Fyall (eds.), *Managing World Heritage Sites,* pp. 147-158, Oxford: Butterworth-Heinemann.

Câmara Municipal de Évora (2005). Estudo sobre o despovoamento dos centros históricos da rede Atlante.

Bardin, L. (1977). *Análise de Conteúdo.* Lisboa: Edições 70.

Berg, B. (1998). *Qualitative Research Methods for the Social Sciences.* Boston: Allyn and Bacon.

Bettman, J.R., Payne, J.W. & Staelin, R. (1986). Cognitive considerations in designing effective labels for presenting risk information. *Journal of Public Policy & Marketing*, **5**, 1-28.

Brakus, J., Schmitt, B. & Zarantonello, L. (2009). Brand experience: What is it? How is it measured? Does it affect loyalty? *Journal of Marketing*, **73**, 52-68.

Branco, F.J. (2006). Uma nova metodologia para a reabilitação urbana: Uma nova oportunidade para o Centro histórico e Baixa do Porto. *Cidades - Comunidades e Territórios, 12/13*, 35-52.

Buhalis, D. & Foerste, M. (2015). SoCoMo marketing for travel and tourism: Empowering co-creation of value. *Journal of Destination Marketing & Management, 4*(3), 151-161.

Chandler, J. A. (2004). Comparing visitor profiles at heritage tourism destinations in Eastern North Carolina. *Journal of Travel and Tourism Marketing*, **16**(1), 51-61.

Chandler, J.A. & Costello, C.A. (2002). A profile of visitors at heritage tourism destinations in East Tennessee according to Plog's lifestyle and activity level preferences. *Journal of Travel Research*, **41**(2), 161-167.

Chen, J. (1997). The tourists' cognitive decision making model. *Revue de Tourisme*, **4**, 4-9.

Choi, S. S. (2016). A study on effect of tourism storytelling of tourism destination brand value and tourist behavioral intentions. *Indian Journal of Science and Technology*, **9**(46), 1-6.

Chronis, A. (2012). Between place and story: Gettysburg as tourism imaginary. *Annals of Tourism Research*, **39**(4), 1797-1816.

Cyrulnik, B. (2009). *Autobiografía de un espantapájaros. Testimonios de resiliencia: el retorno a la vida.* Barcelona: Gedisa.

De Cave, M. & Zaralli, F. (2016). Cultour+ Italy case study. The southern via Francigena, a framework of governance. In M. G.-V. Luis Ochoa Siguencia, *Cultural Management and Tourism in European Cultural Routes: From Theory to Pratice* (pp. 225-235). Poland: Publishing House of the Research and Innovation in Education Institute.

Direção-Geral do Património Cultural. (2018). *Centro Histórico do Porto, Ponte Luiz I e Mosteiro da Serra do Pilar.* Retrieved from http://www.patrimoniocultural.gov.pt/pt/patrimonio/patrimonio-mundial/portugal/centro-historico-do-porto/, 23/04/2018

Drost, A. (1996). Developing sustainable tourism for World Heritage Sites. *Annals of Tourism Research*, **23**(2), 479-492.

Fisher, W.R. (1984). Narration as a human communication paradigm: The case of public moral argument. *Communication Monographs*, **51**(1), 1-22.

Gabbott, M. & Hogg, G. (1994). Consumer behaviour and services: A review. *Journal of Marketing Management,* **10,** 311-324.

Gilmore, A., Carson, D. & Ascenção, M. (2007). Sustainable tourism marketing at a World Heritage site. *Journal of Strategic Marketing,* **15**(2,3), 253-264.

Gubrium, J.F. & Holstein, J.A. (2008). Narrative Practice and the coherence of personal stories. *The Sociological Quarterly,* **39**(1), 163-187.

Hazen, H. (2008). Of outstanding universal value: The challenge of scale in applying the World Heritage Convention at National Parks in the US. *Geoforum,* **39,** 252-264.

Hoch, S. & Ha, Y.-W. (1986). Consumer learning: Advertising and the ambiguity of product experience. *Journal of Consumer Research,* **13,** 221–233.

Holbrook, M. . & Hirschman, E. . (1982). The experiential aspects of consumption: Consumer fantasies, feelings, and fun. *Journal of Consumer Research,* **9**(2), 132-140.

Huh, J. & Uysal, M. (2003). Satisfaction with cultural/heritage sites: Virginia Historic Triangle. *Journal of Quality Assurance in Hospitality & Tourism,* **4**(3,4), 177-194.

Kempf, D.S. & Smith, R. (1998). Consumer processing of product trial and the influence of prior advertising: A structural modeling approach. *Journal of Marketing Research,* **35,** 325–338.

Kerr, T. (2006). Who speaks land stories? Inexpert voicing of place. *Limina,* **12,** 40-51.

Kerstetter, D., Confer, J. & Graefe, A. (2001). An exploration of the specialization concept within the context of heritage tourism. *Journal of Travel Research,* **39**(3), 267-275.

Kim, J. (2010). Determining the factors affecting the memorable nature of travel experiences. *Journal of Travel and Tourism Marketing,* **27**(8), 780–796.

Kolbe, R.H. & Burnett, M.S. (1991). Content-analysis research: an examination of applications with directives for improving research reliability and objectivity. *Journal of Consumer Research,* **18**(2), 243-250.

Lanford, C.J. (2009). Managing for sustainable tourism: a review of six cultural World Heritage Sites. *Journal of Sustainable Tourism,***17**(1), 53-70.

Leask, A. (2006). World Heritage Site designation. In A. Leask & A. Fyall (eds.), *Managing World Heritage Sites,* pp. 147-158, Oxford: Butterworth-Heinemann.

Lee, Y.-S. & Shin, W.-J. (2014). Marketing tradition-bound products through storytelling: a case study of a Japanese sake brewery. *Service Business,* **9,** 281–295.

Li, M., Wu, B. & Cai, L. (2008). Tourism development of World Heritage Sites in China: A geographic perspective. *Tourism Management, 29*, 308-319.

Loureiro, S. C. (2014). The role of the rural tourism experience economy in place attachment and behavioral intentions. *International Journal of Hospitality Management, 40*, 1-9.

Lund, N., Cohen, S. & Scarles, C. (2017). The power of social media storytelling in destination branding. *Journal of Destination Marketing and Management, 8*, 271-280.

Maitland, R. (2010). Everyday life as a creative experience in cities. *International Journal of Culture, Tourism and Hospitality Research, 4*(3), 176-185.

McCabe, S. & Foster, C. (2006). The role and function of narrative in tourist interaction. *Journal of Tourism and Cultural Change, 4*(3), 194–215.

McLellan, H. (2006). Digital storytelling in higher education. *Journal of Computing in Higher Education, 19 (1)*, 65-79.

Mehmetoglu, M. & Engen, M. (2011). Pine and Gilmore's concept of experience economy and its dimensions: An empirical examination in tourism. *Journal of Quality Assurance in Hospitality & Tourism, 12*(4), 237-255.

Mora, P. & Livat, F. (2013, Junho). Does storytelling add value to fine Bordeaux wines? *Wine Economics and Policy, 2*(1), 3-10.

Moreira, M.C. & Cordeiro, J. (2016). The impact of the World Cultural Heritage clasification by UNESCO on the cultural tourist demand in Porto. In C. Henriques., M.C. Moreira. & B.P. César. (Eds.), *Tourism and History World Heritage - The Case Studies of Ibero- American Space* (pp. 40-52). Minho: Interdisciplinary Center of Social Sciences - University of Minho.

Moscardo, G. (2009). Understanding tourist experience through Mindfulness Theory. In K. Metin, A. Decrop & (eds.), *Handbook of Tourist Behaviour: Theory and Practice* (pp. 99-115). New York: Routledge.

Moscardo, G. (2010). The shaping of tourist experience: The importance of stories and themes. In M.P. Lugosi. & J.B. Ritchie. (Eds.), *The tourism and leisure experience: Consumer and management Perspectives* (pp. 3-26). Bristol: Channel View Publications.

Mossberg, L. (2008). Extraordinary experiences through storytelling,. *Scandinavian Journal of Hospitality and Tourism, 8*(3), 195-210.

Mucchielli, R. (1972). *L'analyse de contenu.* Paris: Éd. E.S.F., Coll Séminaires.

Noy, C. (2004). This trip really changed me: Backpackers' narratives of self-change. *Annals of Tourism research, 31*(1), 78-102.

Overend, D. (2012). Performing sites: Illusion and authenticity in the spatial stories of the guided tour. *Scandinavian Journal of Hospitality and Tourism*, **12**(1), 44-54.

Pedersen, A. (2002). *Managing Tourism at World Heritage Sites: A Practical Manual for World Heritage Site Managers*. Paris: UNESCO World Heritage Center.

Pera, R., Viglia, G. & Furlan, R. (2016). Who am I? How compelling self storytelling builds digital personal reputation. *Journal of Interactive Marketing*, **35**, 44-55.

Poria, Y., Butler, R. & Airey, D. (2004). Links between tourists, heritage, and reasons for visiting heritage sites. *Journal of Travel Research*, **43**(1), 19-28.

Poria, Y., Reichel, A. & Avital, B. (2006). Heritage site perceptions and motivations to visit. *Journal of Travel Research*, **44**(3), 318-326.

Poria, Y., Reichel, A. & Cohen, R. (2011). World heritage site - is it an effective brand name? a case study of a religious heritage site. *Journal of Travel Research*, **50**(2), 482-495.

Porto Vivo, S. R. (2013). Plano de Gestão: Centro Histórico Porto Património Mundial. *Conferência Comemoração do 17º aniversário da entrada do centro histórico do Porto na Lista de Património Mundial da UNESCO*.

Remoaldo, P., Vareiro, L., Ribeiro, J. & Marques, V. (2016). Tourists' motivation toward visiting a World Heritage Site: The case of Guimarães. In C. Henriques., C. Moreira & B. P. César (Eds.), *Tourism and History World Herit* (pp. 99-121). CICS-Publicações/eBooks.

Richards, G. (1996). *Cultural Tourism In Europe*. Wallingford: CABI.

Riffe, D., Lacy, S. & Fico, F.G. (2014). *Analyzing Media Messages: Using Quantitative Content Analysis in Research*. Routledge.

Ryans, C. & Higgins, O. (2006). Experiencing cultural tourism: visitors at the Maori arts and crafts . *Journal of Travel Research*, **44**(3), 308-317.

Schmitt, B. H. (1999). *Experiential Marketing: How to Get Customers to Sense, Feel, Think, Act, Relate to Your Company and Brands*. New York: The Free Press.

Seabra, C., Abrantes, J. L. & Kastenholz, E. (2014). The influence of terrorism risk perception on purchase involvement and safety concern of international travellers. *Journal of Marketing Management*, **30**, 874-903.

Smith, L. (2006). *Uses of Heritage*. New York: Routledge.

Strauss, C.H. & Lord, B.E. (2001). Economic impacts of a heritage tourism system. *Journal of Retailing and Consumer Services*, **8**(4), 199-204.

Su, R., Bramwell, B. & Whalley, P. (2018). Cultural political economy and urban heritage tourism. *Annals of Tourism Research*, **68**, 30-40.

Timothy, D.J. (2011). *Cultural Heritage and Tourism: An Introduction.* Bristol: Channel View Publications.

Tivers, J. & Rakic, T. (2012). Introducing the narratives of travel and tourism. In Tivers, J. & Rakic, T. (Ed.), *Narratives of Travel and Tourism* (pp. 1-8). Farnham, UK: Routledge.

UNESCO. (2018a). *Historic Centre of Evora.* Retrieved from Retrieved from United Nations Educational, Scientific and Cultural Organization: https://whc.unesco.org/en/list/361

UNESCO. (2018b). *Historic Centre of Oporto, Luiz I Bridge and Monastery of Serra do Pilar.* Retrieved abril 23, 2018, from UNESCO: http://whc.unesco.org/en/list/755

União das Cidades Capitais de Língua Portuguesa. (2018). *UCCLA.* Retrieved from http://www.uccla.pt/membro/guimaraes, 26/04/2018

VistEvora. (2018). *Onde fica Évora.* Retrieved from VisitEvora: www.visitevora.pt, 24/04/2018.

Wang, Y. (2007). Customized authenticity begins at home. *Annals of Tourism Research,* **34**(3), 789-804.

Winter, Y. (2007). Rethinking tourism in Asia. *Annals of Tourism Research,* **34**(1), 27-44.

Woodside, A.G. (2010). Brand–consumer storytelling theory and research: Introduction to a psychology & marketing special issue. *Psychology & Marketing,* **27**(6), 531–540.

Yavuz, M. C, Sumbul, M., Ergec, N.E. & Derdiyok, C.I. (2016). Storytelling in destination brand communication: A qualitative analysis. *International Interdisciplinary Business-Economics Advancement Journal,* **1**(2), 63-72.

Websites

Câmara Municipal do Porto. (2018). *Património Mundial.* Retrieved, from http://www.cm-porto.pt/cultura/patrimonio-cultural/patrimonio-da-humanidade, 23/04/2018

Câmara Municipal do Évora, (2018). *Câmara Municipal de Évora .* Retrieved from Câmara Municipal de Évora: http://conteudos.evora.net/turismo/pt-pt/, 09/03/2018

Guimarães Turismo - Património Mundial da Humanidade (2017). Retrieved from: https://www.guimaraesturismo.com/, 23/05/2017

Turismo de Portugal (2018). Retrieved from http://www.turismodeportugal.pt , 02/03/2018

Visitportugal (2018). *Visitportugal.* Retrieved from https://www.visitportugal.com/pt-pt , 20/02/2018

Part IV:
Gastronomy Experiences

12 The role of local gastronomy in destination marketing

*Gurel Cetin, Bendegul Okumus and
Zaid Alrawadieh*

The objectives of this chapter are to:

☐   Discuss the role of local food in tourism marketing and explore Istanbul as a culinary destination;

☐   Content analyze hard copy and online official promotional materials;

☐   Determine themes representing Istanbul as a culinary destination informed from the data;

☐   Communicate if culinary resources in Istanbul are sufficiently marketed and represented within the official promotional materials;

☐   Offer a typology of local food representation in destination marketing communications;

☐   Provide suggestions for destination marketing and culinary tourism.

Keywords: Culinary tourism, destination marketing, gastronomy, food, Turkey

Introduction

The quality of a tourist experience is closely related to a destination's capacity to satisfy tourists' needs. Local gastronomy is among the many factors (e.g. climate, service, scenery) that affect tourist decision-making and destination satisfaction (Henderson, 2016; Sotiriadis, 2015; López-Guzmán et al., 2017). Consuming food is both a physical need and socio-cultural activity. Food is consumed by tourists at a destination not only to satisfy their hunger but also to experience the authentic culture and to interact with the locals. The demand for local foods may occur in various stages of intensity (Almeida & Garrod, 2017). However, local foods are usually listed at the top of activities desired by tourists (Okumus & Cetin, 2018). While food consumption may be an extension of the daily experience, it can sometimes turn into a significant part of unique touristic experiences (Quan & Wang, 2004). Recent studies have called for better understanding of local food experiences and their implications for destination marketers (e.g. Alderighi et al., 2016; Tsai, 2016; Björk & Kauppinen-Räisänen, 2016; Almeida & Garrod, 2017). For instance, Folgado-Fernández, Hernández-Mogollón and Duarte (2017) surveyed over 600 participants in two popular Spanish gastronomic festivals and proposed that gastronomic experiences have a positive effect on destination image and loyalty. While the role of local food in enhancing positive tourist experience and eventually fostering favorable behavioral intentions is widely acknowledged (e.g. Alderighi et al., 2016; Tsai, 2016; Andersson et al., 2017), the extent to which DMOs dedicate space for gastronomy in their official promotion materials and the volume, quality, and nature of these elements remain under-studied issues.

As an important element in destinations, local gastronomy has attracted increased attention (Lee & Scott, 2015; Ottenbacher et al., 2016) and has been suggested as an effective component of destination marketing (Okumus et al., 2013; Silkes et al., 2013). Food also makes up a major share of tourist consumption at a destination. According to the World Health Organization (2015), about one-third of overall tourist spending goes to food. Therefore, if gastronomy activities are utilized effectively, food can play a crucial role in marketing destinations (Okumus et al., 2013; Seo et al., 2017; Tellstrom et al., 2005) since tourists spend a respectable share of their time in destinations searching for and consuming local foods (Robinson & Getz, 2014; Sotiriadis, 2015). Moreover, local foods at a destination are not only a physical need but also a source of tourist experience (Beer et al., 2015; Cetin & Bilgihan, 2016; Henderson, 2016; Sanchez-Cañizares & Castillo-Canalejo, 2015).

Istanbul is one of the world's top ten destinations in terms of international visitors, hosting more than 11 million arrivals annually (McCarthy, 2017). Turkey is a transcontinental country that has borders with eight other countries: Georgia to the northeast, Armenia, the Azerbaijan enclave of Nakhchivan and Iran to the east, Iraq and Syria to the south, and Greece and Bulgaria to the northwest. As the trade center of Turkey, exceeding 17 million in population, Istanbul is also a major destination for locals and immigrants (Turkstat, 2016) and thus, it is a good representation of different cultural groups in Turkey. Rich culinary resources in Turkey are already recognized as popular international dishes (Okumus et al., 2007).

Despite diverse culinary resources in Istanbul, research on utilizing local gastronomy in destination marketing is still scant. Recently, there have been debates as to whether Istanbul can harness its rich local food culture and utilize these gastronomy resources more effectively to market Istanbul as a culinary destination. Given this, this chapter evaluates the representation of food within the offline and online official promotional materials. It also offers recommendations for the more effective use of culinary resources in the destination marketing of Istanbul.

Culinary destinations

Foods at a destination might be described as local if the ingredients are locally produced and served (Sims, 2009). Food tourism, also referred to as culinary, gastronomy and gourmet tourism, is primarily motivated by attending food festivals, visiting wineries and farmers' markets, and trying and experiencing cuisine at a destination (Getz, 2000; Hall and Sharples, 2003; Okumus et al., 2007). Food is also one of the significant factors for traveling activities since it physically and mentally prompts all five senses as an experience-intensive tourist activity. Tourists can be categorized into different typologies, ranging from tourists who have less interest in local food to those who search and travel extensively to experience local food (Boyne et al., 2002). Previous studies confirmed that the majority of tourists perceive local food as an essential part of their experience, which influences the holiday decision making-process (Okumus et al. 2007).

The experience of local foods can satisfy travelers' physical (e.g. hunger, safety), psychological (e.g. esteem, relaxation), social (e.g. interaction, entertainment) and intellectual (e.g. culture, ingredients) needs (Bell & Valentine, 1997; Ryu & Jang, 2006). The availability, diversity and authenticity of gastronomic culture can affect tourists' purchasing decisions, pulling them to the destination and generating positive post-purchase behavior – such as the intention to recommend and return (Gursoy & McCleary, 2004; Henderson, 2016). However, the effect of local food experiences may vary based on travelers' preferences and motivations. For instance, Almeida and Garrod (2017) proposed that consuming local foods may be either a peak experience or a secondary experience for tourists. The study also clustered tourists based on their level of engagement with local food.

Food associated with a particular region can be used as a promotional material for all types of tourist activities and destination marketing to create a differentiated image for the destination (Nelson, 2016; Pike 2015; Truong et al., 2017). Food is an important factor for travelers, which makes food tourism a large segment rather than an elite, niche market (McKercher et al. 2008; Spilkova & Fialova, 2013). Although there are different stages of intensity for tourists' food interests, harnessing local cuisines to enhance a positive local image and attract a wide segment of tourists is a viable destination marketing strategy (Boyne et al., 2002; Ab Karim & Chi, 2010; Silkes et al., 2013).

Local food might be treated as a distinct attribute that differentiates the destination and creates a sustainable, competitive advantage (Everett & Slocum, 2013; Horng et al., 2012). Unlike generic tourism resources, such as sun lust, local food cannot be easily imitated, is unique to each specific region, and has few substitutes (Okumus et al., 2007). Although some travelers avoid tasting local dishes (food neophobia), many adventurous visitors are always curious about ethnic and local food (Björk & Kauppinen-Räisänen, 2014). Therefore, local food can be a sustainable way of creating differentiation by stressing both unique physical and cultural characteristics of local gastronomy (Kivela & Crotts, 2005; Silkes et al., 2013). Current research in culinary tourism has concentrated on motivations of tourists, sustainability of local food, and the restaurant industry (Chang et al., 2010; Kim et al., 2009; Kivela & Crotts, 2006; Mak et al., 2012; Telfer & Wall, 2000). However, the tactics for utilizing gastronomy in a holistic destination promotional and marketing strategy are neglected in destination marketing literature.

The local gastronomy, representing unique ingredients, combinations, rituals, cooking styles, eating styles, social environment, atmospherics and representation, might be used as effective elements in destination image and brand formation (Andersson et al., 2017; Bessiere, 1998; Horng et al., 2012; Jolliffe, 2016; Okumus & Cetin, 2018; Silkes et al., 2013). With a well-designed marketing communication strategy, destinations can attract culinary tourists who come to the destination with major motivations other than the local gastronomy (Jalis et al., 2014; Tsai & Wang, 2017; TanSiew & Hashim, 2013). A central marketing strategy supported and facilitated by the local governments can be an important requirement for culinary marketing efforts of destinations (Ottenbacher et al., 2016). Many well-established destinations such as Italy and France and some other emerging tourist destinations such as Thailand and Singapore have already been investing in their culinary resources to differentiate themselves from their competitors and offer unique destination brand experiences (Henderson, 2009; Horng & Tsai, 2010).

Marketing destinations by using local foods

The role of local food experiences in fostering the development of tourism in destinations is widely recognized (Antón et al., 2019; López-Guzmán et al., 2017; Lee & Arcodia, 2011). This recognition stems from the fact that food consumption is a salient factor that enhances tourism experiences by both creating a sense of the "ontological comfort of home" as well as a sense of novelty (Quan & Wang, 2004: 302). Therefore, the demand for local foods has notably grown as experiencing local gastronomic products in destinations has become among the top activities preferred by visitors while on vacation (Okumus & Cetin, 2018). Many mature and some emerging destinations seem to recognize the role of local foods in attracting larger numbers of visitors and extending the length of their stay. This is evidenced by the increasing number of food and wine festivals taking place in several destinations over the globe (Lee et al., 2017).

Tourists collect information about a destination before travelling. They also seek information on local food, restaurants and popular eating venues. Information on local food is particularly important if the destination is unfamiliar to the travelers and if they have a special interest in the local gastronomy (Pawaskar & Goel, 2016). Therefore, both generic information about the local food targeted to mainstream markets and specific information of local gastronomy targeted to culinary tourists should be easily accessible in printed and electronic promotional materials of destinations (Jalis et al., 2014; Silkes et al., 2013). Printed materials are usually available at tourism information offices and visitor centers, whereas electronic materials are available online at several platforms including DMO websites and user-generated-content (UGC) platforms. There is also a shift to utilizing electronic resources from printed material in promoting the destinations. Websites are now more convenient, dynamic and can provide a more complete experience via text, audio and visual messages (Kim et al., 2009). They also offer the ability to search for information and options to interact with other customers and make easy reservations for travelers (Surenkok et al., 2010).

The mission of creating and promoting a culinary image of a destination lies primarily within the responsibility of the DMO rather than the individual stakeholders. Local food festivals, special events and street markets can be marketed through electronic materials in addition to printed materials. This is of significant importance since travelers are more likely to consider official information resources as more credible (Horng & Tsai, 2010; Lin et al., 2011). Therefore, the utilization of electronic promotional tools of DMO, websites, social media and mobile apps is important in order to attract tourists to the destination and improve their culinary experiences.

Turkish food

The variety of local foods is one of the main motivations for tourists who visit Turkey (Okumus et al., 2012; Yuksel, 2001). Turkey boasts different cultures, civilizations, and the legacy of three global empires (Roman, Byzantine, and Ottoman). The country is placed en route to important trade routes (e.g. Silk Road) and religious pilgrimages since the middle ages. The hospitality of the local people creates a welcoming environment for visitors from different cultures and culinary habits (Cetin & Okumus, 2018).

The Turks themselves were based in Central Asia and lived as nomadic tribes using different ingredients available in varied natural environments. They practiced diverse cooking and preservation methods to make the food durable and storable to use during their travels. When Turks came to Anatolia, the region already had a rich culinary background, with a variety of ingredients which created diversity and improved food, as cultural interactions and trade flourished (Biringen et al., 2013; Guler, 2016; Ozdemir et al., 2007). A large portion of the culinary products are already known globally (i.e. yoghurt, Turkish coffee). They are patented and protected by geographic indications. Some culinary goods (e.g. Turkish coffee) are also included in the UNESCO list (Okumus et al., 2013; UNESCO, 2015).

Istanbul, as the capital of two major empires (Byzantine and Ottoman), is located on the trade route between Asia and Europe and is recognized as a business and cultural hub. The city itself attracts more than 11 million international visitors annually (Istanbul Directorate for Culture and Tourism, 2018). Despite these advantages, there have been debates as to whether Istanbul is properly utilizing its culinary potential in destination promotion. Particularly, the effectiveness of the large-scale promotional campaigns is argued (Alvarez, 2010) and the special interest tourism is somewhat neglected (Okumus et al., 2012). Although its significance is acknowledged by various governmental organizations, utilizing culinary resources in the official promotion of the destination is still insufficient and requires further interest and research. Therefore, using this case study, the chapter examines how local gastronomy and food are used as a tool to create a positive brand image by TMoCT (Turkish Ministry of Culture and Tourism) and its representative office in Istanbul.

As a leading international destination, and given its rich culinary resources, Istanbul can be considered an ideal domain to analyze culinary tourism. In this chapter, the printed and electronic gastronomic materials about Istanbul are analyzed in order to evaluate the representation of local gastronomy and the utilization of culinary resources in destination marketing. Based on the content analysis and inter-coder consensus, the content was divided under origin of the food (regional, national and international), atmospherics (scenery, people, entertainment) and content of the representation (raw food, ingredients, entrees, main courses, desserts and drinks). The findings show that food makes up only 8% of the total promotional material of Istanbul. Instead, sun lust tourism, cultural tourism and meetings were highlighted most, as well as various activities like shopping, sports and camping. Food only received space under these headings as a supportive activity, rather than an attraction worthy of standalone attention and design. While several studies highlight the cultural and historical heritage of Istanbul as key assets enhancing its image and, eventually, its competitiveness (e.g. Alvarez & Yarcan, 2010; Sahin & Baloglu, 2011; Kladou & Mavragani, 2015; Alrawadieh et al., 2018), local gastronomy is a key attribute that visitors appreciate as a part of their tourist experience in Istanbul (Alrawadieh et al., 2018; Korzay & Alvarez, 2005). In other words, our findings indicate that the current marketing strategies underestimate the potential of local food as a key factor in enhancing the competitive advantage of the destination. To harness the power of food experience, destination marketers should view food as a 'peak experience' rather than a 'supporting activity' (Quan & Wang, 2004).

The share of food was greater within recent material, which shows a gradual improvement in recognizing the significance of food for Istanbul as a tourist destination. There were also some inconsistencies among different electronic and printed materials. Specifically, content translated from Turkish lacked professional marketing language and design. Yet the new website, introduced by the Ministry of Culture and Tourism (GoTurkeyTourism.com), has represented local gastronomy more professionally. Not surprising given the ability to publish various high-quality contents (e.g. pictures and videos) with low costs, electronic material in general allocated more space to culinary resources in Istanbul than the printed material.

Concerning the origin of the food, national food had a larger share (6%) than regional (2%) and international food (1%) in the promotional material. Regarding the distribution of atmospherics, a major portion of the material included scenery (44%), people (22%), entertainment (12%), and other typologies for representing food. Concerning scenery, the Bosphorus and historic monuments were the most frequently used images. People interacting, dancing, nightclubs and belly dancers were other images often used symbolizing atmospherics with food. The content of the food (Table 12.1) was represented under raw food (21%), ingredients (7%), entrees (17%), main courses (15%), desserts (12%), and drinks (34%).

Table 12.1: Share and representation of food in promotional material

Origin	Percentage of Total	Content	Percentage of Total
International food	1%	Raw food	21%
Regional food	2%	Ingredients	7%
National food	6%	Entrees	17%
Atmosphere		Main courses	15%
Scenery	44%	Desserts	12%
Entertainment	12%	Drinks	34%
People	22%		

The presentation and content of the materials were inadequate due to translation errors, simplistic approaches to descriptions, and the limited number and quality of the images used. Despite the other activities, the visual streams were also missing food. The information about the local and international food and beverage outlets was limited, particularly within DMO web pages, which should be able to offer various alternative venues at the destination to taste local food along with their contact information. Although a detailed list of alternative tourism was provided, food tourism alternatives were scarce. As a result, gastronomic alternatives for the current official promotions are still seen as a supporting activity and not a major tourist motivation for destination marketing in Turkey.

Conclusion

Utilizing tangible and intangible culinary resources and attractions in destination marketing is attracting increased attention. Yet there is limited activity and understanding in some tourist destinations as to how to operationalize local gastronomy and to what extent food should be employed in promotional materials. The chapter explored the representation of gastronomy within the official printed and electronic promotional materials. Istanbul is a suitable domain to explore the role of food in destination marketing. Culinary resources of Istanbul have been overlooked since other strong alternative tourist products are still offered in Istanbul. Currently, food is treated as a supporting attraction that may improve tourists' experience, rather than a principal motivation. However, considering the share of alternative tourism types, culinary tourism should receive more coverage and attention from the government as well as local and private organizations.

The chapter classified food-related materials based on three main typologies: origin of the food (regional, national and international), atmosphere in which food was presented (scenery, people and entertainment) and type of food (raw food, ingredients, entrees, main courses, desserts, drinks). Although the framework is destination-specific (i.e. Istanbul), it may still be adopted by other destinations seeking to assess their culinary marketing. A similar classification might also be used to evaluate destination promotions, and marketers might plan their culinary representation in destination marketing based on the typology offered in this study.

Drawing off the chapter's findings, Turkey is a world leader in the production of grape. Not surprisingly, there are a number of indigenous grape varieties in Turkey. Here is the summary information about the major Turkish grapes that are used to make wine., Istanbul has been, unfortunately, unsuccessful in fully utilizing its culinary resources in destination marketing compared to other tourism activities and alternative motivations. Turkey has more than 1,500 named grape varieties, of which 800 are genetically unique (GoTurkeyTourism.com, 2018). However, culinary resources like these have only lately been leveraged by the government's websites, and not aggressively. Coordinated marketing and private partnership efforts to create holistic culinary marketing have been neglected by the stakeholders, with inadequate utilization of food festivals, events and local farmers' markets. Therefore, more experiential marketing, cooking courses, electronic recipes, interactive maps of local food, and certification and promotion of restaurants and wineries would offer broad and memorable local gastronomy experiences to visitors of Istanbul and other diverse culinary cities in Turkey.

The chapter explained the role of gastronomy in official destination promotion materials for Istanbul. It can be summarized that:

◆ Official destination promotional materials both printed and electronic were content analyzed.

◆ Only eight percent of the promotional material is dedicated to food.

◆ Concerning the type of food, national food was represented more than regional and international food.

◆ Regarding atmospherics, food was depicted with scenery, people and entertainment respectively.

◆ Types of food used in promotional material were classified under raw food, ingredients, entrees, main courses, desserts and drinks.

◆ For a more effective culinary destination marketing, various suggestions with respect to promotional material, their design, and content were offered.

References

Ab Karim, S. & Chi, C.G.Q. (2010). Culinary tourism as a destination attraction: An empirical examination of destinations' food image. *Journal of Hospitality Marketing & Management*, **19**(6), 531-555.

Alderighi, M., Bianchi, C. & Lorenzini, E. (2016). The impact of local food specialities on the decision to (re) visit a tourist destination: Market-expanding or business-stealing?. *Tourism Management*, **57**, 323-333.

Almeida, A. & Garrod, B. (2017). Experiences with local food in a mature tourist destination: The importance of consumers' motivations. *Journal of Gastronomy and Tourism*, **2**(3), 173-187.

Alrawadieh, Z., Dincer, M.Z., Istanbullu Dincer, F. & Mammadova, P. (2018). Understanding destination image from the perspective of Western travel bloggers: the case of Istanbul. *International Journal of Culture, Tourism and Hospitality Research*, **12**(2), 198-212.

Alvarez, M.D. (2010). Marketing of Turkey as a tourism destination. *Anatolia*, **21**(1), 123-138.

Alvarez, M. D. & Yarcan, Ş. (2010). Istanbul as a world city: A cultural perspective. *International Journal of Culture, Tourism and Hospitality Research*, **4**(3), 266-276.

Andersson, T.D., Mossberg, L. & Therkelsen, A. (2017). Food and tourism synergies: perspectives on consumption, production and destination development, *Scandinavian Journal of Hospitality and Tourism*, **17**(1), 1-8.

Bell, D. & Valentine, G. (1997). *Geographies: We are what we eat*. London: Routledge.

Bessiere, J. (1998). Local development and heritage: Traditional food and cuisine as tourist attractions in rural areas. *Sociologia Ruralis,* **38**, 21-34.

Biringen Löker, G., Amoutzopoulos, B., Özge Özkoç, S., Özer, H., Şatir, G. & Bakan, A. (2013). A pilot study on food composition of five Turkish traditional foods. *British Food Journal,* **115**(3), 394-408.

Björk, P. & Kauppinen-Räisänen, H. (2014). Culinary-gastronomic tourism–a search for local food experiences. *Nutrition & Food Science,* **44**(4), 294-309.

Björk, P. & Kauppinen-Räisänen, H. (2016). Local food: a source for destination attraction. *International Journal of Contemporary Hospitality Management,* **28**(1), 177-194.

Boyne, S., Williams, F. & Hall, D. (2002). On the trail of regional success: Tourism, food production and the Isle of Arran Taste Train. In G. Richards & A.-M. Hjalager (Eds.), *Tourism and Gastronomy* (pp. 91–114). London: Routledge.

Cetin, G. & Bilgihan, A. (2016). Components of cultural tourists' experiences in destinations. *Current Issues in Tourism,* **19**(2), 137-154.

Chang, R. C., Kivela, J. & Mak, A. H. (2010). Food preferences of Chinese tourists. *Annals of tourism research,* **37**(4), 989-1011.

Everett, S. & Slocum, S. L. (2013). Food and tourism: An effective partnership? A UK-based review. *Journal of Sustainable Tourism,* **21**(6), 789-809.

Folgado-Fernández, J. A., Hernández-Mogollón, J. M. & Duarte, P. (2017). Destination image and loyalty development: the impact of tourists' food experiences at gastronomic events. *Scandinavian Journal of Hospitality and Tourism,* **17**(1), 92-110.

Getz, D. (2000). *Explore Wine Tourism: Management, development and destinations*. New York: Cognizant Development Corporation.

GoTurkeyTourism.com (2018). Tourism and travel guide to Turkey. https://www.goturkeytourism.com. Retrieved on 15.10.2018

Guler, O. (2016). What is your favorite local food menu? Application of conjoint analysis on the Eastern Mediterranean Cuisine of Turkey. *Journal of Tourism and Gastronomy Studies,* **4**(3), 38-52.

Gursoy, D. & McCleary, K. (2004). An integrated model of tourists' information search behavior. *Annals of Tourism Research,* **31**(2), 353–373.

Hall, M. & Sharples, L. (2003). The consumption of experiences or the experience of consumption? An introduction to the tourism of taste. In M. Hall, L. Sharples, R. Mitchell, N. Macionis & B. Cambourne (Eds.), *Food Tourism around the world: Development, management and markets*. Oxford: Butterworth-Heinemann.

Henderson, J.C. (2009). Food tourism reviewed. *British Food Journal*, **111**(4), 317-326.

Henderson, J.C. (2016). Local and traditional or global and modern? Food and tourism in Singapore. *Journal of Gastronomy and Tourism*, **2**(1), 55-68.

Horng, J.S. & Tsai, C.T.S. (2010). Government websites for promoting East Asian culinary tourism: A cross-national analysis. *Tourism Management*, **31**(1), 74-85.

Horng, J.S., Liu, C.H., Chou, H.Y. & Tsai, C.Y. (2012). Understanding the impact of culinary brand equity and destination familiarity on travel intentions. *Tourism Management*, **33**(4), 815-824.

Jalis, M.H., Che, D. & Markwell, K. (2014). Utilising local cuisine to market Malaysia as a tourist destination. *Procedia-Social and Behavioral Sciences*, **144**, 102-110.

Kim, Y.G., Eves, A. & Scarles, C. (2009). Building a model of local food consumption on trips and holidays: a grounded theory approach. *International Journal of Hospitality Management*, **28**, 423-431.

Kivela, J. & Crotts, J.C. (2005). Gastronomy tourism. *Journal of Culinary Science & Tourism*, **4** (2-3), 39-55.

Kivela, J. & Crotts, J.C. (2006). Tourism & gastronomy: Gastronomy's influence on how tourist experience a destination. *Journal of Hospitality and Tourism Research*, **30**, 354-377.

Kladou, S. & Mavragani, E. (2015). Assessing destination image: An online marketing approach and the case of TripAdvisor. *Journal of Destination Marketing & Management*, **4**(3), 187-193.

Korzay, M. & Alvarez, M.D. (2005). Satisfaction and dissatisfaction of Japanese tourists in Turkey. *Anatolia*, **16**(2), 176-193.

Lee, I. & Arcodia, C. (2011). The role of regional food festivals for destination branding. *International Journal of Tourism Research*, **13**(4), 355-367.

Lee, K.H. & Scott, N. (2015). Food tourism reviewed using the paradigm funnel approach. *Journal of Culinary Science & Technology*, **13**(2), 95-115.

Lee, W., Sung, H., Suh, E. & Zhao, J. (2017). The effects of festival attendees' experiential values and satisfaction on re-visit intention to the destination: The case of a food and wine festival. *International Journal of Contemporary Hospitality Management*, **29**(3), 1005-1027.

Lin, Y. C., Pearson, T. E. & Cai, L. A. (2011). Food as a form of destination identity: A tourism destination brand perspective. *Tourism and Hospitality Research*, **11**(1), 30-48.

López-Guzmán, T., Uribe Lotero, C.P., Pérez Gálvez, J.C. & Rios Rivera, I. (2017). Gastronomic festivals: attitude, motivation and satisfaction of the tourist. *British Food Journal*, **119**(2), 267-283.

Mak, A.H., Lumbers, M., Eves, A. & Chang, R.C. (2012). Factors influencing tourist food consumption. *International Journal of Hospitality Management*, **31**(3), 928-936.

McCarthy, N. (2017). Bangkok was the World's most visited city In 2016. https://www.forbes.com/sites/niallmccarthy/2017/01/04/bangkok-was-the-worlds-most-visited-city-in-2016-infographic/#6ff101952a9c. Retrieved on 23.06.2017.

McKercher, B., Okumus, F. & Okumus, B. (2008). Food tourism as a viable market segment: It's all how you cook the numbers! *Journal of Travel & Tourism Marketing*, **25**(2), 137-148.

Nelson, V. (2016). Food and image on the official visitor site of Houston, Texas. *Journal of Destination Marketing & Management*, **5**(2), 133-140.

Okumus, B. & Cetin, G. (2018). Marketing Istanbul as a culinary destination. *Journal of Destination Marketing & Management*, **9**, 340-346.

Okumus, B., Okumus, F. & McKercher, B. (2007). Incorporating local and international cuisines in the marketing of tourist destinations: the case of Hong-Kong and Turkey. *Tourism Management*, **28**, 253-261.

Okumus, F., Avci, U., Kilic, I. & Walls, A.R. (2012). Cultural tourism in Turkey: A missed opportunity. *Journal of Hospitality Marketing & Management*, **21**(6), 638-658.

Okumus, F., Kock, G., Scantlebury, M.M. & Okumus, B. (2013). Using local cuisines when promoting small Caribbean island destinations. *Journal of Travel & Tourism Marketing*, **30**(4), 410-429.

Ottenbacher, M.C., Harrington, R.J., Fauser, S. & Loewenhagen, N. (2016). Should culinary tourism and hospitality service attributes be defined as primary tourism drivers? An expectancy-fulfillment grid approach. *Journal of Foodservice Business Research*, **19**(5), 425-440.

Ozdemir, S., Gocmen, D. & Yildirim Kumral, A. (2007). A traditional Turkish fermented cereal food: Tarhana. *Food Reviews International*, **23**(2), 107-121.

Pawaskar, R. P. & Goel, M. (2016). Improving the efficacy of destination marketing strategies: A structural equation model for leisure travel. *Indian Journal of Science and Technology*, **9**(15), pp. 1-11.

Pike, S. (2015). *Destination Marketing: Essentials*. Routledge.

Quan, S. & Wang, N. (2004). Towards a structural model of the tourist experience: An illustration from food experiences in tourism. *Tourism management*, **25**(3), 297-305.

Robinson, R. & Getz, D. (2014). Profiling potential food tourists: An Australian study. *British Food Journal*, **116**(4), 690-706.

Ryu, K. & Jang, S. (2006). Intention to experience local cuisine in a travel destination: the modified theory of reasonable action. *Journal of Tourism and Hospitality Research*, **30**, 507-516.

Sahin, S. & Baloglu, S. (2011). Brand personality and destination image of Istanbul. *Anatolia–An International Journal of Tourism and Hospitality Research*, **22**(01), 69-88.

Sanchez-Cañizares, S. & Castillo-Canalejo, A.M. (2015). A comparative study of tourist attitudes towards culinary tourism in Spain and Slovenia. *British Food Journal*, **117**(9), 2387-2411.

Seo, S., Yun, N. & Kim, O.Y. (2017). Destination food image and intention to eat destination foods: a view from Korea. *Current Issues in Tourism*, **20**(2), 135-156.

Silkes, C.A., Cai, L.A. & Lehto, X.Y. (2013). Marketing to the culinary tourist. *Journal of Travel & Tourism Marketing*, **30**(4), 335-349.

Sims. R. (2009). Food, place and authenticity: Local food and sustainable tourism experience. *Journal of Sustainable Tourism*, **17**(3), 321-336.

Sotiriadis, M. D. (2015). Culinary tourism assets and events: suggesting a strategic planning tool. *International Journal of Contemporary Hospitality Management*, **27**(6), 1214-1232.

Spilkova, J. & Fialova, D. (2013). Culinary tourism packages and regional brands in Czechia. *Tourism Geographies*, **15**(2), 177-197

Surenkok A., Baggio R. & Corigliano M.A. (2010) Gastronomy and tourism in Turkey: The role of ICTs. In Gretzel U., Law R., Fuchs M. (eds.) *Information and Communication Technologies in Tourism (pp. 567-578)*. Vienna: Springer.

TanSiew, T. & Hashim, N. H. (2013). An investigation into official tourism websites for promoting food tourism in ASEAN countries. *Asia-Pacific Journal of Innovation in Hospitality and Tourism*, **2**(2), 171-182.

Telfer, D.J. & Wall, G. (2000). Strengthening backward economic linkages: Local food purchasing by three Indonesian hotels. *Tourism Geographies*, **2**, 421-447.

Tellstrom, R., Gustafsson, I. & Mossberg, L. (2005). Local food cultures in the Swedish rural economy. *Socilogia Ruralis*, **45**, 346-359.

Tsai, C. T. (2016). Memorable tourist experiences and place attachment when consuming local food. *International Journal of Tourism Research*, **18**(6), 536-548.

Tsai, C. T. S. & Wang, Y. C. (2017). Experiential value in branding food tourism. *Journal of Destination Marketing & Management*, **6**(1), 56-65.

Turkstat (2016). City Population by years 2000 – 2016. http://www.tuik. gov.tr/PreIstatistikTablo.do?istab_id=1590. Retrieved on 17.06.2017.

UNESCO (2015). Lists of intangible cultural heritage and register of best safeguarding practices. http://www.unesco.org/culture/ich/index. php?lg=en&pg=00011#tabs. Retrieved on 12.03.2015.

World Health Organization (2015). *International Travel and Health*. Geneva: WHO Press.

Yuksel, A. (2001). Managing customer satisfaction and retention: A case of tourist destinations, Turkey. *Journal of Vocational Marketing,* **7**(2), 153–168.

13 Innovations in the wine tourism experience: The case of Marqués de Riscal

Diego Bufquin, Robin M. Back and Jeong-Yeol Park

The objectives of this chapter are to:

☐ Assess the effects of congruence perceptions – between a post-modernist hotel architecture, its surrounding landscape, visitors' self-image, and a winery's brand image – on winery visitors' arousal, delight and behavioral intentions;

☐ Analyze the relationships between substantive and communicative servicescape perceptions, and winery visitors' positive affect, satisfaction, and behavioral intentions, as well as the moderating effects of brand and architectural familiarity;

☐ Investigate the influence of winery tourists' motivations and satisfaction on number of visits and revisit intentions;

☐ Study whether visitors' geographic proximity or distance has an influence on revisit intentions and number of visits;

☐ Examine whether winery tourists' revisit intentions decrease after a certain number of visits, and whether satisfaction postpones such decrease in revisit intentions.

Keywords: wine tourism, servicescape, motivations, satisfaction, delight, revisit intentions

Introduction – winery innovations: The case of Marqués de Riscal

Wine tourism has been gaining importance as a popular form of special interest tourism, with an increasing body of academic literature concentrating on the field, and the United Nations World Tourism Organization holding its first Global Conference on Wine Tourism in the Kakheti Region of Georgia in 2016. While the term 'wine tourism' originally related mainly to visitation of wineries for the purpose of tasting and/or purchasing wine, it has become accepted that wine tourists now desire far more from their wine tourism experience. They also look for innovative products and services such as culinary offerings, lodging, cultural and recreational activities, retail choices and an enjoyable rural landscape (Brown et al., 2006; Bruwer & Alant, 2009; Cohen & Ben-Nun, 2009). This has resulted in many wineries around the world adding additional facilities and attractions beyond the primary wine tasting experience.

There is, however, little academic research on innovations in wine tourism beyond the traditional wine tasting/winery tour experience, yet many wineries have been adding attractions and activities, especially restaurants and accommodation. One such example is Spice Route in Paarl, South Africa, which, besides wine tasting, also offers tastings of beer, gin, chocolate, charcuterie, and preserves, and is home to three restaurants, a delicatessen, a coffee shop, a glass blowing studio, a diamond cutting studio, a gift shop, a pilates studio, and mountain biking trails (Explore Spice Route, 2018). Another is the Spier Wine Farm in Stellenbosch, South Africa, whose facilities include a luxury hotel and spa, conference facilities, four restaurants, a gift shop, a craft market, picnic facilities, Segway tours, and eagle encounters (Spier Wine Farm, 2018).

Such innovations in wine tourism are not confined to 'new world' wine regions, however. Since the mid-2000s, Spain has been marketing wine tourism as an alternative to its better known beach vacations (GBSB Global Business School, 2017). With the shift in wine tourism in recent years from a focus on winemaking and wine tasting to a wider group of leisure and recreational experiences (Brown et al., 2006; Bruwer & Alant, 2009; Cohen & Ben-Nun, 2009; Getz & Brown, 2006), Spain has seen the development of a number of innovative winery attractions, with the Marqués de Riscal winery, on which this case study concentrates, having led the way. Established in the town of Elciego in Spain's Rioja region in 1858, Marqués de Riscal is one of the country's oldest and most respected wineries (see Figure 13.1).

Figure 13.1: Hotel Marqués de Riscal. Photo credit: I-Escape.com.

In 2006, Marqués de Riscal inaugurated its 'City of Wine'. Occupying a 100,000m^2 site and at a cost of some €70 million, the intention was to attract as much attention as possible in order to maximize both tourism and wine sales (Michael, 2015). In addition to the existing historic winery, the 'City of Wine' added a striking post-modernist hotel designed by world renowned architect, Frank Gehry. The 'City of Wine' incorporates two restaurants (one of them Michelin-starred), a wine therapy spa, conference and events facilities, a coffee shop, a shop selling wine and other products, and a museum. While not unique in the world, its sheer scale and cost, together with the diversity of its tourism product offering, differentiate Marqués de Riscal from most other Spanish wineries (Vila et al., 2012). In the City of Wine's first year of operation, visitor numbers to the Rioja region as a whole increased by an astonishing 68 percent (Instituto Nacional de Estadística, 2010; IREA, 2008), which resulted in around twenty applications to local authorities for the construction of new hotels to house the Region's greatly increased number of tourists (Vila et al., 2012). Thus, Marqués de Riscal presents an ideal case for further investigation into innovations in the wine tourism experience.

(In)congruence perceptions, and wine visitors' arousal, delight and behavioural intentions

The hospitality industry has continually been evolving over the past few decades with the development of unique products and services (Vila et al., 2012). The main goal of these innovations is for companies to avoid falling into the trap of commoditization, of which product homogeneity is considered by hotel executives to be the element that contributes the most to a lack of meaningful differentiation (Beldona et al., 2015). Hence, hospitality companies are doing their best to differentiate themselves with the creation of distinguishable products and services in order to surpass customer expectations while delivering memorable experiences.

As mentioned, an example of such product innovations was led by Marqués de Riscal with the inauguration of the 'City of Wine', which includes the Hotel Marqués de Riscal, a postmodernist jewel designed by world-famous architect Frank Gehry and located in the heart of this historic winery. Although the 'Gehry effect' (i.e. the power of Frank Gehry's buildings to transform an entire city) is undeniable, the juxta-position between historic and postmodernist architecture has not seen much investigation in the hospitality literature (Meagher, 2014; Vila et al., 2012). Frank Gehry is known to create architectural landmarks that not only disrupt the local landscape, but are at times a source of con-troversy. For instance, when the Guggenheim museum in Bilbao was inaugurated in 1997, it generated a fair share of criticism for being too imposing and spectacular (Hedgecoe & Whittle, 2012).

Because of the disruptive nature of Frank Gehry's buildings, the first study's objective was to understand how the juxtaposition between historic and postmodernist architecture affects visitors' emotions and behavioral intentions. Second, due to the historic nature of the Marqués de Riscal winery, the authors also wanted to understand how such a groundbreaking and postmodernist hotel may affect customers' brand perceptions of one of the region's oldest and most traditional wineries. Lastly, as Solomon (1983) explains, consumers frequently purchase prod-ucts not solely for their functionality, but also for their symbolic or social significance, with the formation of a 'self-brand connection' (Escalas & Bettman, 2005). Thus, the third objective was to examine how congru-ence perceptions between visitors' self-image and the hotel architecture (i.e. whether they identify with the hotel's architecture) affect winery tourists' emotions and behavioral responses.

In order to achieve such goals, Oliver, Rust, and Varki's (1997) delight model was taken into account, as it implies that surprise and perfor-mance act as antecedents of customer emotions (i.e. arousal and delight) and behavioral intentions. The use of this model allows academics and hoteliers to better understand how a surprise factor, such as Gehry's postmodernist architecture, affects winery visitors, as no study thus far has used disruptive hotel architecture as an 'excitement' element that could improve visitors' arousal, delight and behavioral intentions.

To fulfill the study's objectives, the target sample was defined as tourists who had visited the Marqués de Riscal winery at least once since the inauguration of the Hotel Marqués de Riscal in 2006. A total of 10,500 surveys were distributed and 737 responses were used for analysis. The constructs used in the survey were adapted from previous literature. In order to examine the proposed conceptual relationships, this study followed a two-step approach as suggested by Anderson and Gerbing (1988, 1992). In the first step, the model fit and validity of each construct were tested with confirmatory factor analysis (CFA). Once the validity of all constructs was confirmed, structural equation modeling (SEM) was utilized to evaluate the overall fit of the model and to test the proposed hypotheses. In sum, the current study demonstrated that the perceived incongruence between a postmodernist hotel's architecture and its surrounding historic buildings positively affects winery visitors' arousal and delight. This study therefore demonstrates that perceived architectural incongruence can act as a positive rather than a negative construct, specifically in a hospitality setting where striking modern hotel architecture is viewed against a historic backdrop.

Furthermore, congruence perceptions between the hotel architecture and the brand image of the Marqués de Riscal winery also increased winery visitors' arousal and delight. Thus, when winery visitors believe that the hotel architecture matches the winery's brand, their arousal and delight levels tend to increase as a consequence. This is particularly interesting considering that, prior to the construction of the Gehry-designed hotel, the Marqués de Riscal brand image was perceived as somewhat dull. In the ten plus years since the hotel inauguration, however, the winery's brand image has changed, as it has become associated with striking modern hotel architecture in the minds of consumers.

Congruence perceptions between visitors' self-image and the hotel architecture, on the other hand, were found to affect arousal, but did not influence delight. Moreover, the current study confirmed the significant effect of arousal on delight (Loureiro & Kastenholz, 2011; Oliver et al., 1997). Lastly, arousal and delight were found to significantly improve winery visitors' behavioral intentions, meaning that both emotions lead them to (a) spread positive word-of-mouth, (b) recommend the winery and (c) desire to visit the winery again in the future.

The current study has important implications for wineries, hotel operators and other hospitality firms. More specifically, when guests identify with the design of a building (i.e. there is congruence between their self-image and that of the perceived architecture), and when there are striking contrasts between historic and novel architecture or design, the (in)congruence perceptions resulting from such cognitive processes enhance visitors' arousal and delight, which in turn affect their behavioral intentions. As a result, when designing and implementing new buildings, hospitality firms should always consider the importance of architectural design and how remarkable and unusual architecture may be more impactful in the minds of consumers than the many standard 'cookie cutter' buildings that abound. This study also demonstrated the ability of iconic architecture to transform and redefine the image of a brand with which it is connected. Thus, wineries, hotels, and other hospitality firms should consider how their brands may be transformed by the architecture of unusual buildings, even if the latter are used for different purposes altogether.

Servicescape perceptions, familiarity, and hotel customers' attitudinal and behavioral outcomes

Bitner (1992) coined the term 'servicescape' to refer to the physical environment in which a service firm delivers services to its customers, while the influence of environmental cues on consumer behavior has long been recognized by service businesses as well as by interior designers and architects (e.g., Baker et al., 1992; Gilboa & Rafaeli, 2003; Kearney et al., 2007; Tai & Fung, 1997). A substantial body of research has shown that consumer behavior and emotions can be greatly influenced by the physical environment (Mehrabian & Russell, 1974; Donovan & Rositer, 1982; Turley & Milliman, 2000), and an extensive servicescape literature mostly relates to the substantive staging of the servicescape, or the staged physical environment (Dong & Siu, 2013). Only a handful of studies, however, have investigated the effects of the communicative staging of servicescape, which includes cultural elements and employee communications with customers (e.g., Chang, 2016; Durna et al., 2015; Lin & Mattila, 2010). Additionally, no study to date has been found investigating the effects of servicescape in a postmodernist hotel environment, such as the Hotel Marqués de Riscal. With its flowing ribbons of titanium and unique interior and exterior, it could be argued that there may be few more highly staged servicescapes.

The main objectives of this study were thus (a) to identify the role of substantive and communicative servicescape on hotel customers' positive affect (also known as positive emotions), satisfaction and behavioral intentions, and (b) to determine whether brand familiarity and architectural familiarity have a moderating influence in the relationship between substantive and communicative servicescape and customers' positive affect. To fulfill these objectives, the population of interest was defined as travelers who had visited the Hotel Marqués de Riscal, while the target sample was defined as travelers who had stayed at the Hotel Marqués de Riscal at least once since its opening in 2006.

An online survey was created, with participants randomly selected from the customer database of the Hotel Marqués de Riscal and with the survey link also posted on the hotel's social media pages. Thus, a mix of convenience sampling and self-selection sampling methods were adopted. The scales used in the survey were all adapted from prior studies. A seven-point Likert scale was used for all constructs. A total of 180 surveys were collected. After eliminating errors and missing values, 150 responses were utilized for further analysis. The study utilized Partial Least Squares – Structural Equation Modeling (PLS-SEM), which is known as a causal modeling approach aimed at maximizing the explained variance of the dependent latent constructs (Hair et al., 2011).

Results showed that substantive servicescape and communicative servicescape both have a positive influence on positive affect. However, the influence of substantive servicescape on positive affect was greater than that of communicative servicescape. Further, positive affect had a positive influence on satisfaction, which in turn increased behavioral intentions. Moreover, both brand familiarity (i.e. familiarity with the Marqués de Riscal brand) and architectural familiarity (i.e. familiarity with Frank Gehry's architecture) significantly moderated the relationship between the hotel's substantive servicescape and positive affect, with the positive influence of substantive servicescape on positive affect greater for participants with low familiarity than for those with high familiarity. Neither familiarity dimension, however, had any significant moderating effect in the relationship between communicative servicescape and positive affect, thus showing communicative servicescape to be an important factor in determining the level of positive affect, irrespective of the level of familiarity. Further, a series of post-hoc analyses to determine mediating and indirect effects found that positive affect fully mediates the relationships between the servicescape dimensions and satisfaction, while substantive servicescape had more significant indirect effects on satisfaction and behavioral intentions than communicative servicescape in such a postmodernist hotel setting.

The results of this study have some interesting practical implications for hospitality businesses, particularly full-service hotels with a highly substantively staged servicescape. While most hospitality businesses are aware of the importance to their guests of the physical environment in which services are delivered, this study shows that they should still pay close attention to their communicative servicescape, i.e. how employees communicate with customers and the cultural elements of the guest experience. Both servicescape factors are shown to influence guests' emotional responses, which in turn influence satisfaction and thereby behavioral intentions. In terms of familiarity, renowned brands and iconic architecture may evoke high emotional responses during an initial visit, but customers are shown to have lower emotional responses once they become familiar with the brand and architecture. For such guests, the cultural and customer service aspects of the experience may therefore become more important, as these aspects may vary between visits and are unaffected by familiarity. The more a guest returns to a property, therefore, the more important the communicative staging becomes, and the importance of loyal repeat guests to the success of any business is well documented in the literature (Kandampully & Suhartanto, 2000). A luxury hotel such as the Marqués de Riscal would be advised to ensure a high level of communicative servicescape through excellent staff training together with pleasing non-tangibles, such as atmosphere and ambience, which portray the cultural heritage of Elciego and the Rioja wine region.

Wine tourists' motivations and satisfaction

Given the increase in the popularity of wine tourism and the trend of expanding the amenities, activities and experiences offered by wineries, it becomes important to understand which factors motivate tourists to visit a particular winery for the first time and, even more importantly, which motivations influence both their number of visits and revisit intentions. While there has been previous research into the motivations of tourists to plan a wine tourism vacation (Sparks, 2006), and how demographic differences may affect winery tourists' revisit intentions (Stoddard & Clopton, 2015), no research has investigated motivations to visit a particular winery, and how such motivations influence the number of visits and revisit intentions, which are especially relevant when the experiences offered go beyond the traditional wine tasting and tour.

Wineries that wish to attract tourists must develop appropriate attractions and experiences to attract new customers and to form a loyal visitor base, investing their capital wisely to ensure that visitor numbers not only increase, but that those visitors keep returning. Wineries need to understand their visitors' decision making process, i.e. why do they decide to visit, why they wish to return, and why they actually return? In order to understand visitor behavior, one must understand motivations for destination choice, perceptions of the experience, satisfaction with the experience, and future revisit intentions (Fayed et al., 2016).

This study draws its sample from the population of previous visitors to the Marqués de Riscal winery, and includes both one-time visitors and those who have visited on multiple occasions. The surveying of actual former winery visitors, rather than potential visitors, is an important distinction of this study. This differs from the many studies that treat behavioral intentions as a proxy for actual behavior, which has been shown to frequently not be the case (Ajzen, 1985). A mixture of convenience and self-selection sampling was used, with a link to the survey emailed to randomly selected previous visitors in Marqués de Riscal's database. Screening questions ensured that only actual previous visitors participated in the survey. Of the 2,630 surveys collected, 1,602 usable responses were selected for analysis.

The survey consisted of three sections. In the first section, participants were asked to select their most important motivations to visit the Marqués de Riscal winery. These motivations were adapted from previous studies. Six motivations were provided regarding (1) the reputation, reviews and perceived quality of the winery and the wines, (2) the architecture of the winery's hotel, (3) the location of the winery, (4) the influence of media coverage and advertising, (5) recommendation by others, and (6) spontaneous visits to the winery (e.g. "I was in the area or driving past and decided to visit it").

The second section required participants to evaluate their overall satisfaction with the winery. These items were measured using a 7-point Likert scale. Participants were also asked to indicate their total number of visits since 2006, and their revisit intentions for this winery. The scale for revisit intentions, which was adapted from a previous study, was measured using a 7-point Likert scale.

In the third section, participants were asked to respond to questions regarding their sociodemographic and geographic characteristics. A series of multiple regression analyses was performed to verify the influence of motivations to visit and satisfaction on the number of previous visits and revisit intentions. Due to the fact that the measurement scales for the motivation factors were categorical, five dummy variables were included, and 'spontaneous visits to the winery' was utilized as the reference group.

Results showed that the only motivation factor that showed a significant influence on both the number of previous visits and revisit intentions was the reputation, reviews and perceived quality of the winery and its wines. Participants who were motivated to visit the winery due to media coverage and advertising showed higher revisit intentions. Likewise, participants' overall satisfaction with the winery experience had a positive influence on revisit intentions. With respect to the effects of geographic characteristics, participants from North America showed significantly higher intentions to revisit compared to visitors from Spain, despite Spanish residents visiting significantly more frequently. While the architecture of the hotel was not a significant reason for either revisit intentions or the number of previous visits, media coverage and advertising of the property, which would include the hotel and its architecture in many instances, was a significant reason for revisit intentions, although not for the number of visits. These findings perhaps indicate that while the architecture may inspire visitors to want to come back, it is in itself an insufficient motivation to actually revisit. Finally, it was found that the greater the number of previous visits, the higher the revisit intentions, showing that the more people had visited the winery, the more they desired to return.

Interestingly, it appears that the core winery product, i.e. the wines and winery experience, remains the most important component of the visit. While this should therefore be a primary focus, it should not be seen to negate the advantages of diversifying the wine tourism experience, as the overall winery experience includes all facets of the tourist offering. It is therefore suggested that wineries continue to diversify their tourism product in order to satisfy tourists' desire for a more varied experience. However, it is nonetheless crucial that wineries not lose sight of the importance of maintaining the quality and reputation of their wine and wine tasting, delivering a highly satisfying experience that will keep visitors desiring to come back and actually coming back. It may also be beneficial to recognize repeat visitors, perhaps with a free tasting, loyalty program, gift, or invitations to exclusive events.

Relationship among winery tourists' satifaction, repeat visits, and revisit intentions

Despite the fact that the Marqués de Riscal winery had benefited from increased revenues since the inauguration of the 'City of Wine' in 2006, it was still unclear whether their product and service innovations would continue to attract repeat visitors in the long run or after a certain number of years. Based on the concept of hedonic adaptation, which refers to the perceptual process that affective arousal resulting from a new experience decreases after repeated exposure to the same stimulus (Wang et al., 2009), one of the main goals of this study was to determine whether winery tourists' revisit intentions decrease after an 'optimal' number of repeat visits.

One reason that may explain why winery visitors' recurrent experiences lower revisit intentions over time is the concept of satiation, which refers to a decline in overall enjoyment due to repeated exposure to a stimulus (Galak et al., 2013; Redden, 2008). Even with a great service experience, in which the level of satisfaction is high, customers can eventually become satiated if the experience is repeated too often (Coombs & Avrunin, 1977). When a person is first exposed to a stimulus, he or she starts to learn about the stimulus (Berlyne, 1970). This learning process enhances positive affect, which increases revisit intentions (Mehrabian & Russell, 1974). However, if a person experiences the same stimulus too often, such positive affect tends to decrease due to hedonic adaptation (Wang et al., 2009). In other words, tourists' revisit intentions may increase as the number of visits increases, but revisit intentions may end up decreasing over time if the same stimulus is experienced too many times.

Furthermore, satisfaction is considered a key antecedent leading to customer loyalty (Oliver, 1999), and significantly moderates the relationship between customers' exit intentions and the attractiveness of an alternative relationship or supplier (Ping, 1994). This implies that when consumers are highly satisfied with a specific product or service, they will be less likely to search for similar products or services elsewhere. By applying the aforementioned theoretical framework, it is reasonable to suggest that the rate of decline in revisit intentions, caused by the increasing number of visits by tourists to Marqués de Riscal, could differ according to visitors' levels of satisfaction. Hence, the second main objective of this study was to examine whether satisfaction moderates the relationship between winery tourists' repeat visits and revisit intentions. Lastly, the authors also wanted to assess the winery's attributes and visitors' sociodemographic characteristics that improve visitors' satisfaction the most, as findings regarding such attributes and characteristics are somewhat conflicting and may not apply to the Marqués de Riscal winery specifically.

In order to fulfill the study's objectives, this study also defined the target sample as travelers who had visited the Marqués de Riscal winery at least once since the inauguration of its 'City of Wine' in 2006. A total of 10,500 online surveys were distributed and 2630 surveys were collected. After eliminating errors and missing values, 1378 responses were utilized for further analysis.

At the beginning of the survey, participants were first asked to indicate the number of previous visits to the Marqués de Riscal winery since the inauguration of the 'City of Wine'. Second, participants were asked to choose the winery attributes that they had enjoyed the most – six categories were provided such as 'the quality of wines', 'the winery tour/wine tasting', 'the ambiance', 'scenery and landscape', 'the historic winery' and 'the hotel design/architecture'. The constructs related to satisfaction and revisit intentions were adapted from prior studies and were measured using a 7-point Likert scale. In the final section of the survey, participants were asked to indicate their socio-demographic information, such as gender, age, education, and country of residence.

To identify the relationship between respondents' socio-demographic characteristics, winery attributes, satisfaction, number of visits and revisit intentions, a regression analysis was performed using STATA 14.0. To verify the moderating effect of satisfaction, a moderated regression analysis was employed (Sharma et al., 1981).

Results indicated that the overall revisit intentions of winery v isitors tend to increase as the number of visits increases; but after 4.6 visits, revisit intentions start to decrease significantly. This means that there is indeed an optimal number of visits that maximizes winery visitors' revisit intentions. Moreover, the moderated regression analysis showed that revisit intentions start decreasing after 5.5 repeat visits for 'high satisfaction' visitors, and at a much more rapid pace (i.e. after 3.89 visits) for 'low satisfaction' visitors. Interestingly, the two attributes that contributed the most to high levels of satisfaction were the winery tour/wine tasting experience and the overall ambiance of the winery. Lastly, gender, age, and country of residence had significant impacts on satisfaction as well.

This study has a number of practical implications that winery owners and operators should pay attention to. Winery operators should ensure that the activities and experiences on offer are continually refreshed and updated in order that guests not become satiated by repetition of identical stimuli each time they visit a winery. This may be accomplished by varying the types of wine tasting on offer, updating information imparted during the winery tour, changing restaurant menus and merchandise on offer, and adding new or different activities. Likewise, wineries should not only focus on delivering exceptional wine tastings and tours to their visitors, but should provide such services within an attractive and/or unique servicescape in order to create a desirable ambience. In so doing, there is less likelihood of customers becoming satiated, thereby increasing the possibility of the optimal number of visits continuing to increase. This will ensure that visitors keep returning, and that their revisit intentions remain high. Last but not least, findings suggest that the Marqués de Riscal winery should target its marketing and service efforts toward 'less satisfied' customer segments (e.g. younger, male, and Spanish), in order to increase their satisfaction and thereby revisit intentions and actual repeat visits.

Conclusion

This chapter is based on the findings of four different studies that were conducted at one of the most innovative and reputable wineries in Spain, i.e. Marqués de Riscal, which in 2006 inaugurated its 'City of Wine', a groundbreaking project that includes a 43-room hotel designed by a world-famous architect, among other services and amenities (e.g. wine therapy spa, convention center, shops, and restaurants). The results, obtained via two sets of data (i.e. from both hotel customers and winery visitors), have important implications for winery and hotel owners/operators.

First, since (in)congruence perceptions – between a postmodernist hotel and its historic landscape, visitors' self-image, and the winery's brand image – improved visitors' arousal, delight and behavioral intentions, wineries and similar hospitality companies should carefully plan the design of their new buildings so that they produce strong impressions in the eyes of consumers. This, in turn, will lead to heightened emotions and behavioral intentions (e.g. spread positive word-of-mouth, recommend the winery, and desire to visit the winery again).

Moreover, winery operators should do everything they can to improve the reputation, reviews and perceived quality of their wineries and wines, since these factors were found to significantly affect tourists' number of visits and revisit intentions. With respect to the various services and amenities offered at Marqués de Riscal, the winery should focus on delivering amazing winery tour/wine tasting experiences and an overall ambiance that positively impacts visitor satisfaction. The winery should also try to improve their marketing and service efforts toward 'less satisfied' customer segments (e.g. younger, male, and Spanish) in order to increase their satisfaction. Indeed, despite the fact that Spanish visitors tended to visit the winery more frequently than tourists from North America, the latter tended to have higher revisit intentions. Despite this, it was revealed that winery tourists' revisit intentions tend to decline after a certain number of visits. However, the more winery tourists are satisfied with their visits, the less rapidly their revisit intentions tend to decrease over time. Hence, wineries should not only focus on delivering exceptional wine tastings and tours for their visitors, but they should provide such services within an attractive and/or unique servicescape in order for tourists to return more frequently.

Lastly, the findings revealed that not only the substantive servicescape of a hotel impacts customers' positive affect, satisfaction, and behavioral intentions, but that the communicative servicescape plays a major role as well. As a result, hoteliers should prioritize the design of their hotels and also pay close attention to their communicative servicescape, which includes (a) how employees communicate with customers and requires good staff training, and (b) cultural elements of the guest experience. Since the stunning architecture of the Hotel Marqués de Riscal was likely to have less impact on guests familiar with Frank Gehry's architecture, the hotel's management team should therefore ensure high levels of staff training for quality staff/guest interactions and top notch staff presentation.

Summary

♦ The perceived (in)congruence between the architecture of a post-modernist hotel, the local landscape, visitors' self-image and the winery's brand image positively affects visitors' arousal and delight. Arousal influences delight and both of these emotions significantly increase winery visitors' behavioral intentions.

♦ Both substantive and communicative servicescape improve hotel customers' positive affect, which has a positive influence on satisfaction, which in turn significantly increases behavioral intentions.

♦ Architectural and brand familiarity moderate the relationship between substantive servicescape and positive affect, with the influence being greater for participants with low brand and architectural familiarity than for those with high familiarity.

♦ Among tourists' motivations, the reputation, reviews and perceived quality of the Marqués de Riscal winery and its wines significantly affect the number of visits and revisit intentions, while media exposure affects revisit intentions.

♦ While visitors' geographic proximity to the winery increases the number of visits, distance from it increases revisit intentions.

♦ There is a decline in winery visitors' revisit intentions after a certain number of visits. However, the more winery visitors are satisfied with their visits, the less their revisit intentions tend to decrease over time.

◆ Winery tour/wine tasting and the overall ambiance of the winery positively impact visitors' satisfaction, as well as tourists' age, gender, and country of residence.

References

Ajzen, I. (1985). From intentions to actions: A theory of planned behavior. In Kuhl, J. & Beckmann, J. (Eds.), *Action Control* (11-39). Berlin: Springer.

Anderson, J.C. & Gerbing, D.W. (1988). Structural equation modeling in practice: A review and recommended two-step approach. *Psychological Bulletin*, **103**(3), 411-423.

Anderson, J.C. & Gerbing, D.W. (1992). Assumptions and comparative strengths of the two-step approach: Comment on Fornell and Yi. *Sociological Methods & Research*, **20**(3), 321-333.

Baker, J, Levy, M. & Grewal, D. (1992). An experimental approach to making retail store environmental decisions. *Journal of Retailing*, **68**(4), 445-460.

Beldona, S., Miller, B., Francis, T. & Kher, H. V. (2015). Commoditization in the U.S. lodging industry: Industry and customer perspectives. *Cornell Hospitality Quarterly*, **56**(3), 298-308.

Berlyne, D.E. (1970). Novelty, complexity, and hedonic value. *Perception & Psychophysics*, **8**(5), 279-286.

Bitner, M.J. (1992). Servicescapes: The impact of physical surroundings on customers and employees. *Journal of Marketing*, **56**(2), 57-71.

Brown, G.P., Havitz, M.E. & Getz, D. (2006). Relationship between wine involvement and wine related travel. *Journal of Travel and Tourism Marketing*, **21**(1), 31-46.

Bruwer, J. & Alant, K. (2009). The hedonic nature of wine tourism consumption: An experiential view. *International Journal of Wine Business Research*, **21**(3), 235-257.

Chang, K.-C. (2016). Effect of servicescape on customer behavioral intentions: Moderating roles of service climate and employee engagement. *International Journal of Hospitality Management*, **53**, 116-128.

Cohen, E. & Ben-Nun, L. (2009). The important dimensions of wine tourism experience from potential visitors' perception. *Tourism and Hospitality Research*, **9**(1), 20-23.

Coombs, C.H. & Avrunin, G.S. (1977). Single-peaked functions and the theory of preference. *Psychological Review*, **84**(2), 216.

Dong, P. & Siu, N.Y.-M. (2013). Servicescape elements, customer predispositions and service experience: The case of theme park visitors. *Tourism Management*, **36**, 541-551.

Donovan, R. J & Rossiter, J. R. (1982). Store atmosphere: An environmental psychology approach. *Journal of Retailing, **58**(1), 34-57.

Durna, U., Dedeoglu, B.B. & Balikçioglu, S. (2015). The role of servicescape and image perceptions of customers on behavioral intentions in the hotel industry. *International Journal of Contemporary Hospitality Management, **27**(7), 1728-1748.

Escalas, J. & Bettman, J. (2005). Self-construal, reference groups and brand meaning. *Journal of Consumer Research, **32**(3), 378-389.

Explore Spice Route (2018). Retrieved from www.spiceroute.co.za, 02/03/2019

Fayed, H.A.K., Wafik, G.M. & Gerges, N.W. (2016). The impact of motivations, perceptions and satisfaction on tourists' loyalty. *International Journal of Hospitality & Tourism Systems, **9**(2), 14-25.

Galak, J., Kruger, J. & Loewenstein, G. (2013). Slow down! Insensitivity to rate of consumption leads to avoidable satiation. *Journal of Consumer Research, **39**(5), 993-1009.

GBSB Global Business School (2017). *Enotourism: The growth of wine tourism in Spain.* Retrieved from www.global-business-school.org/announcements/enotourism-growth-of-wine-tourism-spain, 19/06/2018

Getz, D. & Brown, G. (2006). Critical success factors for wine tourism regions: A demand analysis. *Tourism Management, **27**(1), 146-158.

Gilboa, S. & Rafaeli, A. (2003). Store environment, motions and approach behaviour: applying environmental aesthetics to retailing. *International Review of Retail, Distribution and Consumer Research, **13**, 195-211.

Hair Jr, J.F., Hult, G.T.M., Ringle, C. & Sarstedt, M. (2011). PLS-SEM: Indeed a silver bullet. *Journal of Marketing Theory and Practice, **19**(2), 139-151.

Hedgecoe, G. & Whittle, H. (2012). Bilbao's Guggenheim continues to divide. *Deutsche Welle.* Retrieved from www.dw.com/en/bilbaos-guggenheim-continues-to-divide/a-15904659, 19/06/2018.

I-Escape.com (n.d.). *Hotel Marques de Riscal: Elciego, The Basque Country, Spain.* Retrieved from: www.i-escape.com/hotel-marques-de-riscal, 19/06/2018.

Instituto Nacional de Estadística. (2010). *Encuesta de ocupación hotelera.* Madrid: Instituto Nacional de Estadística.

IREA. (2008). *Informe Hoteles & Resorts, El mercado de inversión hotelera en España.* Madrid: IREA.

Kandampully, J. & Suhartanto, D. (2000). Customer loyalty in the hotel industry: The role of customer satisfaction and image. *International Journal of Contemporary Hospitality Management, **12**(6), 346-351.

Kearney, T., Kennedy, A. & Coughlan, J. (2007). *Servicescapes: A review of contemporary empirical research*. Sixteenth Annual Frontiers in Service Conference, San Francisco, California.

Lin, I.Y. & Mattila, A.S. (2010). Restaurant servicescape, service encounter, and perceived congruency on customers' emotions and satisfaction. *Journal of Hospitality Marketing & Management*, **19**, 819-841.

Loureiro, S.M.C. & Kastenholz, E. (2011). Corporate reputation, satisfaction, delight, and loyalty towards rural lodging units in Portugal. *International Journal of Hospitality Management*, **30**(3), 575-583.

Meagher, D. (2014). The Gehry effect transforms a city. *Weekend Australian*. Retrieved from www.theaustralian.com.au/life/wish/the-gehry-effect-transforms-a-city/story-e6frg8io-1227114764412, 19/06/2018

Mehrabian, A. & Russell, J. A. (1974). *An Approach to Environmental Psychology*. Cambridge, MA: The MIT Press.

Michael, C. (2015, April 30). The Bilbao effect: Is 'starchitecture' all it's cracked up to be? A history of cities in 50 buildings, day 27. *The Guardian*. Retrieved from www.theguardian.com/cities/2015/apr/30/bilbao-effect-gehry-guggenheim-history-cities-50-buildings, 19/06/2018

Oliver, R.L. (1999). Value as excellence in the consumption experience. In: M. B. Holbrook, (Ed.), *Consumer Value: A Framework for Analysis and Research*. London: Routledge.

Oliver, R.L., Rust, R.T. & Varki, S. (1997). Customer delight: Foundations, findings, and managerial insight. *Journal of Retailing*, **73**(3), 311-336.

Ping, R.A., Jr. (1994). Does satisfaction moderate the association between alternative attractiveness and exit intention in a marketing channel? *Journal of the Academy of Marketing Science*, **22**(4), 364-371.

Redden, J.P. (2008). Reducing satiation: The role of categorization level. *Journal of Consumer Research*, **34**(5), 624-634.

Sharma, S., Durand, R.M. & Gur-Arie, O. (1981). Identification and analysis of moderator variables. *Journal of Marketing Research*, **18**(3), 291-300.

Solomon, M.R. (1983). The role of products as social stimuli: A symbolic interactionism perspective. *Journal of Consumer Research*, **10**(3), 319-29.

Sparks, B. (2006). Planning a wine tourism vacation? Factors that help to predict tourist behavioral intentions. *Tourism Management*, **28**(5), 1180-1192.

Spier Wine Farm (2018). Retrieved from www.spier.co.za, 19/06/2018

Stoddard, J.E., and Clopton, S.W. (2015). Exploring the differences between new and repeat visitors to North Carolina wineries: Implications for winery marketing strategy development. *Journal of Wine Research*, **26**(3), 225-240.

Tai, S.H.C. & Fung, A.M.C. (1997). Application of an environmental psychology model to in-store buying behaviour. *The International Review of Retail, Distribution and Consumer Research,* **7**(4), 311-337.

Turley, L.W. & Milliman, R.E. (2000). Atmospheric effects on shopping behavior: A review of the experimental evidence. *Journal of Business Research,* **49**(2), 193-211.

Vila, M., Enz, C. & Costa, G. (2012). Innovative practices in the Spanish hotel industry. *Cornell Hospitality Quarterly,* **53**(1), 75-85.

Wang, J., Novemsky, N. & Dhar, R. (2009). Anticipating adaptation to products. *Journal of Consumer Research,* **36**(2), 149-159.

14 Understanding memorable enogastronomic experiences: A qualitative approach

*Arlindo Madeira, Antónia Correia and
José António Filipe*

The objectives of this chapter are to:

☐   Introduce those factors that make a memorable enogastronomic experience for tourists visiting a destination;

☐   Present qualitative findings that reveal that gastronomy and wines play a major role in the way that visitors experience a destination and indicate that some travellers would return to the same destination to savour its unique gastronomy.

Keywords: Food, wine, tourism, enogastronomy, memorable experiences.

Introduction

In recent decades, studies related to the culinary arts and wine have been receiving increasing attention from researchers in fields such as sociology, anthropology and tourism (Mason & Paggiaro, 2012). Gastronomy can be understood as an 'art of living', the possession of skills and knowledge relating to food and drink and to their choice, which enhances the pleasure and enjoyment of eating and drinking (Santich, 2004). The fact that gastronomy (the art of selecting, preparing, serving and enjoying food) has been celebrated for centuries elucidates that eating-related pleasures go beyond nutrition and subsistence (Macht et al., 2005). Wine culture has also accompanied the history of humanity, being the most consensual drink (besides water) to pair with the majority of regional cuisines around the world (Harrington, 2005; Koone et al., 2014). In fact, wine has been giving people pleasure for over 8000 years (Charters,2006). Indeed, it may have been significant in human life even before bread was being made (McGovern et al., 2003).

There is a general perception of the link between the enjoyment of food and wine; as Louis Pasteur claimed, "a meal without wine is like a day without sunshine" (Pettigrew & Charters, 2006). A wider-ranging interpretation is given by Gillespie et al. (2002) who states that gastronomy is about the recognition of a variety of factors relevant to the foods and beverages eaten and consumed by a group, in a locality, region or even a nation. This interpretation helps to establish a connection between enogastronomy, tourism and development of niche travel and niche destinations (Kivela & Crotts, 2009).

It is now widely accepted that food and wine are an integral part of contemporary tourism (Cohen & Avieli, 2004; Henderson, 2009; Hillel et al., 2013; Hjalager & Richards, 2002). Enjoying food while travelling is not new, but the role of food in tourism has dramatically gained importance among tourism researchers in recent decades, going from an obvious necessity for travellers to the appearance of various tourism designations related with wine and gastronomy (Stone et al., 2017). Although, there is no agreement on a definition of food-related tourism, designations such as 'food', 'culinary', 'gourmet' and 'gastronomic' tourism mention beverages and wine in particular in their definitions (Okumus et al., 2007).

Nowadays, memorable enogastronomic experiences represent a new benchmark for destinations, and tourism businesses must seek to deliver these as they are pivotal to becoming and remaining competitive in the marketplace (Stone et al., 2017). Food and beverage experiences are crucial to destinations because they strongly influence feelings of involvement and place attachment (Henderson, 2009). Whatever the reason for visiting a tourist destination, enogastronomic experiences play a role in determining perceptions and satisfaction with the overall travel experience, influencing tourists' attitudes, decisions and behaviour (Macionis, 1998; Hjalanger & Corigliano, 2000). Understanding the visitor's enogastronomic memories is determinant, so the destinations must adapt to the preferences of the visitors (Björk & Kauppinen-Räisänen, 2016; Sthapit, 2017). Perceiving the elements that visitors experience most related to food and wine enables destinations to deliver experiences in which tourists are emotionally attached to the destination, which eventually influences their intentions of revisiting (Gross & Brown, 2006; Kivela & Crotts, 2006). Thus, it is crucial to understand what the elements are of the wine and food experiences that visitors most value during their stay.

Most of the existing studies on enogastronomic experiences use quantitative approaches, not allowing participants the opportunity to use their own words to describe the elements that have marked the experience (Carmichael, 2005; Cohen & Ben-Nun, 2009; Kivela & Crotts, 2006; Pikkemaat et al., 2009; Quadri-Felitti & Fiore, 2012). The use of qualitative methods in tourism-related research is useful because it allows the research process to be humanized, embodying the researcher, humanizing the research process and inviting more critical playfulness with data by including the visitor's own words (Wilson & Hollinshead, 2015). In this chapter, we intend to perceive which words are most used by visitors to express the feelings resulting from the experience in the destination visited.

Literature review

Enogastronomy

According to Kivela and Crotts (2006), gastronomy encompasses culinary elements (dishes, food and the methods to prepare them) as well as all that is related to enology, so local wines are considered as forming an integral part of a given type of gastronomy.

Gastronomy relates to the social, cultural and historical aspects of food and eating, encompassing the study of cuisines, restaurants and dining, food and wine matching, tourism and gastronomic writing (Santich, 2004). The fact that gastronomy is the expression of a region and its culture means that it can be used as a differentiating factor for a destination in an increasingly competitive global marketplace (Hall & Sharples, 2004). On the one hand, gastronomy is simply related to the hedonism of enjoying good food and drinks and on the other, it is a complex discipline that encompasses everything into which food enters, including all the things we eat and drink (Scarpato, 2003). This link between gastronomy and wine is called enogastronomy (Miranda & Tonetto, 2014; Corvo, 2016). This link is not only justified by the tradition of wine-producing countries in consuming wine with meals, but also by the chemistry of the elements; that is, wine in all its versions (white, red, rosé, fortified, late harvest and sparkling) is a natural option for paring with food and thus emphasizes the organoleptic properties of most regional cuisines (Harrington, 2008). In making a food and wine pairing choice, this effect is many times the ultimate objective – the wine and food combine to create a totally new and superior gastronomic effect (Harrington, 2008). Regardless of the type of tourism, food and wine have become important travel motivators in their own right, sometimes representing the primary attraction in a country or region (Henderson, 2009).

Definitions of gastronomy, wine and tourism

Food and tourism have a very close relationship and food is a critical tourism resource (Quan & Wang, 2004). It is vital for physical sustenance and all tourists have to eat when travelling, but food can be a major draw and primary motivator for some, which satisfies a multiplicity of physiological and other needs and wants (Tikkanen, 2007).

Gastronomy is classified as the primary motivation for tourists who travel specifically to experiment with the local cuisine or to taste the dishes of a celebrity chef, and as a secondary motivation when the tourist considers the local cuisine as an important option, but not the only one among other attractions available in the chosen destination. (Lopez-Guzman & Sanchez-Canizares, 2012). Tourist food consumption is a unique form of eating in a foreign context (Cohen & Avieli, 2004). Local food consumption can connect tourists with a destination's landscape and unique way of life (Mason & Paggiaro, 2012), cultural impressions and insights (Andersson et al., 2017) and local people (Baldacchino, 2015). As pointed out by several authors, there is a natural connection between wine and food that leads to enogastronomic experiences (Hjalager & Richards, 2002; Mitchell & Hall, 2003; Wolf, 2014). Designations such as food tourism, cuisine tourism, gastronomic tourism, culinary tourism or gourmet tourism mention the integration of gastronomy and wine, which suggests that contemporary travellers search for unique enogastronomic experiences (Table 14.1).

Table 14.1: Definitions around gastronomy, wine and tourism

Designations	Definition	Based on
Food tourism	A visit to primary and secondary food producers, food festivals, restaurants and specific locations for which food tasting and/or experiencing attributes of special food production region are the primary motivation factor for travel.	Hall et al,1996; Wolf,2006; Hall & Sharples,1998; Hall & Macionis,1998; Hall & Sharples,2003; Henderson,2009;
Wine tourism	A visit to vineyards, wineries, wine festivals and wine shows, for which wine tasting and/or experiencing the attributes of a wine region are the prime motivating factors for visitors.	Hall et al.,2000; Getz,2000; Charters & Al-Knight,2002; Stewart et al.,2008; Bruwer & Alant,2009
Gastronomic tourism	This refers to a wider interest in food and wine, which may include expensive products, typically related to interest in the broader dimensions of wine and food and the cultures and landscapes that produce them.	Hjalager & Corigliano, 2000; Richards,2015;Sims,2009; Kivela & Crotts,2006; Smith & Costello, 2009
Cuisine tourism	A similar concept to gastronomic tourism, although it reflects special interests in specific types of cuisine, whether national or regional.	Scarpato & Daniele,2003; Ignatov & Smith,2006; Hall & Mitchell, 2007; Wolf,2014
Gourmet tourism	Characterized by visits to expensive, and/or highly rated restaurants, wineries and gastronomic festivals, with the participation of renowned Chefs. Usually includes tasting expensive and exclusive products.	Hall & Sharples,2003; Hall et al.,2003; Hall & Mitchell, 2007; Beer, Ottenbacher & Harringtom, 2012;
Culinary Tourism	It refers not only to gastronomy, but also to the social context in which food is prepared, and implies a transfer of knowledge about the people, culture, traditions and identity of the place visited. In this typology, wine and /or culinary-related experiences contribute significantly to the reason for travelling to the destination.	Cohen & Avieli,2004; Hall & Mitchel,2007; López-Guzmán & Sánchez-Cañizares,2012; Sohn & Yuan,2013; Stone, Migacz & Wolf, 2018

Memorable enogastronomic experiences

Gastronomy is not just about the consumption of food products, but also involves an experience composed of food, wine heritage and landscape (Mason & Paggiaro, 2012).

Memorable tourism experiences have primarily considered a destination or trip as a whole, but individual elements (such as dining or drinking) are the source of many memories (Stone et al., 2017). Indeed, experiencing the food of destinations, whether it is the aromas, tasting, or gazing upon the preparation is an integral aspect of tourism (Gregorash, 2018). Nowadays, gastronomy is part of tourism products and is being used to attract more tourists (Robinson & Getz, 2014). Gastronomy and wine offer a myriad of differentiation opportunities for destinations (Chang et al., 2011). In fact, gastronomy experiences have increasingly been promoted as a combined 'attraction' by many destinations (Kivela & Crotts, 2006; Stewart et al., 2008). Thus, food and drink experiences can strongly impact the development and crystallization of destination image (Harrington & Ottenbacher, 2013). Memorable food and drink experiences are linked to an increase in travel satisfaction and positive word of mouth (Stone et al., 2017). Food and drink related memories can make tourists emotionally attached to the destination, enhancing their level of involvement with it and eventually influencing revisit intentions (Sthapit, 2017). Once they experience local gastronomy, travellers express a higher level of attachment to the destination, as food unites visitors with the local culture (Tsai, 2016). From the earliest studies on food tourism or culinary tourism, the authors refer to the importance of food and drink experiences during the stay at the destination. Long (2004) used the term 'culinary tourism' for the first time to express the idea of experiencing other cultures through food. Wolf (2002), however, defines culinary and gastronomy tourism as travel in order to search for and enjoy prepared food and drink and unique and memorable gastronomic experiences. These culinary or gastronomic experiences are based on the consumption of autochthonous foods, original and authentic dishes, representing the local food culture (Björk & Kauppinen-Räisänen, 2016). The consumption of local food elicits emotional reactions, both positive and negative, such as anger, disappointment, happiness, joy, pleasure and excitement (Mak et al., 2012). Travel often provides this element of novelty by presenting varied food in varied settings with different people (Stone et al., 2017).

Tasting novel foods during a holiday is a mark of an authentic experience that most visitors crave to participate in (Wijaya et al., 2013). Enogastronomic experiences have the power to modify the food preferences and tastes of the visitors, as well as to allow them to experience the culture and customs of the destination (Kivela & Crotts, 2006; Kivela & Crotts, 2009). Culinary and gastronomic 'experience-scapes' serve as suitable settings for evoking emotions such as those related to consumption (Sthapit, 2017). This suggests that feelings and memories consuming food and beverages when on holiday are very special and attractive, because they become transposed into experiences that are often very personal (Stone et al., 2017). Experiences stored in the human memory are of great importance, as travellers often reflect on their trip experiences (Sthapit, 2017). Furthermore, the symbolic and emotional components of meals may be intensified during travel and thus add to the perceived clarity of the memories in the context of the experience (Lashley et al., 2003).

The elements of memorable enogastronomic experiences

Today, memorable experiences represent a new benchmark that destination managers and tourism businesses must seek to deliver (Kim et al., 2012). However, little is known about the elements that contribute to the memorability of tourists' enogastronomic experiences. For Schmitt (2010), the elements that compose the experience result from the interaction of sensory (sense), affective (feeling), cognitive (thinking), behavioural (acts) and social (relating). Many authors have studied the experiences related to food and wine, from the Pine & Gimore's (1999) experience economy model, based on the four E's of the experience (Carmichael, 2005; Pikkemaat et al., 2009; Quadri-Felitti & Fiore, 2013). Björk and Kauppinen-Räisänen (2014) concluded that food experiences are multidimensional in nature and unfold into five characterizing dimensions: food, social behaviour, external environment, service place and time. Quan and Wang (2004) state that the major motive for this type of tourism is to search for novelty and change in food consumption. Hansen et al. (2005) highlight the design, the atmosphere and social interaction where the experience happens as determinants of the enogastronomic experience. For Kim et al. (2012), there are seven decisive factors for a memorable gastronomic experience: hedonism, involvement, local culture, refreshment, meaningfulness, knowledge and novelty. Chandralal and Valenzuela's (2013) study showed that experiencing actual local lifestyle, food, cultures, hospitality, social interactions, staff professionalism, novelty and surprises makes an experience memorable. Sthapit's (2017) study revealed that a memorable gastronomic experience would often be recalled through seven experiential dimensions: local specialties and food attributes (taste), authenticity, novelty, togetherness and social interaction, hospitality and servicescape (including food souvenirs). Richards (2015), describes in detail the elements that define enogastronomic experience: the food and beverages products, eating practices, the art and customs of preparing and eating, the origins of food, the sensory elements (taste, smell, touch, look), the food preparation (techniques of cooking), the origins of food (organic food, ethnic cuisines, locally produced food, etc.), forms of serving (fast food, slow food, street food, etc.) and the context in which it is served and consumed (restaurants, bars, markets, food quarters, streets, etc.). For Stone, et al. (2017), the elements that define a memorable food and drink experience include a particular food or drink, the location or setting (where the experience occurred), companions (social interactions among visitors), the occasion and the touristic elements (authenticity, novelty or nostalgia). From the review of the literature, a table is presented with the most relevant enogastronomic experiential elements mentioned by the authors.

Table 14.2: Possible elements that define memorable enogastronomic experiences

Elements	Definition	Based on
Wine and food	Wine and food are identify by several authors as 'la raison d'être' of food related tourism. Tourists travel to destinations to experience food or drink in intense ways.	Henderson (2009); Wolf (2006); Hjalager & Richards (2002); Hall & Mitchell (2004); Kivela & Crotts (2006); Smith & Costello (2009); Tsai (2016)
Hedonism	The hedonic consumption paradigm suggests that in many situations consumers seek fun, amusement, fantasy, arousal, sensory stimulation and enjoyment.	Getz (2000); Hall & Sharples 2003); Kivela & Crotts (2006); Bruwer & Alant (2009); Sthapit (2017)
Local food culture	Food culture is heavily imbued with elements of cultural capital. Local food culture is a means to express a destination's culinary identity, cultural heritage, shared gastronomy value, and lifestyle of a place.	Ignatov & Smith (2006); Sims (2009); Kim, Ritchie & McCormick (2012); Bessière (2013); Fieldhouse (2013); Lai, Khoo-Lattimore & Wang (2018)
Design/ atmosphere	Facilitates immersion into the food and drink experiences through the use of design elements, architecture, art and intimacy, and the landscape where the experience happens.	Hansen, Jensen & Gustafsson (2005); Kim (2014); Stone et al., (2017);
Service quality	Service quality is recognized by travelers when the staff is hospitable, courteous, helpful, friendly and willing to exceed their duties.	Thach & Olsen (2006); O'Neill & Charters (2006); Chang, Kivela & Mak (2011), Chandralal & Valenzuela (2013); Kim (2014)
Social interaction	Relates to whether food and drink experiences foster social interaction between visitors and residents, as well as visitors and their travelling party.	Hansen, Jensen & Gustafsson (2005); Carmichael (2005); Chandralal & Valenzuela (2013); Sthapit (2017)
Novelty	Refers to the extent to which local food/drink experiences provide an intensification of daily life experiences by offering novel, fresh and original features.	Kim, Ritchie & McCormick (2012); Chandralal & Valenzuela (2013); Quan & Wang (2014); Stone et al. (2017)

Authenticity	Connotes traditional culture and a sense of genuineness. The sense of authenticity is also related to tasting local products (food and beverages). Travellers are typically motivated by a desire to experience the 'real' life of the local people.	Sims (2009); Chang, Kivela & Mac (2011); Björk & Kauppinen-Räisänen (2014); Richards (2015); Sthapit (2017);
Involvement	Enhances not only an individual's sensitivity to certain activities and his or her perception of a particular activity's importance, but also enhances the individual's commitment to specific services or places.	Lockshin & Spawton (2001); Hall & Mitchell (2004); Sparks (2007); Bruwer & Alant (2009); Kim, Ritchie & McCormick (2012)
Education	Plays a fundamental role in creating memories and consequent satisfaction among visitors when learning about food, wine and its production, about history, culture and gastronomy.	Charters & Ali-Knight (2000); Thach & Olsen (2006); Getz & Carlsen (2008); Bruwer & Alant (2009); Fountain & Charters (2010); Quadri-Felitti & Fiore (2013)
Entertain-ment	Occurs when the tourists participate actively or passively in a series of cultural and educational activities.	Ali-Knight & Carlsen (2003); Carmichael (2005); Oh et al. (2007); Quadri-Felitti & Fiore (2013); Carlsen & Boksberger (2015)

Methodology

The objective of this study is to understand what are the determinant elements of enogastronomic tourist experiences, from the visitor's perspective. The work describes visitors' enogastronomic experiences through their declarations. Data was collected in 2017, face-to-face from visitors aged above 18 years old in 16 wineries established in the Lisbon wine region (Portugal). Lisbon has a very rich and diverse local cuisine which is complemented with wines produced in the newly created wine region. The Lisbon wine region is composed of nine denominations (or sub-regions), grouped into three characteristic blocks. The south, near Lisbon, with the denominations of Bucelas, Colares and Carcavelos. In the centre of the region loom the denominations of Alenquer, Arruda, Lourinhã, Obidos and Torres Vedras, while in the north stands Encostas d'Aire. There are only a few sub-routes (Oeste, Alenquer, Colares, Bucelas and Carcavelos) which are characterized by initiatives of some local producers. At the end of data collection, 314 complete questionnaires were obtained. The first step was to analyse the answers obtained through the questionnaires with NVivo software. The second step, named the 'open coding process', aimed to open up respondents' description data by fragmenting it, identifying the experience elements and using constant comparison to scrutinize the data for every meaning (Glaser, 1992). The coding process conceptualizes "data by constant comparison of incident with incident, and incident with concept, to emerge more categories and their properties" (Glaser, 1992). *Constant comparison* is "the exploration of similarities and differences across incidents in data" (Goulding, 2002) and occurs where incidents are coded for properties and categories that connect them (Glaser, 1992). Initial codes are labelled "to generate concepts" which are "clustered into descriptive categories" (Goulding, 2002). Once concepts have been identified they are analysed in more depth and are grouped under more abstract "higher order" concepts (Strauss & Corbin, 1998). At this stage, incidents are compared to incidents recalled from experience, memos written during the data collection and analysis process and from the literature.

This systematic comparison sensitizes the researcher to properties and dimensions in the data that might have been overlooked (Strauss & Corbin, 1998). The third step was word counting, illustrated through 'word clouds' which allow an easy and objective reading of the results. A word cloud, also called a 'tag cloud' or 'weighted list', is a visual depiction of the frequency tabulation of the words in any selected written material in which the more frequently used words are effectively highlighted by occupying more prominence in the representation (Miley & Read, 2011). Word clouds can be useful tools for preliminary analysis and for validation of previous findings (McNaught & Lam, 2010). All the samples obtained need to be considered as convenience samples. This is a qualitative follow-up study by Madeira, Correia and Filipe (2019), also carried out in Lisbon, with the aim of defining a conceptual model that structures the boundaries and variables that pave enogastronomic experiences.

Findings

Sociodemographic profile of the sample

Data was collected from questionnaires applied to tourists who visited Lisbon wine producers with the purpose of having enogastronomic experiences. The majority of respondents were reported to be males (63.7%), holding a college degree (44.2%) or a master's or doctoral degree (25.8%). Respondents were divided between foreign visitors (51.9%), and Portuguese (44.9%). Further, the majority of them declared that they were in Portugal to experience gastronomy and wines (70.4%). Furthermore, the vast majority stated that they had already visited Portugal or other countries for the purpose of tasting gastronomy and wines (70.4%). In addition, most respondents were repeat visitors (68.8%) and travelled with friends (35.7%), family (37.9%), or in group (20.1%).

Table 14.3: Socio-demographic characteristics of the sample (n=314)

	Frequency	Valid Percent		Frequency	Valid Percent
Are you over 18?			**Education Level**		
Valid Yes	314	100	High school or lower	60	19.1
Gender			College	146	46.5
Male	200	63.7	Bachelor´s	28	8.9
Female	114	36.3	Master or PhD	80	25.5
Are you in Portugal to experience W & G?			**Repeat visit**		
No	93	29.6	No	98	31.2
Yes	221	70.4	Yes	216	68.8
Repeat visit?			**Travel companion**		
No	98	31.2	Alone	15	4.8
Yes	216	68.8	Family	119	37.9
Nationalities			Groups	64	20.3
Portuguese	141	44.9	Friends	112	.35.7
Foreigners	173	55.1	Missing	4	1.3

What do enogastro tourists value the most?

From the descriptions in answer to the open-ended questions made to visitors, it was possible to analyse the contents according to the elements that define the memorable experiences, researched in the literature review. After that, using line-by-line coding, descriptions which had similar features or core categories as described in the codebook created for this research in relation to the ten elements were grouped together and then put in one type and those with other features into another type and so on (Table 14.4). Line-by-line coding helps the researcher to take an analytic stance towards their work (Charmaz, 1996).

Table 14.4: The line-by-line coding process

Line-by-line coding	Selective coding	Main experiential elements
"Fresh products and well prepared. It is not the most popular gastronomy but it is very good. Good seafood and fish. Good restaurant, service and wines and at a reasonable price".	Fresh, products, well prepared, gastronomy, good, seafood, fish, wines, price.	Wine and food
"Local gastronomy is one of my favorites. It's one of the reasons to come back to Portugal."	Local, gastronomy, favorite, reason, Portugal.	
"There are a lot of typical dishes from the regional cuisine, and others adapted from different regions. Lisbon is where the best restaurants are, with exception of the Algarve region".	Lisbon, Algarve, regional, cuisine, traditional dishes, adapted, restaurants.	Authenticity
"In Lisbon we had different experiences: in some cases modern cuisine and others traditional. All good in general."	Modern, traditional, cuisine, good, experiences.	
"What a good surprise. Today at the winery, we had homemade food. Amazing products prepared by a very creative Chef".	Good surprise, winery, homemade food, amazing products, prepared, creative, Chef.	Novelty
"it was really a nice discovery. Local gastronomy is much more rich and complex than just cod fish dishes and sardines".	Nice discovery, local gastronomy, rich, complex, cod fish, sardines.	
"Good and tasty gastronomy. An explosion of flavors, colors and textures".	Good, tasty gastronomy, explosion, flavors, colors, textures.	Hedonism
"Beautiful country, good food and excellent wines. A feast to the senses".	Beautiful country, good food, excellent wines, feast, senses.	
"Amazing modern winery with a modern architecture and beautiful design furniture that mixes contemporary and classic elements. The tasting room was perfectly integrated with the view"	Amazing, modern winery, architecture, design, furniture, contemporary, classic elements, dining room, perfectly, integrated, view.	Design/ atmosphere
"We loved the old winery in Colares. Seems that the time had stopped. It was the perfect atmosphere to taste old wines from this producer".	Loved, old winery, Colares, time, stopped, perfect atmosphere, taste, old wines, producer.	
"The Portuguese are irremediably related to the history of food, the recipes that led to the four corners of the world and the ingredients they brought to Europe. Also in the history of wine, the Portuguese have a prominent role, by the stories that relate to some of its most emblematic wines, such as Madeira, Carcavelos or Port wine".	Portuguese, history, recipes, world, ingredients, Europe, excellent, wine, food, emblematic, stories, gastronomy	Local food culture

Table 14.4: The line-by-line coding process (continued)

Quote	Codes	Category
"It is a country with excellent food and wine, a lot of history and culture that is also related to gastronomy and wines".	Country, excellent food, wine, history, culture, gastronomy, wines.	
"Yesterday we found a small restaurant, just by luck. It was such a nice place managed by a couple that welcomed us so well that we felt at home".	Small restaurant, nice place, welcomed, felt at home.	Service quality
"Portuguese cuisine is one of my favorites. fantastic fish and seafood. excellent wines and above all, great service. Yesterday, dinner in Lisbon. A classic restaurant that we always revisit when we're in Lisbon.	Portuguese cuisine, favorites, fantastic, excellent, great service, classic restaurant, revisited, Lisbon.	
"We come in an tour organized by the hotel, with people that we never had met before and all of them were so nice. The wine tasting was so much fun".	Tour, hotel, people, never met before, nice, wine tasting, fun.	Social interaction
"Dinner with friends at a *tasquinha* (typical small restaurant). simple, good. Genuine and tasty food in a very happy atmosphere".	Dinner, friends, restaurant, genuine, tasty food, happy atmosphere.	
"A very good experience. We chose a small producer to visit because usually it not so crowded and we can learn more about wines. The enologist was very knowledgeable about Portuguese wines".	Good experience, small producer, visit, learn about wines, knowledgeable enologist, Portuguese.	Education/ Knowledge
"Two nights ago we went to a Michelin starred restaurant. In the end, the maître invited us to meet the Chef, who is not only a good cook, but also a very knowledgeable person who explained us some techniques used".	Michelin star restaurant, Chef, good, knowledgeable, techniques explained.	
First time in Lisbon and I love it. It is a trendy and exciting city with a lot things to see and activities to participate in. We went to a winery and we had a very good experience: tasting the wines produced with some food and the enologist's explanation."	Lisbon, love, trendy, exciting city, activities, participate, winery, good experience, tasting food, wines, produced, enologist, explanation	Involvement
"I felt at home in Lisbon. Friendly people, great food and amazing wines and lots to see. We will definitely recommend a visit to our friends.	Home, Lisbon, friendly people, great food, amazing wines, recommend, visit, friends.	
"We had dinner at Adega Machado (fado restaurant). Good food, wine and good fado show".	Dinner, fado, restaurant, show, food, wine	Entertainment
"Yesterday, we had dinner in a small place in Bairro Alto. It was good with nice live music".	Dinner, place, good, live music	

From the review of the literature, eleven main elements were considered in order to analyse memorable enogastronomic experiences: food and wine (Hall & Mitchell, 2007; Kivela & Crotts, 2006), authenticity (Sims, 2009; Richards, 2015), novelty (Bruwer & Alant, 2009; Chandralal & Valenzuela, 2013; Stone et al., 2017), hedonism (Hall & Sharples 2003;), design and atmosphere (Hansen et al., 2005); Kim, 2014), service quality (Thach & Olsen, 2006; Kim, 2014), social interaction (Hansen et al., 2005; Sthapit, 2017), education and knowledge (Charters & Ali-Knight (2000); Fountain & Charters, 2010), involvement (Kim et al., 2012; Sparks, 2007;), food culture (Ignatov & Smith, 2006; Lai et al., 2018) and entertainment (Quadri-Felitti & Fiore, 2013; Carlsen & Boksberger, 2015). Three word clouds were then composed from the analyses of 6654 words. The first word cloud (Figure 14.1) is organized from the visitors' opinions regarding destination cuisine. The question raised was "How would you describe the cuisine at this destination?". From the answers given it is possible to summarize the words most mentioned by respondents. The word 'good', without specifying any particular connection, appears in the cloud as the most cited by the respondents. This result can be explained by the fact that the word in question is an adjective, synonymous of something positive, used to express different ideas such as:

"Good fresh fish and shellfish. Good wines. I don't eat meat, because I am vegetarian."

"Good cuisine with soul, using good local products."

Figure 14.1: Word cloud from the local cuisine opinion

Results also suggest that words such as 'diverse', 'exotic', 'intense', 'elegant', 'amazing', 'sophisticated', and 'surprisingly' may be related with sensations of novelty in the descriptions. In addition, words like 'tasty', 'delicious', 'comfort' and 'flavors' can be associated with hedonism, as the respondents' words stated:

"We had dinner a restaurant in Chiado with an elegant and sophisticated cuisine. It was an amazing experience".

"I'm enjoying local gastronomy very much. Fish and seafood are very tasty and fresh, cooked in a simple way".

"Local cuisine is exotic and very tasty. I have tasted the best fish I remember".

"I find local cuisine surprisingly tasty, with good products at a reasonable price".

Other words that stand out were 'rich', 'fresh', 'products', 'identity', 'genuine', 'creative', 'gastronomy' and 'chefs' which it is easy to relate to the attributes of any regional cuisine. Some descriptions of the interviewees reinforce the idea of respondents' opinions about the local cuisine and what gives it a character of authenticity, while the words 'culture', 'history' and 'Mediterranean' connect with culture and local food history:

"Rich cuisine, full of identity that not only uses excellent products but also cooks it in a genuine way".

"The cuisine is evolutive, modern and tasty, interpreted by a new generation of young and creative chefs".

"Mediterranean-based cuisine, full of history with lots of flavor and a mixture of ingredients".

"The gastronomy of Lisbon is in its essence a mixture of gastronomic cultures, brought from other parts of the country and also of dishes created by people who came from other countries".

The second word cloud (Figure 14.2) relates to the views of visitors connected with the experience of eating out at the destination. The question asked was "What do you remember from your last experience of eating out?". The word that stands out most is Portuguese. This may be explained by the fact that the study was carried out in Portugal:

"I really like Portuguese cuisine. It has some similarities with ours (Spanish). Very well-seasoned and nicely presented".

"…When dining out I have a tendency to revisit the typical Portuguese dishes, which can be presented in a more modern way".

Also, there are many words that allude to the food consumed in the restaurant visited, such as: 'codfish', 'seabass', 'roasted lamb', 'suckling pig' and so on. There is also a set of words where 'wine' is identified, which suggests the relationship between food and this beverage during the consumption of the meal:

"I tried the roasted lamb with a full bodied red Douro. It was delicious".

"From my last eating out experience I remember the tasty traditional codfish and good local wine".

"My last experience was a tasting menu (12 dishes) in a fine dining restaurant with wine pairing".

Figure 14.2: Word cloud from the eating out experience

The words 'fado' and 'show' suggest that some restaurants had entertainment activities for the guests. Furthermore, the words 'service, 'staff' and 'welcoming' suggest the importance of quality of service in memorable experiences:

"We had dinner at a fado restaurant. Good food, wine and good fado music".

"A fado restaurant, good show, good food but not excellent with ordinary and expensive wines".

"Our last dining out was in the hotel restaurant good experience of modern Portuguese cuisine with good wine and excellent service".

"In our last dining experience, the food was ok, not enough for the expected standards. Service was kind and courteous".

Finally, the words 'friends' and 'group' leads us to the importance of social interaction during the experience:

"From the last dinner experience, I remember the camaraderie between the group, the atmosphere of the restaurant, the good service and the full satisfaction, justified by the quality of the food, which combined with the other interactions caused a feeling of well-being".

"Today in a "tasquinha" (tavern) with childhood friends. Simple dishes that I keep in my mind when I'm not in Portugal".

Figure 14.3: Word cloud from respondents' points of view about the enogastronomic destination

The third word cloud (Figure 14.3) was based on the question "Do you have any other views about Portugal as a wine tourism destination?", which asked the respondents to express their opinion on other points about Portugal as an enogastronomic destination. Words that stand out were, unsurprisingly, 'wine', 'food', 'gastronomy', 'country', which are naturally related to the question, and words such as 'knowledgeable' and 'learning', leading to the notion of education during the experience:

"In Quinta do Sanguinhal we were received by the winemaker very knowledgeable about their wines. We tasted the wines with local food, accompanied by an explanation".

"We visited the property and sampled the wines in the winery with an explanation of each one. Learning about wine is a passion for me".

The words 'activities', 'vibrant', 'attractions', 'favorite', 'recommend' may be related with guests' involvement with the destination. Furthermore, words like 'design', 'landscape', and 'atmosphere' are associated with the creation of an atmosphere that favours a memorable experience, either through construction features or integration with the landscape:

"… The cellar had a modern design with excellent facilities, well integrated into the landscape".

"…We visit the Adega Cooperativa of Colares, which is integrated in a very beautiful landscape. The winery has an old architecture, which gives it a very special atmosphere".

"First time in Lisbon and I love it. It is a trendy and exciting city with lot things to see and activities to participate".

"I felt at home in Lisbon. Friendly people, great food, amazing wines and lots to see. We will definitely recommend a visit to our friends".

Conclusions

From the visitors' descriptions about their experiences regarding local cuisine, eating out and their points of view about Lisbon as an enogastronomic destination, it was possible to analyse each sentence through a coding process and each word, using the word cloud process. Qualitative results from the content analysis and the word clouds reveal that the most relevant elements of the gastronomic experience, according to the literature review, are present in this study. Thus, eleven main elements were identified: food and wine, hedonism, authenticity, novelty, design and atmosphere, service quality, social interaction, education and knowledge, involvement, local food culture and entertainment. Naturally, food and wine elements stand out, as well as the adjectives used to describe the local gastronomy. These are consistent with the essence of enogastronomic experiences, whose main objective is to taste food and drinks (mainly wine) and with the need to describe the sensations transmitted by these elements (Kivela & Crotts, 2006).

The search for pleasant sensations through the consumption of food and wine is also very present in the respondents statements, which leads us to the concept of hedonism (Bruwer & Alant, 2009). References to the local enogastronomy history and culture are also identified in the content analysis, which shows the importance of elements of the destination's culinary identity (Igantov & Smith, 2006). Novelty and authenticity are referred to by researchers as fundamental elements of the tourism experience related to food and wine, are also mentioned by the respondents of this study, in words that give the feeling of surprise about the characteristics of authenticity of the products tasted (Chandralal & Valenzuela, 2013; Richards, 2015).The importance of the creation of an atmosphere conducive to food consumption through design and architecture elements is equally present in respondents' statements (Kim, 2014). References to the live performance during the consumption of food and wine indicate the importance of entertainment during the enogastronomic experiences (Carlsen & Boksberger, 2015). Other descriptions report the importance of getting visitors involved with local activities or places during their enogastronomic visit, as a way of maximizing the experience (Kim et al., 2012). Finally, there are also elements related to the importance of quality of service, as well as social interaction and education within the experience-scape setting (Carmichael, 2005; Fountain & Charters, 2010; Thach & Olsen, 2006). Thus, this research shows the complexity of the elements that compose a memorable enogastronomic experience, which goes far beyond the core products (gastronomy and wines). Of course, each scenario where the experience occurs is unique, which can lead to different combinations of all these elements, that is, in some cases there are elements that stand out more than others and vice versa. The visitor's socio-demographic characteristics are equally important in the perception of the experience by the visitor. Therefore, we consider that future research should take into account the type of cuisine (traditional, contemporary), the type of service (fine dining, traditional restaurant), the type of entertainment provided and cultural factors of the demographic sample (there are cultures that give more importance to some elements of experiences to the detriment of others).

References

Andersson, T. , Mossberg, L., & Therkelsen, A. (2017). Food and tourism synergies: Perspectives on consumption, production and destination development. *Scandinavian Journal of Hospitality and Tourism*, **17**(1), 1-8, DOI: 10.1080/15022250.2016.1275290

Ali-Knight, J., & Carlsen, J. (2003). An exploration of the use of 'extraordinary' experiences in wine tourism. In *Colloquium in Wine Marketing*, Adelaide July (26-27).

Beer, C. L., Ottenbacher, M. C., & Harrington, R. J. (2012). Food tourism implementation in the Black Forest destination. *Journal of Culinary Science & Technology*, **10**(2), 106-128.

Baldacchino, G. (2015). Feeding the rural tourism strategy? Food and notions of place and identity. *Scandinavian Journal of Hospitality and Tourism*, **15**(1-2), 223-238.

Bessière, J. (2013). 'Heritagisation', a challenge for tourism promotion and regional development: an example of food heritage. *Journal of Heritage Tourism*, **8**(4), 275-291.

Björk, P. & Kauppinen-Räisänen, H. (2014). Culinary-gastronomic tourism–a search for local food experiences. *Nutrition & Food Science*, **44**(4), 294-309.

Bruwer, J. & Alant, K. (2009). The hedonic nature of wine tourism consumption: an experiential view. *International Journal of Wine Business Research*, **21**(3), 235-257.

Carlsen, J., & Boksberger, P. (2015). Enhancing consumer value in wine tourism. *Journal of Hospitality & Tourism Research*, **39**(1), 132-144.

Carmichael, B. (2005). Understanding the wine tourism experience for winery visitors in the Niagara region, Ontario, Canada. *Tourism Geographies*, **7**(2), 185-204.

Chandralal, L. & Valenzuela, R. (2013). Exploring memorable tourism experiences: Antecedents and behavioural outcomes. *Journal of Economics, Business and Management*, **1**(2), 177-181.

Chang, C., Kivela, J. & Mak, H. (2011). Attributes that influence the evaluation of travel dining experience: When East meets West. *Tourism Management*, **32**(2), 307-316.

Charmaz, K. (2006) *Constructing Grounded Theory, a practical guide through qualitative analysis*. London: Sage.

Charters, S. (2006). *Wine and Society: The social and cultural context of a drink*. Routledge.

Charters,S. & Ali-Knight, J. (2000).Wine tourism - a thirst for knowledge?. *International Journal of Wine Marketing*, **12**(3), 70-80.

Cohen, E. & Avieli, N. (2004). Food in tourism: Attraction and impediment. *Annals of Tourism Research*, **31**(4), 755-778.

Cohen, E., & Ben-Nun, L. (2009). The important dimensions of wine tourism experience from potential visitors' perception. *Tourism and Hospitality Research*, **9**(1), 20-31.

Corvo, P. (2016). *Food Culture, Consumption and Society*. Springer.

Fieldhouse, P. (2013). *Food and Nutrition: Customs and Culture*. Springer.

Fountain, J. & Charters, S. (2010). Generation Y as wine tourists: their expectations and experiences at the winery cellar door. In Beckendorff, P., Moscardo, G. & Pendergast, D (Eds.). *Tourism and Generation Y* (pp. 47-57). Location: CAB International.

Getz, D. (2000). *Explore Wine Tourism: Management, development & destinations*. Cognizant Communication Corporation.

Getz, D. & Carlsen, J. (2008). Wine tourism among Generations X and Y. *Turizam: međunarodni znanstveno-stručni časopis*, **56**(3), 257-269.

Gillespie, C., Cousins, J. & Pelham, P. (2002). European gastronomy into the 21st century. *Food Service Technology*, **2**(2), 107-107.

Glaser, B. (1992). *Basics of Grounded Theory Analysis: Emergence vs Forcing*. Sociology press.

Goulding, C. (2002). *Grounded Theory: A practical guide for management, business and market researchers*. Sage.

Gregorash, B. (2018). Examining gastronomic experiences using auto-driven photo-elicitation. In R. Nunkooo (Ed.), *Handbook of Research Methods for Tourism and Hospitality Management*, Cheltenham: Edward Elgar, pp. 212-221.

Gross, M. J., & Brown, G. (2006). Tourism experiences in a lifestyle destination setting: The roles of involvement and place attachment. *Journal of Business Research*, **59**(6), 696-700.

Hall, M, & Macionis, N. (1998). Wine tourism in Australia and New Zealand. In R. Butler, M. Hall, & J. Jenkins (Eds.), *Tourism and Recreation in Rural Areas*. Wiley.

Hall, M. & Mitchell, R. (2004). Consuming tourists: Food tourism consumer behaviour. In M. Hall, L. Sharples, R. Mitchell, N. Macionis & B.

Cambourne (Eds.), *Food Tourism around the World: Development, management and markets*. Oxford: Butterworth-Heinemann, 72-92.

Hall, M. & Mitchell, R. (2007). Gastronomic tourism: Comparing food and wine tourism experiences. In M. Novelli (Ed.) *Niche Tourism: Contemporary issues, trends and cases*, 87-102. Routledge.

Hall, M. & Sharples, L. (2003). The consumption of experiences or the experience of consumption? An introduction to the tourism of taste. In M. Hall, L. Sharples, R. Mitchell, N. Macionis & B. Cambourne (Eds.), *Food Tourism around the World: Development, management and markets*. Oxford: Butterworth-Heinemann.

Hall, M., Longo, M., Mitchell, R., & Johnson, G. (1996). Wine tourism in new Zealand. In *Proceedings of Tourism Down Under II: A research conference* (pp. 109-119). Dunedin: University of Otago.

Hall, M., Sharples, L., Cambourne, B. & Macionis, N. (eds) (2000) *Wine Tourism Around the World: Development, management and markets*. Oxford: Butterworth-Heinemann.

Hansen V., Jensen, Ø. & Gustafsson, I. (2005). The meal experiences of á la carte restaurant customers. *Scandinavian Journal of Hospitality and Tourism*, **5**(2), 135-151.

Harrington, R. (2005). The wine and food pairing process: Using culinary and sensory perspectives. *Journal of Culinary Science & Technology*, **4**(1), 101-112.

Harrington, R. & Ottenbacher, M. (2013). Managing the culinary innovation process: The case of new product development. *Journal of Culinary Science & Technology*, **11**(1), 4-18.

Henderson, J. (2009). Food tourism reviewed. *British Food Journal*, **111**(4), 317-326.

Hjalager, A. & Corigliano, M. (2000). Food for tourists – determinants of an image. *International Journal of Tourism Research*, **2**(4), 281-293.

Hjalager, A. & Richards, G. (2002). Still undigested: Research issues in tourism and gastronomy. In A. M. Hjalager & G. Richards (Eds.), *Tourism and Gastronomy*. London: Routledge.

Hillel, D., Belhassen, Y. & Shani, A. (2013). What makes a gastronomic destination attractive?. Evidence from the Israeli Negev, *Tourism Management*, **36**, 200-209.

Ignatov, E. & Smith, S. (2006). Segmenting Canadian culinary tourists. *Current Issues in Tourism*, **9**(3), 235.

Kim, J., Ritchie, B. & McCormick, B. (2012). Development of a scale to measure memorable tourism experiences. *Journal of Travel Research*, **51**(1), 12-25.

Kim, J. (2014). The antecedents of memorable tourism experiences: The development of a scale to measure the destination attributes associated with memorable experiences. *Tourism Management*, **44**, 34-45.

Kivela, J. & Crotts, J. (2006). Tourism and gastronomy: Gastronomy's influence on how tourists experience a destination. *Journal of Hospitality & Tourism Research*, **30** (3), 354-377.

Kivela, J. & Crotts, J. (2009). Understanding travelers' experiences of gastronomy through etymology and narration. *Journal of Hospitality & Tourism Research*, **33**(2), 161-192.

Koone, R., Harrington, R., Gozzi, M. & McCarthy, M. (2014). The role of acidity, sweetness, tannin and consumer knowledge on wine and food match perceptions. *Journal of Wine Research*, **25**(3), 158-174.

Lai, M., Khoo-Lattimore, C. & Wang, Y. (2018). A perception gap investigation into food and cuisine image attributes for destination branding from the host perspective: The case of Australia. *Tourism Management*, **69**, 579-595.

Lashley, C., Morrison, A. & Randall, S. (2003). Hospitality as an emotional experience: Exploring special meal occasions. In *Twelfth CHME Research Conference Proceedings*, 285-302.

Lockshin, L. & Spawton, T. (2001). Using involvement and brand equity to develop a wine tourism strategy. *International Journal of Wine Marketing*, **13** (1), 72-81.

Long, L. (2004), *Culinary Tourism*, Lexington: University Press of Kentucky.

López-Guzmán, T. & Sánchez-Cañizares, S. (2012). Culinary tourism in Córdoba (Spain). *British Food Journal*, **114**(2), 168-179.

Macht, M., Meininger, J. & Roth, J. (2005). The pleasures of eating: A qualitative analysis. *Journal of Happiness Studies*, **6** (2), 137-160.

Macionis, N. (1998). Wine and food tourism in the Australian capital territory: Exploring the links. *International Journal of Wine Marketing*, **10**(3), 5-22.

McGovern, P., Fleming, S. & Katz, S. (Eds.). (2003). *The Origins and Ancient History of Wine: Food and nutrition in history and anthropology*. Routledge.

McNaught, C. & Lam, P. (2010). Using Wordle as a supplementary research tool. *The Qualitative Report*, **15**(3), 630-643.

Mak, A., Lumbers, M., Eves, A. & Chang, R. (2012). Factors influencing tourist food consumption. *International Journal of Hospitality Management*, **31**(3), 928-936.

Mason, M. C. & Paggiaro, A. (2012). Investigating the role of festivalscape in culinary tourism: The case of food and wine events. *Tourism Management*, **33**(6), 1329-1336.

Miley, F. & Read, A. (2011). Using word clouds to develop proactive learners. *Journal of the Scholarship of Teaching and Learning*, **11**(2), 91-110.

Miranda, R. & Tonetto, L. (2014). Designing the immaterial: Design of pleasant experiences through enogastronomic stimuli. *Strategic Design Research Journal*, **7**(1), 15-22.

Mitchell, R., & Hall, M. (2003). Consuming tourists: Food tourism consumer behaviour. In C.M. Hall, L. Sharples., R. Mitchell, N. Macionis & B. Cambourne (eds.) *Food Tourism around the World: Development, management and markets*, 60-80.

Okumus, B., Okumus, F. & McKercher, B. (2007). Incorporating local and international cuisines in the marketing of tourism destinations: The cases of Hong Kong and Turkey. *Tourism Management*, **28**(1), 253-261.

O'Neill, M. & Charters, S. (2006). Service quality at the cellar door: A lesson in services marketing from Western Australia's wine-tourism sector. In Prideaux, B., Moscardo, G. and Laws, E. (Eds) *Managing Tourism and Hospitality Services: Theory and international applications*, CABI, Wallingford, 251-261.

Pettigrew, S. & Charters, S. (2006). Consumers' expectations of food and alcohol pairing. *British Food Journal*, **108**(3), 169-180.

Pikkemaat, B., Peters, M., Boksberger, P., & Secco, M. (2009). The staging of experiences in wine tourism. *Journal of Hospitality Marketing & Management*, **18**(2-3), 237-253.

Pine, J., & Gilmore, J. (1999). *The Experience Economy: Work is theatre & every business a stage.* Harvard Business Press.

Quadri-Felitti, D. & Fiore, A. (2013). Destination loyalty: Effects of wine tourists' experiences, memories, and satisfaction on intentions. *Tourism and Hospitality Research*, **13**(1), 47-62.

Quan, S. & Wang, N. (2004). Towards a structural model of the tourist experience: An illustration from food experiences in tourism. *Tourism management*, **25**(3), 297-305.

Richards, G. (2015). Evolving gastronomic experiences: From food to foodies to foodscapes. *Journal of Gastronomy and Tourism*, **1**(1), 5-17.

Robinson, R., & Getz, D. (2014). Profiling potential food tourists: An Australian study. *British Food Journal*, **116**(4), 690-706.

Santich, B. (2004). The study of gastronomy and its relevance to hospitality education and training. *International Journal of Hospitality Management*, **23**(1), 15-24.

Scarpato, R. (2003). Gastronomy as a tourist product: The perspective of gastronomy studies. In A.-M. Hjalager & G. Richards (eds.) *Tourism and Gastronomy* (pp. 65-84). Routledge.

Scarpato, R. & Daniele, R. (2003). New global cuisine: Tourism, authenticity and sense of place in postmodern gastronomy. In C.M. Hall, L. Sharples., R. Mitchell, N. Macionis & B. Cambourne (eds.) *Food Tourism around the World: Development, management and markets*, pp 296-313.

Sims, R. (2009). Food, place and authenticity: local food and the sustainable tourism experience. *Journal of Sustainable Tourism*, **17**(3), 321-336.

Smith, S. & Costello, C. (2009). Segmenting visitors to a culinary event: Motivations, travel behavior, and expenditures. *Journal of Hospitality Marketing & Management,* **18**(1), 44-67.

Sohn, E. & Yuan, J. (2013). Who are the culinary tourists? An observation at a food and wine festival. *International Journal of Culture, Tourism and Hospitality Research,* **7**(2), 118-131.

Sparks, B. (2007). Planning a wine tourism vacation? Factors that help to predict tourist behavioural intentions. *Tourism Management,* **28**(5), 1180-1192.

Stewart, J. , Bramble, L., & Ziraldo, D. (2008). Key challenges in wine and culinary tourism with practical recommendations. *International Journal of Contemporary Hospitality Management,* **20**(3), 303-312.

Sthapit, E. (2017). Exploring tourists' memorable food experiences: A study of visitors to Santa's official hometown. *Anatolia,* **28**(3), 404-421.

Stone, M., Soulard, J., Migacz, S. & Wolf, E. (2018). Elements of memorable food, drink, and culinary tourism experiences. *Journal of Travel Research,* **57**(8), 1121-1132.

Strauss, A. & Corbin, J. (1998). *Basics of Qualitative Research.* Thousand Oaks: Sage.

Thach, E. & Olsen, J. (2006). The role of service quality in influencing brand attachments at winery visitor centers. *Journal of Quality Assurance in Hospitality & Tourism,* **7**(3), 59-77.

Tikkanen, I. (2007). Maslow's hierarchy and food tourism in Finland: five cases. *British Food Journal,* **109**(9), 721-734.

Tsai, C. (2016). Memorable tourist experiences and place attachment when consuming local food. *International Journal of Tourism Research,* **18**(6), 536-548.

Wijaya,S., King, B., Nguyen, T. H. & Morrison, A. (2013). International visitor dining experiences: A conceptual framework. *Journal of Hospitality and Tourism Management,* **20**, 34-42.

Wilson, E. & Hollinshead, K. (2015). Qualitative tourism research: Opportunities in the emergent soft sciences. *Annals of Tourism Research,* **54**, 30-47.

Wolf, E. (2002) Culinary Tourism: A Tasty Economic Proposition, Retrieved from http://www.culinarytourism.org

Wolf, E. (2006). *Culinary Tourism: The hidden harvest: A dozen hot and fresh reasons how culinary tourism creates economic and community development.* Dubuque: Kendall/Hunt.

Wolf, E. (2014). Introduction to the food tourism industry. Have Fork Will Travel. A Practical Handbook for Food and Drink Tourism Professionals. World Food Travel Association. Portland.

15 Conclusion

Antónia Correia, Alan Fyall and Metin Kozak

Born in Casablanca, Morocco in 2017, the book comprises chapters from those scholars who attended 'The Art of Living Together' conference, in addition to those who express a deep curiosity on the subject of experiential consumption and marketing in tourism generally, and the art of living together more precisely. In particular, the book sought to raise the profile of experiential marketing by analyzing and critically reporting on the facilitation, celebration and sharing of culture through tourism experiences. As culture is so often the reason for travel and consumption, tourism can enable and threaten culture and its practices. Questions such as what are the best opportunities and practices to follow, what are the aims and pitfalls and mistakes of those tourism operations in this arena already, and what forces and disruptors of change, such as huge growth of the outbound Chinese market, are likely to impact (for better or for worse) experiential consumption and marketing in the future? In addition, how may different tourists be engaged in exploring and learning by cultural experiences? To answer these questions, the book started with a discussion of the four realms of a tourism experience in different contexts, these being namely education, escape, entertainment and aesthetics. In turn, the book was broken down into four key sections: destination experiences; motivations and identity; narratives and storytelling; and gastronomy experiences.

Part I: Destination Experiences

In the first part of the book, Chapter 2 explored staisfaction and place attachment in a mature destination, that of Benalmádena in Spain. The chapter presented information about residents' opinions regarding satisfactory and unsatisfactory aspects of tourism and determined levels of place attachment. The chapter concluded that the aspect of tourism that most satisfied the population of Benalmádena was the creation of employment and economic growth in the city, with residents noting that pollution, dirt and noise were those aspects of tourism that bothered them the most. Interestingly, while those residents under 20 years of age and Benalmádena natives were the groups most comfortbale with tourism as an engine of the economy and a generator of employment, while those over 65 years of age and those who did not have high levels of educational attainment expressed worries about the negatives, mostly pollution, caused by tourism. Overall, the population of Benalmádena has a high level of place attachment which is a positive outcome as the chapter concludes that the level of support for tourism development from the host community would decrease if the community perceives that the total effects of tourism are negative.

The tourism experience starts at the destination. However, the destinations has a life cycle which can be challenging when reaching the maturity stage – destinations such as Benalmádena. Such destinations can not be new and unique forever, with the residents serving as those who are most aware of the destination's strengths and weaknesses. Chapter 2 thus represents a good example of how so-called mature destinations can avoid the typical decline of a mature destination. The compliance of residents to facilitate the tourists' experience thus comes about with a compromise of a more sustainable approach to tourism development by which tourists, destinations and residents may benefit.

Key research question: How can a more experiential approach to destination management and marketing be applied for the equal benefit of residents, the destination and its visitors?

Chapter 3 took a slightly different direction in that it evaluated the relationship between servicescapes and tourists' evaluation of shops. In this chapter, the subjects' evaluation was found to be influenced by the features of the shops in various manners. First, commercial manipulations (interior decorations, products for tourists, and shopkeepers' openness to tourists) were found to contribute to their touristic and active atmosphere. In addition, a shop's exterior's openness and Okinawa style had a positive effect on the active atmosphere and were thus found to be beneficial in its formation. However, excessive manipulation (organization) of the shops' interiors was suggested to have a negative effect on their touristic and active atmosphere. As such, although the presentation of the local lifestyle and shopkeepers' openness to tourists are important for shops to function as places for tourists' shopping or appreciation of local culture, the decoration and organization of the interiors and assortment of touristic goods might be regarded as too distracting vis-à-vis the local authenticity. Thus, servicescape of shops must be reconsidered carefully depending on whether the place intends to foster tourists' shopping activities or enhance their experience of local culture.

Key research question: How do shops and shop owners accommodate locals and tourists with a servicescape that enhances the experience of local culture for tourists yet maintains a sense of local authenticity for resident customers?

The experience theme continued in Chapter 4 whereby the authors determined and examined the role of tour guides and the contribution of guide's interpretation to the tourist experience and satisfaction. This chapter revealed that all educational, esthetic, entertainment and escapist experiences are relevant in package tours. Moreover, the communication skills of the guides, their personality, ability to create a sense of escape, represent the locals and show the unseen were experiential guiding characteristics of particular significance. It comes as no surprise, therefore, that communication skills, an ability to create a sense of escape, an ability to interpret various artistic details, and an ability to teach and create a fun environment, were identified as the guide related roles that explain the variance satisfaction levels.

Key research question: What are the most beneficial forms of training and certification for guides to follow to embrace a more experiential approach to tour guiding and how can more educational institutions incorporate such approaches in their own curriculum development?

The importance of place safety was introduced in Chapter 5 where terrorism, sadly, comes to the discussion of the interaction of the guest with the place. Terrorism tends to happen in the most vibrant destinations, but exactly where and when it will happen is impossible to predict. On the one hand, tourists tend not to travel to places where they feel threatened. On the other hand, tourists tend to visit places where their peers enjoy visiting to be in conformity with the others, consequently they end up visiting places that are very well known. Well known destinations are then more likely to be chosen as targets for terrorists. These conflicting motives lead some destinations to a more vulnerable form of safety, that could damage the image of the destination. Unfortunately only when terrorism happens is the destination then perceived as unsafe. The question is, shall destinations announce safety as a competitive advantage when all the world is vulnerable to terrorism?

Key research question: What strategies can destinations adopt to demonstrate their state of 'terrorist-readiness' as a strength to tourists, without compromising what tourists may perceive as increased vulnerability to such unpredictable events?

Senses have been proven to be an important part of the tourism experience, with Chapter 6 emphasizing them as the ultimate form to provide an identity to the destination. The chapter concluded that tourist perceptions are created from stimuli being captured by human senses, thus making the study of the senses from a consumer perspective an important area of research, with online reviews serving as a proxy of tourist experience. In addition, sensory features were identified and analysed from a large number of visitor comments extracted from TripAdvisor with regard to accommodation, restaurants and tourist attractions in the nine islands of Cape Verde, a small island developing state. The visual sense was by far the most predominant one, followed by gustatory and auditory senses. Most notable visual sensory elements were beach, sea, sand, water and green while music and quietness were frequently mentioned as auditory sensory impressions.

Key research question: How can destinations that attract such varied cultural segments use the five senses in their destination marketing plans to good effect?

Considering that the human dimension is the most critical part of tourism experiences, Chapter 7 approaches the service performance of hotels shared on TripAdvisor. The conclusions were not surprising in that staff (language, assurance, responsiveness, reliability) were deemed to be the most important determinants of tourists' satisfaction, although hotel design and location, facilities and services, room experience, food and beverage and price were also part of tourists' experiences, that usually ends with browsing or shopping around.

Key research question: How best can this research be replicated in other sun and sea destinations (mature or not) and other relevant platforms, in order to assess if a similar bundling of attributes occurs in hotels and/or other types of accommodations business within tourism?

Part II: Motivations and Identity

One of the key questions raised in this book was to understand what Eastern (Asian) tourists are willing to experience and why, with Chapters 8 and 9 contibuting to further the body of knowledge of Chinese tourists.

Chapter 8 sought to shed light on those factors that better explain the motivations that drive tourists' intention of traveling to Macau, with it demystifying the Chinese propensity to gambling while on holidays. Gamblers and non-gamblers value culture, value for money, socialization, relaxation and nightlife while on holidays. These results demonstrate that even if emerging, the four realms of a tourism experience drives their willingness to travel. The results presented in the chapter supported the notion with six motivational factors accounting for tourists' traveling intention, namely cultural, sports, nightlife, relaxation, value for money, and prestige. Culture, sports, and nightlife were found to be the main drivers of tourists in general. Interestingly, gamblers and non-gamblers tourists did not differ in terms of their motivation for visiting Macau, with culture the single most important driver of tourism expenditure in Macau. In recent years, Macau has established a strong and salient image of cultural attractions and international sports events to complement its more traditional gambling product (and global reputation). Looking to the future, the chapter asserts that culture, sports, nightlife activities, special events, and cuisine, really should be added to marketing campaigns.

Key research question: How best can a destination with such a strong reputation for a single product (i.e. gambling) add to its destination portfolio through culture, sports, nightlife activities, special events, and cuisine without damaging the core product upon which its reputation and tourist dollars are built?

Chapter 9, meanwhile, approached Chinese tourists' attitudes, unveiling inappropriate behaviors that although explained may create resistance in the destinations that receive them. The widespread image of Chinese tourists lead to embarrassment at the national government level, with proposals to ensure that tourists behave more appropriately while visiting other destinations in the future. These negative images affect tourist self esteem that, in turn, tend to moderate their behavior. Furthermore, the chapter also concluded that there needs to be more receptiveness to Chinese tourists as there are cultural differences that need to be understood by receiving destinations.

Key research question: How best can destinations more appropriately educate and accommodate Chinese tourists to the benefit of all stakeholders including tourists from other Asian and non-Asian countries?

Part III: Narratives and Storytelling

The question "how can different tourists be engaged in exploring and learning by cultural experiences" is central to Part III. Chapter 10, for example, concluded that heritage managers should continue to view narratives and storytelling as critical to the visitor experience with the heritage sector clearly able to benefit from the further adoption of concepts in the experiential co-creation literature to complement existing management practices. Co-creative opportunities should be considered as a viable management strategy for heritage marketers and managers while developing exhibitions and interpretation, with successful narrative co-creation leading to a more engaging, individualised and memorable visitor experience. For this to succeed, co-created narratives need to capitalize on collaboration, personalisation, control and emotional connectivity to drive more engaging, individualised and memorable visitor experiences.

Key research question: How can the heritage sector best adopt experiential approaches to visitor management while at the same time preserving the richness and authenticity of the heritage being experienced?

Chapter 11 continued this theme by analysing the pre-tourist storytelling experiences in World Heritage Historical Centers in Guimarães, Oporto and Évora, through the content analysis of the information provided by their official websites. The chapter concluded that websites are important pre-experience storytellers and that Oporto and Évora are two cities whose information strategies is particularly complete and educational, providing visitors with rich architectural, artistic and geographical information. Implications drawn from this chapter include the need for managers and owners of such heritage sites to fully understand the importance of storytelling in the creation of the tourist pre-experience. In addition, they need to be aware of the crucial role that experiential marketing plays in the creation of memorable experiences in tourists. Tourists are emotional consumers who look for pleasurable experiences based on five sensory dimensions. Through stories, the destination can create desirable meanings regarding its attributes. Storytelling adds value to the destinations, because through it historical and cultural heritages can be promoted.

Key research question: How best can the heritage sector analyze the stories told by tourists in social media platforms like travel blogs and others, and bring them together in a cohesive unified visit experience?

Part IV: Gastronomy Experiences

Chapter 12 explained the role of gastronomy in official destination promotion materials for Istanbul. In the specific context of Istanbul, it was interesting to note that only eight percent of promotional material was dedicated to food with national food represented more than regional and international food. Regarding atmospherics, food was depicted with scenery, people and entertainment respectively with the types of food used in promotional material classified under raw food, ingredients, entrees, main courses, desserts and drinks.

Key research question: What strategies can destinations adopt to be a more effective 'sensory' culinary destination?

Wine tourism and the wine tourism experience was the subject of Chapter 13, where the perceived (in)congruence between the architecture of a post-modernist hotel, the local landscape, visitors' self-image and the winery's brand image were found to positively affect visitors' level of arousal and delight. Arousal influences delight and both of these emotions significantly increase winery visitors' behavioral intentions. Both substantive and communicative servicescapes were found to improve hotel customers' positive affect which, in turn, was found to have a positive influence on satisfaction. This, in turn, was then found to significantly increase behavioral intentions. Interestingly, there was a decline in winery visitors' revisit intentions after a certain number of visits, though the more winery visitors were satisfied with their visits, the less their revisit intentions tended to decrease over time. The chapter concluded that winery tour/wine tasting and the overall ambiance of the winery positively impact visitors' satisfaction, as well as tourists' age, gender, and country of residence.

Key research question: As wine tourism moves from a very small niche to a more established niche tourism activity in many countries, how can wineries further enhance their experiential dimensions in the face of increased competition locally, regionally and internationally?

Finally, Chapter 14 took a qualitative approach to understanding memorable enogastronomic experiences. The chapter introduced those factors that make a memorable enogastronomic experience for tourists visiting a destination and presented qualitative findings that reveal that gastronomy and wines play a major role in the way that visitors experience a destination and that some travellers would return to the same destination to savour its unique gastronomy.

Key research question: What is the best means for wineries to attract repeat visitors and how can wineries truly differentiate themselves to cross-cultural groups?

To close, this book demonstrated that experiential marketing is a complex and multidimensional force to which tourists, locals, destinations, professionals and government are called to contribute. Furthermore, the contribution of all of them are not enough, as emotions, senses and motivations of tourists moderate the form they experience and share the destination; this complexity and subjectivity bringing to light the fact that experiential marketing truly is an *art of living together*.

Index

Printed in the United States
By Bookmasters